The Interpretation of Ritual

Contributors

R. G. ABRAHAMS *Lecturer in Social Anthropology,
University of Cambridge*

EDWIN ARDENER *Fellow of St John's College, Oxford, and
Lecturer in Social Anthropology, University of Oxford*

ELIZABETH BOTT *Psychoanalyst and social anthropologist*

RAYMOND FIRTH *Emeritus Profressor of Anthropology,
University of London*

ESTHER GOODY *Fellow, and Lecturer in Social Anthropology,
New Hall, Cambridge*

P. H. GULLIVER *Professor of Anthropology, University of Calgary*

J. S. LA FONTAINE *Reader in Anthropology,
London School of Economics*

EDMUND LEACH *Provost of King's College and Reader in Social
Anthropology, University of Cambridge*

AIDAN SOUTHALL *Professor of Anthropology,
University of Wisconsin*

MONICA WILSON *Professor of Social Anthropology,
University of Cape Town*

A. I. RICHARDS

The Interpretation of Ritual

ESSAYS IN HONOUR OF A. I. RICHARDS

EDITED BY **J. S. La Fontaine**

TAVISTOCK PUBLICATIONS

First published in 1972
by Tavistock Publications Limited
11 New Fetter Lane, London EC4
Printed in Great Britain
in 11/13 point Baskerville
by Butler and Tanner Ltd, Frome and London

SBN 422 73880 8

To Audrey
with affection and respect

Contents

viii *Contents*

Introduction

J. S. LA FONTAINE

The essays in this book have been written as a tribute to the work of Audrey Richards. As such they obviously refer to the stimulus that each contributor has found in her work, but in order to give a focus to the contributions, the organizers and editor felt it necessary to select in advance a single theme from her interesting and varied corpus of writing. In this way we hope to have provided a book that will show more clearly the importance for the development of anthropological thinking of Audrey Richards's own contribution in this field.

One of the problems facing us was that it was clearly impossible to choose a theme that would allow all her many colleagues and admirers to contribute, but the subject of ritual seemed to offer the widest scope. From among those who were asked to contribute there were some who felt that the theme was not close enough to their interests or who were prevented from contributing by research or teaching commitments; ill-health prevented another contribution. Among those who originally promised articles for the book are Professor P. H. Gulliver and Dr P. Kaberry who, with myself, were the organizers of the volume. However, Professor Gulliver has contributed the bibliography of Audrey Richards's work and Dr Kaberry has contributed substantially to the Introduction.[1] Both would wish to be closely associated with the volume's intention, as would others whose names do not appear as the authors of articles. The contributors then are a selection from among the many anthropologists who would wish to demonstrate publicly their affection and admiration for Audrey Richards.

Audrey Isabel Richards was born in England in 1899. Her early childhood was spent in India, but she was educated at Downe House and then at Newnham College, Cambridge, where she took her degree in natural sciences in 1922. She did her graduate work in London and in 1930, as a pupil of Malinowski, went to do field research among the Bemba in what was then Northern Rhodesia. It is difficult to imagine now what courage and initiative must have been required forty years ago for a woman to undertake intensive fieldwork alone in Africa, for our tradition of research has become firmly established and generally accepted.

Audrey Richards obtained her Ph.D. in 1931 with 'Hunger and work in a savage tribe'. She held a lectureship at the London School of Economics until 1937, and undertook further research among the Bemba in 1933–4. In 1938 she went to South Africa, taking over the senior lectureship in anthropology at the University of Witwatersrand from Mrs Hoernle. Here she began some more fieldwork, this time among the Tswana of the Northern Transvaal. In 1941 she broke off her fieldwork to come back to England and work in the Colonial Office, returning to the LSE in 1944. She was appointed Reader in 1946 and continued her teaching until 1950. During this time she was active as secretary of the Colonial Social Science Research Council, to which she had been appointed in 1944, and was one of those responsible for drawing up a post-war programme of anthropological research. In 1948 the Council established an Institute of Social Research in East Africa as part of its research programme. The Institute was attached to Makerere College in Uganda, then a university college affiliated to London University. In 1950 Audrey Richards, who had taken a large share in its planning, was appointed Director and she remained there for five years. She received the CBE in 1955 in recognition of her work. Having retired from the Institute in 1956, she took up the Fellowship offered her by her old college, Newnham, and became Director of Studies in Anthropology. She took an active part in teaching and later founded the African Studies Centre in Cambridge, establishing there a series of interdisciplinary seminars. She also resumed her place on the CSSRC for another six years. From 1962 until her retirement in 1967 she held the Smuts Readership in Anthropology. In 1962 she and E. R. Leach launched the study of an Essex village which, as well as providing interesting field data, gave some postgraduate students the privilege of being trained by her in fieldwork techniques. Although officially retired, she is still an active presence in the anthropological world and has a number of important works in preparation.

The honours accorded Audrey Richards are evidence of the esteem she has won for herself in the academic world. In 1941 she was awarded the Wellcome Medal and in 1945 the Rivers Memorial Medal for distinguished field research. She delivered the Munro Lectures in 1956, and in 1958 the Mrs Willy Gordon Lecture, the Mason Lectures, and the Jane Harrison Lecture. In 1963 she gave a Royal Institution Discourse and in 1965 the Frazer Lecture. In addition, as visiting Professor or Lecturer she taught at Northwestern University, the University of Ghana, Cape Town University, the University of Chicago, and McGill University. For three years from 1963–66 she was President of the African Studies Association and from 1959 to 1961 the first (and to date the only) woman President of the Royal Anthropological Institute. She is also a Fellow of the British Academy.

In the course of this distinguished and varied career, Audrey Richards has made many contributions to anthropology. Her work at the Institute of Social Research showed clearly her ability to initiate and carry out plans for long-term research, while recognizing the contribution that social scientists could make to the solution of problems of practical urgency that concerned the governments of the three East African territories. At the Institute, and again as Director of the African Studies

Centre in Cambridge, she showed her belief in and her flair for organizing interdisciplinary collaboration; the joint contributions of anthropologists, economists, historians, and psychologists under her leadership have resulted in some notable publications. Her personal qualities enabled her to make a community in Makerere of the different and often disparate personalities associated with the Institute. She handled with characteristic skill the sometimes difficult relations between the Institute, the College, and the government of Uganda. As Director, she held firm ideas as to the value of planning so that comparative studies might be possible, both in terms of particular theoretical problems and in order to clarify regional variations in culture and social organization. Her deep conviction of the value of field studies for all social sciences added a new dimension to the work of many members of the Institute, whose research tradition was different from that of anthropology. Yet she was not dogmatic, and the research done under her direction bears no recognizable Institute stamp, as to either problems or methods. As an extremely junior research student, I was always made to feel that my research contributions carried the same weight as that of my senior colleagues and that we were all free to concentrate on the problems that interested us, with the assurance that we would receive attention and generous help from the Director when we needed it.

As a teacher and colleague Audrey Richards has never sought to impose her own ideas, but rather to share her passionate enthusiasm for understanding society. She combines extreme generosity in her contributions to solving the intellectual problems of her students and colleagues with a scrupulous acknowledgement of such help from others. Her awareness of common humanity, her concern for people in societies she has studied is obvious, not only in the way she writes but in her involvement with research that might achieve practical and beneficial results. Hence her insistence that the boundaries between intellectual disciplines, particularly between psychology and anthropology, are less important than the joint contributions they can make to the solution of particular problems, and her enthusiasm for multidisciplinary research.

The width and scope of Andrey Richards's studies are remarkable: nutrition; politics; ritual; kinship; economics; socialization; and ethics are among the topics on which she has written. Some of her finest work consists of analyses of ethnographic data; she is the antithesis of the 'armchair anthropologist' for her data are drawn from her own research. Yet it is in the course of her interpretation of the life of particular societies that her most important contributions to theory have been made. As Leach (1961, p. 4) has already pointed out, her analysis of family structure among the matrilineal peoples of central Africa is an essential teaching text. The work on initiation to which many of these essays refer is another example of the enduring theoretical significance of her writing.

To characterize Audrey Richards's theoretical position is difficult, for her wide interests and lack of polemic show a mind open to new ideas. Having been trained by Malinowski, the clear influence of his teaching shows in her first writing, but her later work just as clearly indicates her development from the functionalism of that early period towards a more structural approach. Moreover it is also true that the theoretical significance of what she has written has often been overlooked; since her ideas emerge from her solutions to the problems of interpreting particular ethnographic data, they have not generally been presented as 'theoretical contributions'. This is not the place for a full-scale appreciation of the nature of Audrey Richards's contribution to anthropology for that contribution is not yet complete. It is sufficient to indicate the qualities that make it outstanding – wide scope and variety, combining in each work detailed observation with penetrating analysis, so that the understanding of the society that she conveys makes the exposition seem deceptively simple. It is an achievement often ignored but rarely equalled.

An appreciation of Audrey Richards would not be complete without some record, however inadequate, of her personality, which inspires affection in her friends as her work compels admiration in her colleagues. Her presence at the East African Institute made Kampala a port of call for many distinguished social scientists whose visits enlivened seminars and other less formal gatherings, while her own gaiety and wit made Institute parties a notable feature of Kampala life. Only a Director with Audrey Richards's deep appreciation of the ridiculous would have coped so well with the daily hazards of the first years of the Institute, which included such varied and human problems as the Institute mechanic's loss of his nose by walking through a plate-glass window; her cook's attempt, late one night, to force his wife's head into an empty marmalade tin;[2] and the bland courtesies of the Ganda landlord on whose land a corner of the Director's new house was inadvertently built. Her unfailingly polite responses to his frequent visits 'to enjoy the view from *our* verandah' earned her the admiration of all. Only a Director with her wisdom and her reputation for practical acumen as well as scientific integrity would have coped with the many demands made upon her by administrators as well as academics. Who but Audrey Richards, some years later, would have contributed to an examination on East African ethnography a question that read: What advice would you have given the Governor of Uganda on the Ganda question in 1953?

Personalities such as Audrey Richards's create legends, and stories multiply. Her vagueness has been the subject of many anecdotes, but it enhances rather than conceals a shrewd observer's eye and an acute perception of character. Her generosity and help to students and friends in trouble has always been unstinted and she has never expected thanks or even acknowledgement for it. Perhaps Audrey Richards's most endearing quality is her complete lack of self-importance; she relishes telling and elaborating stories against herself. One that she particularly enjoys concerns her first experience at the Colonial Office. Having been introduced to her new job with instructions that stressed the necessity of taking action herself when possible, she was shown her new office where she opened her first file, determined to follow her instructions to the letter and shirk no decision, however difficult. Imagine, she says, her distress when the first item proved to be a prison report that read 'From the Governor of the Seychelles to the Colonial Office: I am pleased to report that the public conveniences installed last year continue to give satisfaction.' After twenty minutes' agonized academic debate, she reports that she took up her pen and wrote, in a firm hand, the single word 'seen'. One can hardly better this light-hearted record of a vivid personality to whose warmth and zest this preface is a tribute, as the book is in honour of her more sober academic qualities.

The central theme of the book, the interpretation of ritual, obviously refers mainly to that important but curiously neglected work *Chisungu*, a masterly study of girls' initiation ritual among the Bemba. Some contributors to this volume have cited other writings on ritual by Audrey Richards, but the most general reference is to *Chisungu* (1956), a book which is greatly valued by her colleagues as teaching material, yet, less often cited in the literature on primitive religion. While its influence on particular authors will become clear to the reader from the essays themselves, it is worth making some general points here. The outline of the analysis set out in *Chisungu* is in terms of initiation as a *rite de passage* with significance for the social relations and roles of this matrilineal society; it is thus structural in general approach. Yet it presents a most careful and detailed interpretation of the symbolic acts, songs, and speech that make up these long and complicated rituals. Thus it pioneers the study of symbolism, which has led to some of the most interesting recent developments in the study of primitive religion. The author distinguishes the different types of interpretation of symbolism that can be obtained: from the 'ordinary' participant; from the ritual specialist; and from the observer. In this she prefigures the systematic distinction of levels of exegetical analysis that is an important part of Turner's approach to ritual (1962). Her emphasis on the polyvalence of symbols and symbolic objects (*Chisungu*, p. 165) relates to the concept of a 'fan' of referents, the concept that Turner has so fruitfully used in his analysis of Ndembu initiation rites. Indeed, much of what was new in *Chisungu* is now so generally accepted, even taken for granted, that its origin is forgotten.

An important element in *Chisungu* is the author's awareness of the emotional element of ritual behaviour. Thus she includes data on the emotional atmosphere that accompanied different stages of the rituals, while distinguishing carefully between the anthropologist's awareness of common socially induced emotions and the psychoanalyst's interpretation of symbolism and individual emotion. The final section of this book consists of essays that juxtapose psychoanalytical and anthropological interpretations of ritual, showing these distinct but mutually illuminating methods of analysing a single corpus of data. Bott's analysis of the Kava ritual amply justifies Audrey Richards's statement (1956, pp. 153–4) that the problems of psychoanalysts and anthropologists are distinct, but it also demonstrates the value she has claimed for multiple explanations of ritual symbolism.

While all the contributors to this volume have accepted the imposition of a common topic as a central theme, it is clear even from a glance at the table of contents that the problems chosen for discussion vary widely, as do the approaches taken. Thus while Firth and Goody both consider the ritual of greeting, Goody is concerned to show the significance of the ritual within one society, pointing her analysis by a comparison within the same area. Firth's method is that of cross-cultural comparison. Writing on twin rituals and belief in Uganda, Southall and Abrahams discuss quite different aspects of similar ethnography – the former concentrating on the association and distribution of different elements of a single cultural complex, the latter showing the significance of twin ritual in one society.

However, certain common themes emerge from the essays that justify the claim that this book presents the modern

approach to the study of ritual, many-sided though that may be.
An important assumption is that 'ritual' refers to all symbolic
behaviour and is not to be confined to actions associated with
religious institutions. Indeed, the problem of defining ritual is
no longer important. In my own essay I have briefly set out
what seems to me to be a distinction between ceremonial
behaviour, such as that described by Firth and Goody, and
ritual, in terms of symbolic elaboration. The distinction I make
is, however, less important than the recognition, implicit in
all the essays, that ritual expresses cultural values; it 'says'
something and therefore has meaning as part of a non-verbal
system of communication. In this respect greeting behaviour
can be analysed in the same terms as a formal ritual, such as
the kava ritual or a wedding – as a set of cultural statements.
Monica Wilson's essay demonstrates how the adoption of
symbolic objects from another culture requires that they be
adapted to fit into an already existing set of cultural values.
All these essays are concerned to elucidate the symbolism of
ritual behaviour as a statement of basic cultural themes.

A further important theoretical assumption concerns the
relation between beliefs and ritual action. It is clear that
anthropology has long since outgrown any crude assumptions
that either is determined by or derivative of the other. In this
book ritual actions are seen as exemplifying in another medium
the cultural values that find verbal expression in statements
about the world, society, man – statements which we call
beliefs and which are elaborated in narratives or myths. The
relation between belief and ritual action is thus derived from
their common relation to underlying cultural elements, which
they both express. The one must then be used to amplify the
other. Gisu beliefs about blood illuminate the symbolic significance of blood in rituals of the person; Bakweri beliefs about
the forest as opposed to the village are given greater significance by the rituals of spirit possession.

As a consequence of this concern to relate both beliefs and
symbols to a deeper structure underlying both, some of the

anthropologists writing in this book indicate the influence that Lévi-Strauss has had on anthropological thought. This influence is clearest in the essay by Leach, whose position is initially that of Malinowski in that he sees myth as providing a charter for ritual and, hence, an elucidation of the myth provides a key to the meaning of the ritual. Yet he analyses the myth by the structuralist method, and uses it, as Lévi-Strauss would not, to understand the symbolic system of the associated ritual. Ardener, Southall, and I also use the principles that, as Lévi-Strauss has demonstrated, organize the structure elements of myth, in order to show their significance in structuring symbolic clusters that, together with their attached beliefs, reveal some of the cultural themes expressed in ritual. It is this modification of the structuralist method that is one of the major indices of such progress as has been made since *Chisungu's* publication.

Thus these essays contain varied anthropological problems analysed in different ways. There is unity, but not uniformity – a justification of Audrey Richards's own belief that 'Single explanations of ritual behaviour . . . deny the nature of symbolism itself'. The book can now be offered to her as a symbolic object, for it combines 'fixity of form with multiple meanings, some of which are standardized and some highly individual'.

NOTES

1. I acknowledge gratefully the help of other colleagues who have contributed to the biographical sketch in this Introduction, particularly Professors R. Firth, M. Friedman, and W. Whiteley.

2. She attempted to calm the alarmed Institute residents who assembled at the scene with the soothing words 'It's all right; it's a seven-pound tin'!

REFERENCES

LEACH, E. R. 1961. *Rethinking Anthropology*. London: Athlone Press.
RICHARDS, A. I. 1956. *Chisungu: A girls' initiation ceremony among the Bemba of Northern Rhodesia*. London: Faber & Faber.
TURNER, V. W. 1962. Three Symbols of Passage in Ndembu Circumcision Ritual. In Gluckman, M. (ed.), *Essays on the Ritual of Social Relations*. Manchester: Manchester University Press.

Verbal and bodily rituals of greeting and parting

RAYMOND FIRTH

Formalized behaviour in greeting and parting has been recorded for many societies, but no systematic study of these rituals has yet been made. This essay, dedicated to Audrey Richards in acknowledgement of her own thoughtful analyses of ritual, is not intended to be such a definitive study, but only to make some broad generalizations and draw attention to possibilities for further inquiry.[1]

Greeting is the recognition of an encounter with another person as socially acceptable. Parting, in a social sense, is the recognition that the encounter has been acceptable. Both involve a concept of a positive social quality in the relationship. Encounter of a physical kind may take place without such social relationship – as by two persons rubbing shoulders in a bus. They recognize the physical presence of each other but the encounter is not socially acceptable, the existence of each is not incorporated into the social universe of the other. A social relationship is then created only by some exchange of signs, as by a word or a nod. Forms of greeting and parting are symbolic devices – or signs if they are specifically descriptive – of incorporation or continuance of persons in a social scheme. A greeting or parting sign is often represented as conveying information and/or expressing emotion – an announcement of presence or intended departure, a statement of pleasure at someone's arrival, or of sadness at his going away. Granting that this may often be so, the informational or emotional content of the sign may be highly variable, even minimal. What is of prime relevance is the establishment or perpetuation of a social relationship, the recognition of the other person as a social entity, a personal element in a common social situation. That this is so is indicated by reverse behaviour, that of 'cutting' a person who is already known but found objectionable – the refusal of a greeting to him is a denial of him as a social entity in what would otherwise be a shared situation. So also when two people are 'not on speaking terms' they do not greet each other and so reduce the area of their common relationship to as small a compass as possible. As with all social relationships, reciprocity is important; an expectation in greeting is that it will elicit social recognition in return.

There is great variety of custom in greeting and parting behaviour across the world.[2] But this variety occurs through a range of relatively few, simple sets of words and non-verbal acts, involving usually speech organs, head, hands, and body. Limited as these components are, with few cultural accessories, their expressive power is considerable and their social implications of great sensitivity. Greeting and parting signs, though highly conventionalized, are not merely formal empty recognition procedures. Perception of them can be instrumental in modifying the behaviour of a person to whom they are directed. There is usually no suggestion that the procedures in themselves have any independent effect, though historically some accompaniments of greeting or parting behaviour have implied a peculiar virtue of their own, as in the giving of a blessing.

In this essay I restrict myself primarily to consideration of verbal and bodily greeting and parting behaviour, with only incidental reference to accessories. Formalized use of body and limbs in signals of greeting and parting very strongly suggests analogies in animal behaviour studied by ethologists under the head of ritualization. This is routine communicative behaviour, usually of display, which is characteristic of members of a given species in given situations, and is adaptive, with the effect of signalling relevant information on, for example, sexual accessibility or territorial defence. The range of ritual behaviour in man, its complexity, and especially its considerable verbal component, has often made parallels with non-human animal behaviour seem remote. But in human greeting and parting behaviour, conventions of formal use of body and limbs play such a major sign-role that animal parallels easily come to mind.

If by ritual is meant symbolic action relating to the sacred, the term is inappropriate for the formal behaviour of greeting and parting. But in the broader sense of formal procedures of a communicative but arbitrary kind, having the effect of controlling or regularizing a social situation, the term is relevant. Otherwise greeting and parting conventions may be regarded as a mild variety of what Elsie Clews Parsons characterized as *crisis ceremonialism*, a term which she regarded as the equivalent of Van Gennep's *rites de passage* – 'ceremonial to signalize or allow of the passing from one stage of life to another'. Perhaps, following her lead, one might coin the term *telectic rites*, from the Greek concept of putting off the old and putting on the new, for such behaviour as greeting and parting, where the major stimulation is provided by the arrival or departure of a person from the social scene (Parsons, 1916, p. 41). But I am concerned here with content rather than with definition.

STRUCTURE AND QUALITY OF GREETING AND PARTING SITUATIONS

Group rituals of greeting and parting on social occasions such as weddings, funerals, or peace-making have been described by anthropologists in detail, with accounts of their symbolic significance. But these rituals are relatively infrequent by comparison with individual greeting and parting rituals, the main theme of this essay.

Forms of greeting and parting vary not only according to differences in culture, but also according to types of social situation: individual or group confrontation; formality or informality of the occasion; prior acquaintance or not of the parties; conventional emotional quality ascribed to the occasion; face-to-face or distant communication. Even between individuals, the relative formality of the occasion may affect the form of greeting or parting behaviour. With the circumscribed stiff, laconic welcome of host and hostess at a public 'reception' can be contrasted their relaxed, jovial, expansive greeting as they circulate among their personal friends in the gathering at a later stage. Even if the occasion is not classed as a formal one by the nature of the invitation, the presence of casual acquaintances may have an inhibiting effect on greeting or parting behaviour by tending to restrain more exuberant manifestations of interest. American or English people who might exchange a kiss in private greeting may refrain from such intimacy in public. But this is a highly cultural matter – a Frenchman in office may bestow a kiss on another on a formal public occasion when he would not do so at an informal private meeting.

In ordinary social intercourse formality may be enhanced when the person to be signalized in greeting is previously unknown to the signalizer. A simple form of this may be observed often in travel, especially perhaps in the United States. When two men previously unknown to each other are seated side by side in an aeroplane, an informal social relationship of an elementary order may be established in getting to and from seats (remarks about the weather, etc.). But after casual exchanges may come formal identification. 'I'm James Brown,' says one man, extending his hand, whereupon the other normally follows suit with his own name and handclasp. Search may be made for further points of contact – home town, business, common acquaintance. But, though presumably gratifying, this is not of primary relevance. What is of main significance is the act of identification, which has been sealed by the clasp of hands. Indeed, once the name has been uttered the hand gesture is almost automatic; as an experiment, one may disconcert such a casual acquaintance by uttering one's name but withholding the hand movement! Yet in materialist terms the act is almost meaningless – the men are seated side by side, have already talked, and could continue to talk; they will probably never meet again; neither wants anything of the other except his temporary companionship, which is already available. The name given may even have been false. But what matters is that *some* name has been given, and *some* personal manual contact made. The accidental travel neighbour has been socially pinpointed, and the handshake is the formal symbol of a social relationship established, of the reduction of an unknown to a (putatively) known social position. The handshake has been interpreted as equivalent to a disclaimer of aggression, as a residual pledge against resort to arms. But in such modern conditions the risk of physical assault is minimal. If a threat is conceived it is of interference with the personality, not with the person, and the handshake has a much more subtle function of serving to reduce social uncertainty.

In such a situation the social identification has been provided by the two parties immediately concerned. The relationship is casual, the identification nominal. But it is not automatic; if neither party takes the initiative no formal greeting takes place. Moreover, it is status-regulated. A handshake is primarily behaviour between male equals or those making a show of equality; my guess is that it occurs much less frequently between men and women. Between women no handshake at all may be exchanged, though other identificatory signs may be. In the growing informality of western society exchanges of names seems to be common with no other greeting sign, but in more formal conditions an intermediary may be used. Traditionally, in sophisticated European circles, greeting between two persons not previously acquainted should be prefaced by an introduction by a third party known to both; without being 'introduced' the two people should not address each other. This rule was especially severe when a man and a woman were concerned. Though the rule has now been relaxed, except in the most formal circumstances, an intermediary is

still often employed. 'Will you introduce me to . . .' can still be an intelligible and appropriate request in some social situations. The role of the third party here is twofold: he (or she) is both the social bridge, the mediator who facilitates the social contact of the two parties, and he may be also an ostensible guarantor of their social identity and, up to a point, of their reliability.

In the past, rules of introduction in European society have been elaborate, and status considerations have played an important part in them. In the game of status and power manipulation within the rules it may be very important to be introduced to someone by A rather than by B. In general the rule has been that a person of lower status is introduced to a person of higher status, in the particular social context. A young man is introduced to an elder man, a man to a woman, an unmarried woman to a married woman, a commoner to a member of the royal family. But one rule may override another. In formal circumstances, immediate role considerations may be more significant than general status considerations. So an elderly clerk may be introduced to a younger man who is his branch manager, a member of the royal family to the head of the college where he or she is becoming a student. But the conditions of such modification are usually narrowly defined by the role situation, and the type of greeting restricted to it accordingly. So, in a formal degree-conferring ceremony, an officiating dean introducing candidates may address the head of the university as 'Chancellor' and tip his headgear in salute, though if they are friends a few minutes later, when they have unrobed, he may address him familiarly by his first name. (Ex-President Eisenhower, just before the inauguration of President Nixon, is reported to have said to him. 'This is the last time I will call you Dick for some while.')

Modern anthropological idiom stresses the communicative function of ritual. Ritual behaviour may also be expressive for the actor, irrespective of the information it conveys to the other party. This is often so with rituals of greeting and parting.

But the situation is complex. In western countries there seems to be, in popular estimation, a strong implication of emotional involvements, even if low-keyed, in greeting and parting situations. Greeting behaviour is expected to express pleasure, parting behaviour to express sadness. It is a matter of common knowledge that the reverse may sometimes be the case, or at least that the parties may be indifferent. Popular jokes make play of the incongruity between outward behaviour and inward feeling on parting, or at least between behaviour before and behaviour after the moment of parting. Yet while such incongruity is admitted, there is a general demand that the forms of emotional interest be preserved; to omit them gives offence. Politeness consists in not allowing incongruity to be overtly perceptible. In reflective comment, then, the forms of greeting and parting can be regarded as 'empty', as 'meaning-less'. But as a means of communication in a social context they are significant. 'Pleased to meet you' on introduction and 'How good of you to have come' at parting, may not add to anyone's social assets, but what they express is a willingness to enter into or continue a social relationship. Their simulation of emotional involvement or moral approval may be only part of the conventional 'small change' of social intercourse, but it has an emollient quality. It is a 'softener' of the social relationship because, by linguistic convention, it sets the relationship in a status frame, implying respect by the speaker to the personality of the recipient.

Such attitudes to the viability of social relationships lie deep in customary behaviour. In English linguistic usage to *greet* some-one is often rendered as to *welcome* him. Now, literally, 'welcome' means 'It is good that you have come' or 'You have come in a good state', and implies a positive attitude of acceptance. Parting is expected to correspond to an analogous attitude, generated by the withdrawal of the person – the cessation, if only temporary, of the relationship. The oft-quoted *partir, c'est mourir un peu* expresses in vivid form the sense of loss of part of one's identity on such an occasion. Yet to signalize a departure is not the mirror image of 'welcome', which would presumably be 'ill-go', but a goodwill term, 'farewell'. So in English historical usage, as in many other languages, rituals of greeting and parting stress the positive, favourable aspect of the social relationship.

The parallelism between greeting and parting emerges also in another way. Not all societies emphasize the positive emotional aspects of the situations in approving language. A Tikopia, on greeting someone who has returned after a long absence, may say the equivalent of 'It is good that you have come.' But is it much more likely that he will open his greeting by '*E aue toku soa!*' (Oh, alas my friend!). An identical expression of what sounds like dismay is uttered when such a friend departs. On very formal occasions of greeting, as well as at parting, a lament type of song might be chanted. Here what is being expressed overtly is not goodwill primarily, but emotional disturbance.[3] The arrival is represented as a moving event, analogous in this sense to a departure. Emphasis is placed not on the contrast between the joy of greeting and the sorrow of parting, but on their similarity – both are disruptive of normal emotional routine: regret for past severance and regret for future severance are aligned in behaviour (cf. Radcliffe-Brown, 1964, pp. 239–41).

In many societies emotional expressions do not seem to be represented in conventional greeting and parting behaviour; granted that they occur, they are muted by the customary verbal forms. One common mode of recognition of a person arriving or leaving is a restatement of the obvious, a verbal equivalent or description of the bodily action. An ordinary Maori greeting of welcome is *haere mai*, 'walk hither'; while two people who have met in the street greet each other with *tena koe*, 'there you are'. They may clasp hands and press noses, but the verbal greeting is laconic. Saying goodbye is of the same order; the person who is going says 'stay there' to the other, who replies 'go there'. In Tikopia a common greeting to a person who has just entered a house is 'so you've come'. A person about to leave says 'I am about to go', to which the conventional reply is 'go then' or simply 'go'. This seems a very curt comment, almost explosive in the way in which it is uttered, but it is meant as a simple aquiescence in the decision announced. Diamond Jenness has recorded in parallel fashion 'The Eskimos had no word for farewell in their language, but came and went without ceremony . . . "I am going" I said again, using their only greeting of farewell; and they answered together "You are going" ' (1964, pp. 61, 245). In neither instance do the ordinary verbal forms of greeting and parting embody any overt expressions of pleasure or sadness. But there are two points to be made about this. The first is that neither the Tikopia nor the Eskimo *say nothing at all* on such occasions. There may be societies where no words of greeting or parting are said at all, but they are probably rare. Usually some verbal recognition is made, if only a grunt, to record arrival and departure on any but the most casual and informal social occasions. The second point is that since on many social occasions words are regarded as inadequate to express feelings anyway, the actual form of words used is not important, and even a brusque phrase will serve as a communication signal. 'Language speaks peremptorily when it gives up trying to express the thing itself . . . The empirical use of already established language should be distinguished from its creative use', wrote Merleau-Ponty (1964, p. 44) in an essay on 'Indirect Language and the Voices of Silence'.

SIGNIFICANCE OF VERBAL STATEMENTS

Rituals of greeting and parting commonly have both verbal and non-verbal elements, but sometimes these serve as alternatives or substitutes for one another. In a moment of tension a handclasp between friends may act instead of a spoken greeting. But some interesting points arise about the verbal component alone.

Conventional English greetings may commonly be in any one of three linguistic forms: a question; an interjection; or an affirmation. The question form, now mainly used by members of an elder generation, 'How do you do?' is formal and requires not a literal answer but an acknowledgment in equally formal, even identical, terms. The interjection 'Hallo!' (American, 'Hello' or 'Hi') is less formal and more common in the younger generations, a straight recognition signal with no putative informational content. But the tone and manner of utterance may convey a more general message than simple greeting. 'When a husband comes home from the office, takes off his hat, hangs up his coat and says "Hi!" to his wife, the way in which he says "Hi", reinforced by the manner in which he sheds his overcoat, summarizes his feelings about the way things went at the office. If his wife wants the details she may have to listen for a while, yet she will grasp in an instant the significant message for her; namely, what kind of an evening they are going to spend and how she is going to have to cope with it' (Hall, 1961, p. 94). The third type, the affirmation, is also fairly formal, but purportedly conveys information rather than inquires about it. Moreover, unlike the other two types, it modulates over time. This is the series 'good morning', 'good day', 'good afternoon', 'good evening' and 'good night'. Three points are noticeable about this type of greeting. The first is that it is a form of assurance, not a conveyance of information of a meteorological kind. One says 'good morning' even though it may be raining heavily. (This discrepancy is often noted and remarked upon wryly in ensuing conversation; it may even be incorporated into the greeting phrases.) The second point is that while all forms of greeting can take differences of stress according to circumstances, those which 'pass the time of day' can be prolonged in ways that reduce their uniformity. A crisp 'good morning' to a business acquaintance is very different from the 'good m-o-o-orning' that one may drawl out to a farmer looking over a gate in a country lane. The latter indicates a kind of familiarity or sociability in a more relaxed atmosphere. The third point is that in English, though not apparently in some other European languages, the time-of-the-day series as *greeting* commonly stops at the evening. Most greeting signals can also be used as parting signals. But 'Good night' in English tends to be an after-sundown *parting* rather than greeting salutation. It is appropriate to use in a country lane to serve as both greeting and parting signal to a passer-by, but if a host greeted his guests with 'good night' they would think it rather odd. A further point – different cultures which use the same general time-frame for ordinary affairs may stress different sectors of it for greeting purposes. The French, unlike the English or the Germans, do not ordinarily involve 'morning' in their greetings, and neither French nor Germans ordinarily use 'afternoon' in a greeting signal.

Lack of informational content is characteristic of greeting in other societies too, as in the Maori 'there you are', which does 'not sound very gracious' as Best put it (1952, p. 124; cf. Smith & Dale, 1920, vol. 1, pp. 362–3). But what is sociologically significant is the acknowledgement of the presence of the other person, which can often be more discriminating than in English if different pronouns can be used for singular, dual, and plural.

Even when greetings assume the form of a question the answer expected by convention is not normally what logic would seem to require. Amused comment has often been passed in England on the (alleged) reply of an enthusiastic foreigner to the question 'How do you do?' by giving an account of his state of health. The apparently analogous 'How are you?' is appropriate as a genuine inquiry between friends, but even here a fairly routine statement such as 'I am very well' is usually taken as a sufficient reply. Even when the reply seems logical it may be in quite formal style. A common Malay greeting is the question 'What news?' which should be met by 'Good news', even if the news is *not* good; bad news is given later. Here the notion is clearly that of not disturbing initially the equable character of what is a somewhat delicate relationship – that of meeting another person. Only when the relationship is firmly established can disturbing information be safely trans- mitted (Zainal-'Abidin, 1950, p. 47). A Chinese traditional greeting variously translated as 'Have you eaten your rice?' or 'Have you eaten your food?' was answered in country districts (where the external forms of etiquette were maintained longer than in the cities) by 'I have been so selfish.' Whether, as has been argued, this greeting and reply were oriented to a community for whom hunger was an ever-present threat or whether, as an anthropologist might think, it was the social aspects of commensalism that were implied, these were polite salutations that were not expected to yield any significant information (cf. Danton, 1963, p. 90; Cormack, 1935, p. 131; Mallory, 1926, p. 1).

The informational content of greeting is not always lacking. This may be so in greetings that involve reference to movement. In the traditional greeting of both Tikopia and Kelantan Malays, a common opening has been to ask a passer-by the question 'Where are you going?' The reply to this might be aptly specific or it might be a rather vague statement 'I am going for a stroll.' Although formal, this latter did have informational relevance. Yet in a sense what was given was negative information. In village situations the formal question often embodies a real curiosity as to the movements of the person greeted, and a specific reply is often a matter for gossip. The reply 'just strolling' or an equivalent phrase serves two functions. It returns the recognition signal and gives assurance that the social relationship is in working order. But it also either conceals the destination of the passer-by from inquisitive ears, or at least indicates that even if the destination is known or guessed it is not being notified officially to casual inquiry.

Though conventionalized, forms of greeting and parting have often been recorded as changing over time. For instance, the common Malay salutations for the time of day, *selamat pagi*, good morning, etc., and for arrival and departure, *selamat datang*, welcome, etc., are stated on good authority (Zainal-'Abidin, 1950, p. 46) to have been of recent growth, adapted from colloquial Indonesian Malay, possibly in the 1920s on the model of an earlier ritual holiday salutation, *selamat Hari Raya*.

An interesting instance of change of greeting pattern with adaptation of local concepts to an alien social frame is given by modern Tikopia practice. In recent years, with the conversion of the whole population to Christianity, the traditional form of greeting has been almost completely abandoned in favour of a direct translation of English forms. As I heard continually in 1966, Tikopia in greeting one another, as well as Europeans, used the forms 'good morning' etc. – in Tikopia: *E laui te pongipongi, e laui te aoatea; e laui te afiafi; e laui te po.* This followed the English times of day precisely, except that quite often the particle *nei* (this) was added. Because of such an addition the Tikopia expression has to be translated in slightly different form from our ordinary English one, since the general has been converted into the specific: 'Good is this morning (day, evening, night)' instead of 'good morning' etc. Although these expressions were used by Tikopia with reference to the particular period, e.g., one was greeted with *e laui te pongipongi nei* in the morning, *e laui te afiafi nei* in the afternoon and evening – in fact they were formal only, with no reference either to the state of the weather or that of the society. But, unlike English practice, 'good night' in its Tikopia form, though not often heard, could be a salutation of greeting as well as of parting. Moreover, *aoatea* – the Tikopia equivalent of the English 'day' in greeting – had a narrower time range, referring primarily to midday. So in its Tikopia form this greeting was more specific and more restricted in time period than in English; the two time-frames were slightly different.

A peculiar feature of English and probably of most other European greeting forms which refer to periods of time is that they are restricted to the compass of a *day*. In taking over this system the Tikopia made an interesting extension – *e laui te vasia nei*, meaning literally 'this time period is good'. Its creation indicated the capacity of the Tikopia to appreciate and develop the principle of the English system, and did away with a possible difficulty of non-comparability of time-phases in the two linguistic systems. In English we can say 'good day' but not 'good midday'; conventionally in Tikopia one can say 'good midday', but one does not normally say 'good day' – which would be *e laui te ao nei* – though one can say 'good night'. A plausible reason for 'good midday' is that the Tikopia *pongi-pongi, aotea, afiafi,* and *po* are all *sequential* phases in the same series of progressive time periods – morning, noon, afternoon, night; whereas *ao* and *po* are *opposed* phases in another series – of alternated time periods or indeed states – daylight, darkness. *Po* is used in both, but *ao* and *aoatea,* though closely related, can be used separately and only the latter is used in the greeting series. Moreover, *po* also may have additional claim to use in greeting since the Tikopia normally count not by days as we do but by nights. In the greeting series *vasia* can refer to almost any time period, long or short; as an expression of flexible usage it can therefore serve especially as a greeting in cases where the time of day is on a borderline between two Tikopia time periods.

What the Tikopia have done is to convert their traditional space-movement reference type of greeting to a time-movement type. They have also converted an invariant style to a variant style; the traditional greeting could be used unaltered at any time of the day, whereas the modern greeting modulates as the day proceeds. They have also replaced a question on the part of the person opening the greeting by an affirmation. The specific steps in their doing this are not fully known to me, but I think that through the (Anglican) Melanesian Mission came the idea of following more up-to-date foreign ways in greeting, with perhaps also the idea that the new forms were less brusque than the old and so more suited to the new way of life. All this substitution of categories would seem to have involved a considerable modification of Tikopia concepts, and concomitant effects in the non-verbal aspects of greeting behaviour might have been expected. But from my observation the new greeting forms seem to have been adopted smoothly, without strain. It is true, however, that children, with their school training, were the major users of the new style. The substitution of an affirmation about the goodness of the time of day for a question as to where one is going has superficially implied a reduction in aggression towards the person greeted. But since the traditional question was often only a formal inquiry this effect may not really be significant. Moreover, apart from the verbal change, Tikopia seemed to behave in just the same way as before to people whom they meet – with bodily contact, hospitality invitations, inquiries for news. What emerges from this example is once again the use of verbal utterance as a greeting signal rather than as a conveyer of information in the form of words used.

In many languages the formal quality of the words of greeting is illustrated by the way in which these can be abbreviated to a set of syllables which would be meaningless without this context. The English 'good morning' can be heard often as 'gmon', 'how do you do?' as 'hadedoo'; the Tikopia *ka poi kifea?* as *poife?*; the Kelantan Malay *hendak pergi kamana?* as *gewano?* Each of these is capable of eliciting an appropriate courteous reply. It is not merely that enough of the correct sound pattern is heard to allow the hearer to fill in the rest from common knowledge and attribute the meaning; the sound pattern may be incorrect by conventional standards and still fulfil the same function. The important sociological fact is the utterance of sounds bearing an approximate likeness to those expected in greeting. Great flexibility is allowed, and the precise correspondence of the sounds produced to those ideally significant is not relevant. Linguistically, this is a commonplace, but it is the relative uniformity of the greeting situation which allows the linguistic pattern such variability.

I can best illustrate this by an experience I had many years ago in a rural area in that part of the Tyrol which is in north Italy. One local greeting in the area (common to the Austrian/south German region) was, and still probably is, *Grüss Gott!* Staying with me at the time in a priest's house was a fellow New Zealander who spoke no German, and who found great difficulty with this salutation, especially the *umlaut*. So I suggested to him that for it he substitute a slurred form of an exclamation once common in New Zealand but now old-fashioned – 'Great Scott!' This worked admirably. By a slight alteration in tone from surprise to recognition he was able to greet people quite passably and felt comfortable, while the local peasants responded cheerfully to what must have appeared to them to be simply a rather garbled version of their traditional expression. That the phonetic pattern differed in several respects, and that the German expression meant 'Greet God!' in piety, while the English one was equivalent to 'Goodness me!' in surprise, was not relevant. Whether the Tyrolese peasants *heard* the expression as '*Grüss Gott*' or whether they regarded it as a rather clumsy effort to pronounce these words and heard it otherwise did not matter; they responded in the same way.

There are two points to make on this. The first is that historically the English form 'Great Scott' is probably either a meiotic rendering of or a substitute for a reference to God, and therefore in a circuitous way my friend's greeting was actually roughly equivalent to the German usage – though I doubt if he knew this. The second point is that the sociological significance of the substituted greeting depended upon a set of recognitions or conceptual assumptions by both parties. My New Zealand friend had to be prepared to use the expression 'Great Scott' as a greeting and not as an exclamation of surprise; if it had been used as the latter his tone might have inhibited the appropriate response. The Tyrolese peasants in complementary fashion had to be prepared to accept a slurred version of 'Great Scott' as a slurred version of '*Grüss Gott*', or alternatively to accept a set of foreign vocables for their intent and not their sound.

Greeting rituals imply a positive acceptance of the person met, a willingness to establish a social relationship; parting rituals imply a recognition that the relationship has been established, and some hint that it could continue. (To 'refuse to say goodbye' is one way of indicating a severance of relationship.) Consequently the verbal forms of greeting and parting seem to involve in many societies a reference to some condition of viability or serenity. In cultures of Judaic tradition, including

Islam, the ritual pronouncements invoke peace. The Hebrew form *shalom aleichum* – to which the response is the same phrase in reverse – has its analogue in Arab and other Muslim societies. Expressions such as the Malay *selamat jalan*, 'peace be on your journeying', to which the response is *selamat tinggal*, 'peace be on your remaining', can be termed literally benedictions – welfare sayings. They have a manifest suggestion of strengthening the social relationship between the parties by projecting it conceptually beyond the immediate occasion through assigning good fortune to the future. Of different etymology but parallel significance are the English 'goodbye', which dictionaries give as a contraction of 'God be with you/ye', and the French *adieu*, consigning a person to God's care. In earlier times, when faith was stronger, all such expressions reflected the quasi-magical virtue attributed to the religious formula.

Yet acceptance of a person by greeting may be modified according to social status. Behavioural codes in many societies specify who may address whom, the style in which the person addressed is to be cited, and the actual words of greeting. Except on very formal occasions, in western society initiative in greeting between persons already known to each other is commonly taken by either, though in polite society the convention that the lady greets first was designed to allow her discretion in the recognition of her acquaintances. In formal contexts generally, senior greets first. In many societies of small scale the mode of address follows kinship conventions and no difficulties arise; in others personal names are used freely. In English society, as elsewhere in the west, the differentiation of names into surnames and personal names, with patronymics as well in Slavic countries, has given scope for fine shades of recognition of status; this has been further complicated by the system of titles in some countries.[4] It is well known that in modern times, with changes in the class structure, these conventions have been greatly relaxed, especially in much freer use of personal first names in greeting; less clearly realized are the problems that have arisen thereby for members of the older generations.[5] Yet as examples from Southeast Asia or Polynesia can show, variance in form of greeting according to relative status can still be relevant (e.g. in High Javanese/Low Javanese; 'chief's language' of Samoa), and use of a 'wrong' form may create acute social tension.[6]

INSTRUMENTAL USE OF THE BODY IN GREETING AND PARTING

The human body is far more of a social instrument than is often suspected.[7] In the main, such instrumentality is symbolic, in that the physical effects are usually small. Occasionally a greeting gesture may be primarily of physical import, as when a host opens a door or unlatches a gate for a guest, though even here the physical act of admission may also be a symbolic act of welcome, a throwing wide of defences which has other obvious physical analogies.

The body as a whole can be a greeting or parting instrument in three main respects: by maintaining a distance gap between the parties; by adopting an overall posture; and by moving to meet or farewell the other party.

Degree of spatial distance kept between the parties is broadly an index to degree of social distance between them. In western societies this operates unsystematically, but in societies with a developed caste system, especially where notions of pollution by contact occur, bodily relationships may be strictly regulated, even to measurable index, and greeting behaviour structured accordingly (e.g. see Aiyappan, 1937, pp. 18–19).

Bodily posture is important in many greeting conventions. One mode of showing respect is sinking to the ground, conveying a depreciation of the self, symbolizing humility and recognition of superior status. Hence in ordinary social intercourse a mutuality of esteem is expressed by mutual bodily lowering. Nadel has recorded how Nupe men of equal rank greet each other by sinking low (his word is 'cowering' which hardly seems apt) for half a minute or longer while exchanging salutations. If they are well acquainted, they stretch out their hands several times in succession and lightly touch each other's fingers. A man of lower rank when meeting his social superior will bow very low or kneel down, and only if difference of rank is slight or obviated by personal intimacy will he venture to offer his hand. If he is on horseback he will dismount, if he is wearing sandals he will take them off, though this may take place on the road, and put them beside him. The man of higher rank will stand or sit still, make a short perfunctory gesture of bowing, and hardly move his arm to meet the other man's hand (Nadel, 1942, p. 129; cf. Mangin, 1921, pp. 18–19 for a description of the analogous 'Mossi salute'). Clearly, in such forms of greeting the lower the status of the person making the greeting, the more the disturbance to which he subjects himself – a principle that seems of very general application. Yet such severe bodily displacement has often offended people of other cultures. Mangin, who noted the ease and grace of the Mossi traditional greeting, which he states was formerly in vogue in all the black empires of the Sudan, especially Ghana, Mali, and Gao, notes also how foreigners entering Mossi country were shocked to see men thus lower themselves before others. A generation later, as I myself observed, similar opinions were being uttered about the 'degrading', 'undemocratic' usage of Hausa in Northern Nigeria by Europeans and Americans who saw it for the first time without realizing the local concepts involved. Examples of body-lowering in Far Eastern societies, such as the Chinese 'kow-tow', have provoked a kind of shocked contemptuous interpretation from westerners, who for the most part ignore the occasional practices of kneeling, crouching, and even prostration that still occur, if rarely, in some western societies.[8]

Even where status differences are not highly marked in ordinary social intercourse, as in the west in modern times, and etiquette demands equalization of posture in greeting between social equals, some modulations are still observable. Frequently, a sitting man rises to his feet to greet another who has just entered the room. But a lady is entitled to remain seated in greeting a man who stands before her and, conversely, a man who is manager of a firm may not rise in saying good morning to his woman secretary ('lady' and 'woman' here being indices to status according to context). Such differences in greeting posture correspond to recognized if minor status differentials. Yet ambiguity can occur, especially if the categories are mixed, and modern practice allows considerable personal discretion. So a manager may rise to greet his woman secretary when she first comes in, in recognition of the general sex rule that a gentleman should not remain seated when a lady is standing; or he may stay in his chair as an expression of his professional situation; or he may be guided by some rule-of-thumb to solve his uncertainties – remain seated if the secretary is a young girl and rise if she is a mature married woman, or rise when she first comes in and remain seated thereafter. What is significant here is how, in what we would like to regard as ordinary practical business conduct, other codes are still allowed to intrude; but even more, how in such questions of 'manners', which are supposedly matters of delicacy, we use our bodies in a lump, as it were, in crude mass, as expressions of the social relationships. Moreover, we tend to do this as a matter of course, as if manipulation of the bodily mass is the equivalent of an agreed language.

The significance of accompanying movement or simultaneous progression in greeting or farewell is not formally expressed in western society (except perhaps in diplomatic protocol and the most ceremonious exercises of a university or a royal court), but tacitly it is fairly well understood in higher business and professional circles. To be conducted into a business man's office by a secretary is usual, but gradations of being farewelled – at your host's desk, at the door of his inner sanctum, in the outer office, at the door of the lift, down at the front door of the building – are recognized status indicators. As with the Nupe, the degree of disarrangement of the one party indicates the relative status of the other. In traditional Chinese officialdom gradations were expressed with much greater finesse and had much more specific status significance.

BODILY GESTURES

Gestures are commonly regarded as movements particularly of the hands and face that accompany speech for purposes of emphasis – a kind of italicized speech, as Macdonald Critchley has put it (1939, p. 11). But some gestures may serve as substitutes for speech, especially when they act as a general means of communication or expression for which no simple speech equivalent can be found. In the translation of movement of parts of the body into symbolic gestures of greeting or parting the range is wide. If one includes what may be called the 'receptor-parts', which are involved as platforms or bases against which the action is performed – e.g. breast to which a person is clasped, or back or buttocks which may be patted, very many major external features may serve.[9] Even the feet, which one is inclined to associate primarily with gestures of rejection or contempt (spurning with one's foot, stamping in disapproval), may serve as receptor, as in the oriental gesture of 'kissing the feet'. But I confine myself here to examination of the use of the head and hands and features of these.

As a prime sensory centre the head may perhaps be expected to serve as a major medium for gestures of greeting and parting, which involve recognition of another person, usually by visual means. In fact some movement of the head, linked with eye movement, is a characteristic recognition and greeting signal in many societies, either with or without verbal utterance. Cultural nuances occur here. Commonly in western societies an upward nod is a recognition/greeting signal, whereas a downward nod is a signal of assent in reply to a question. And in some circles by convention an upward lift of both eyebrows is a recognition signal to someone in a crowd whereas a raised single eyebrow is a quizzical comment. But among Melanesians of the Solomons an upward lift of both eyebrows is a common sign of assent.[10] Generally, the greeting or parting function of the eyes is expressed by the *look*, which would seem to be produced primarily by subtle local muscle movements around the eye and not by the eye itself (cf. modern psychological studies by Michael Argyle and others on eye movement). Tears present a special problem. They may be associated with greeting and parting when emotions are deeply stirred. In western culture they are regarded as being spontaneously generated, though capable of control to some degree. (Is blinking 'to keep the tears back' a real check, or does it merely dissipate them?) But in some other societies, for example in Polynesia, tears as an accompaniment to weeping in many scenes of greeting and parting appear capable of being induced to a considerable degree. In any case, they hardly fall within the category of gesture.

Most features of head and face as well as eyes seem to have symbolic use in some cultural contexts as greeting and parting expressions. The values attached to hair are so explicit (cf. Leach, 1958; Hallpike, 1969) that one might expect to find it involved in some greeting and parting situations. In traditional Tikopia society, where men wore their hair long, it was usual for a man to remove his hair fillet when he entered the presence of his chief with a message, letting his hair hang loose. An interpretation of this might be that in contrast to having his hair bound up for work by removing the tie he was symbolizing the placing of himself at the disposal of his chief. This act, though incorporated in a greeting situation, was a symbol of status acknowledgement rather than a greeting symbol as such. But removal of facial hair, and in particular cutting of the hair of the head by men, was one of the traditional Tikopia symbols of mourning, a gesture of parting practised in former times when people left for a long absence abroad, and not only when they died. (Tikopia traditional custom contradicts Hallpike's idea (1969, pp. 260–1) that long hair is a symbol of being outside society.)

In Polynesian societies the nose is the main organ traditionally used in greeting, and this is even so nowadays, though 'nose rubbing' has been supplemented by the handclasp (Firth, 1969). The tongue seems an unlikely greeting medium apart from speech use. But putting out the tongue symbolically as a greeting gesture has been well authenticated for the Tibetans (apparently without aggressive significance), and for the Maori (as part of their aggressive greeting dances). Although the cheek is a relatively immobile part of the face it plays quite an important role as the site for delivery of a large proportion of kisses, and as a lip-substitute in cheek-to-cheek greeting gestures of familiarity which are not so intimate as to require use of the mouth. Only the ears, as far as I can judge, seem not to be involved symbolically in any greeting or parting gesture. Though not less mobile than the nose, and in modern civilized life far more involved in recognition of objects, their position at the sides of the head away from the eyes has seemed to disqualify human ears from any significant cultural use as greeting signals. (The ears of most animals seem to fill such a function much more directly.)

Apart from the importance of the mouth as a focus of interest for verbal greeting, its use in greeting gesture is twofold. In all human societies the curious gesture of drawing back the lips and baring the teeth – the smile – is one of the major signs of welcome. The significance of this in non-human primates has been extensively studied, and also in children. But as far as I known no systematic study has yet been undertaken of smiling by adults, in different cultural settings.[11] At a crude level of differentiation it seems clear that the baring of the teeth when they are tightly clenched is a sign of anger or other strain, not of pleasure, and it is an inference that smiling as a greeting may be related developmentally to baring of teeth in defence. It would seem also that the more subtle interpretation of the meaning of a smile demands attention to other muscular behaviour of the face – around the eyes, at the corners of the mouth – as well as to type of lip position and movement, and the degree to which the teeth are displayed. Subtle differences of this kind account in western society for our reading of mouth gestures as: the fixed smile, indicating stress or underlying unease; the secret smile, indicating private thoughts; the dubious smile, indicating only partial acceptance of what has been said; the sneering smile, indicating contempt; as well as the welcoming smile. It will probably be agreed by anthropologists that familiarity with people of alien cultures does allow them to interpret behavioural clues in such terms in all societies, though this is rather an article of faith than of demonstration. However, while greeting in the range of societies studied by anthropologists is probably by no means always expressed by smiling, the smile seems to be one of the most characteristic mouth-greeting signs in most if not all societies. Smiling in pleasure at greeting, crying in sadness at parting, would seem to be part of basic social demonstrative rituals.

Yet all mouth gestures are not universal. A type of gesture which is thoroughly built into the conventions of western society is the kiss. Primarily a lip gesture, the kiss is susceptible of a great many modifications. Linked with the sensitivity of lips is their function in erotic contact, which introduces a possible ambiguity into their use in gestures that are intended to signalize social but non-erotic greeting. It is presumably for this reason that while many non-western societies ignore the kiss as a conventional mode of greeting and confine themselves to its analogue in the lip-play of mother on babe, some, as in India, regard it with distaste and even treat it as immoral.[12] By contrast with the tender associations of the kiss in western eyes, reinforced by many literary references, may be cited counter-views such as that in Junod's report from the Thonga. Kissing was formerly unknown to them and laughing at Europeans the Thonga would say 'Look at these people! they suck each other! They eat each other's saliva and dirt!' (1927, vol. 1, p. 352). But even when established as a greeting, the kiss is subject to many variations. In England the normal convention over the last century has been that women kiss women, but men do not kiss men, except in intimate family circumstances as in greeting and parting between father and son – and even then it is optional. In circumstances of some familiarity, such as close kinship, men and women may greet one another by kissing; and both men and women may kiss young children, over a broader range of circumstances, with no prior tie at all (e.g. the classic 'kissing of babies' by parliamentary candidates). In the past the rules have been fairly clear, and at the periphery could be invoked to justify familiarity, as when a man might claim a kiss from a girl on the ground that she was a cousin. But in modern times these rules have been considerably relaxed. Kissing between men and women friends has become much more common, in line with the general relaxation of social norms in favour of individual freedom of action and less perturbation about possible erotic implications. In England the idea seems still to hold that except in special circumstances of family life kissing between men is a sign of effeminacy. But it is well recognized also that in some other European countries, for instance France and Russia, kissing between men is a definite part of social conventions of greeting, especially on public occasions.[13]

The kiss has various subtle modifications. An accompaniment to kissing in many social circumstances is the embrace by the arms, and it is the arm-breast contact rather than the lip-lip or lip-cheek contact that appears to be of major significance. The greeting-hug, not the greeting-kiss, seems to be the gesture that gives prime satisfaction to the participants and prime demonstration of amity to the public. The kiss itself presents several forms, graded roughly according to type of social relationship. Lovers (always) and spouses (mostly) greet each other with a lip-to-lip kiss which may vary in duration and intensity. Parents and children may greet lip-to-lip, but kinsmen and close friends usually greet lip-to-cheek – normally on one cheek, but sometimes on both if moved by affection or continental comparison. But while among members of the immediate family and close kin or friends the erotic implications of a kiss are expected to be absent or subliminal, they may have overt interpretation between people of more distant relationship. (I have noted a recent letter to an American newspaper in which a young woman asked for guidance – she had greeted her husband's father with a kiss on the cheek but he had insisted on a kiss on the lips, which shocked her.) So, in some circles there is a custom of what may be called cheek-to-cheek kissing – an embrace without use of mouth at all. This delicate gesture of greeting may have an emotional charge, but removed from the more erotic zones. In some sections of European continental society a still more delicate if more elaborate usage is that of a man taking a lady's hand and bringing it up before his lips as he bends over it. 'Kissing the hand' need not involve any actual contact of lip with hand, though the simulated gesture of brushing the lip over the lady's fingers can be made to serve a variety of purposes from respectful to erotic messages. A further simulacrum, in which the respect motif of greeting is uppermost, is the substitute for the actual kissing motion of a verbal statement of the 'I kiss your hand, Madame' type.[14]

It would seem that the significance of the lips as erogenous zones has given kissing a kind of danger-quality as a greeting. It is regarded as a form of greeting in western society for which above all permission may have to be asked. To kiss someone is held to be an intrusion on the personality more intimate than that of any other form of greeting. ('May I shake your hand?' is a more frank respect signal, but my impression is that there is a rather formal literary quality about it.) So, kissing on special occasions, such as birthday or wedding, or in congratulations for some honour gained, takes on a special quality of exchange of personalities, in which the sub-erotic qualities of the lip-contact may be a significant component.[15] So too, granted that in western society kissing is an acceptable form of greeting between given categories of persons, a number of associated patterns have been developed to mitigate its side-effects and reduce to a minimum any suggestions of erotic elements in the exchange. What is of particular interest here is the way in which western societies are prepared to skate upon thin ice in juxtaposing so closely an erotic and a merely social gesture, while most other societies seem to have avoided this problem.

In some circumstances a kiss is a respect signal rather than a greeting signal. Such instances as kissing a bishop's ring, kissing the toe of St Peter's statue in Rome, 'kissing hands' of the sovereign before taking up a diplomatic appointment, exemplify this. But the gesture also conveys a sense of greater intimacy than others – some elements of self-involvement of an emotional kind in the relationship. The point here is that the involvement is one way; the gesture in such contexts is not a reciprocal one, hence the emphasis is on respect rather than on greeting as such. It is from this point of view that the most notorious kiss in history – or mythology – that of Judas, carries its shock effect: the gesture of respect shown in the kiss, and shown intimately, was incompatible with the repudiation of respect and of intimacy shown in the betrayal. Incidentally, this example demonstrates a significant function of the kiss in some circumstances – that of being a marker of social position. A critical social indicator may be provided by who in a group is greeted in this way.

Comparable in mobility with the mouth as a greeting instrument is the hand with the arm. Here too considerable variety of gesture is shown, both cross-culturally and in any single society. Broadly, greeting and parting gestures may be conveyed by salutation with one hand, by joining one's hands, or by joining hands with the other party. Here avoidance of physical contact between the parties in the one case and seeking it in the other may be symptomatic of deeper attitudes about the nature of personality and the degree to which it can be compromised or reinforced by intrusion of another personality upon it. One-handed greeting may be made with open or closed fist. In the west we regard the clenched fist as primarily a sign of aggression and defiance, and it has been conventionalized into a communist greeting on such a basis. But in Northern Nigeria it has been used as an ordinary greeting, devoid of any such aggressive significance; it is a token of amity (Firth, 1963,

p. 23). Open-handed salutation may vary from the casual wave of greeting to a passing acquaintance or the more regular flapping of an uplifted wrist in farewell, to the precise military salute. The last in particular is formalized, and designed to indicate and support differences in rank.

Traditionally, in the east, a person has joined his own hands in greeting, either clasped in front of him in Chinese style, or set palm to palm in front of the face, as in India and many parts of Southeast Asia. In some of these societies the height at which the hands are held or to which they are raised is a measure of the social status of the person greeted – another of the simple physical indices that can be made to be of great symbolic importance. In the west tradition has been for each person to proffer a hand to the other, and the greeting to consist of a handclasp or handshake. A variant of this may be 'hand-joining', with both parties using two hands, one (normally the junior) placing his hands palm to palm within the similarly held hands of the other. In Malaya, for instance, such hand-joining has rules governing who, according to sex, age, and difference of rank, may properly join hands with whom. Only elderly women, not young women, should traditionally join hands with men, in respect and motherly or sisterly affection, and by custom a clean layer of cloth should be placed between the hands (Zainal-'Abidin, 1950, p. 47). Another form of two-handed salutation, clapping, is significant partly because it is commonly non-reciprocal (though there are exceptions to this) and partly because, as a form of percussion, it is one of the simplest accessories to bodily movement in a field that uses a variety of noise-making instruments of salutation (cf. Needham, 1967).

Some societies have used the single handclasp as a greeting. Rattray has noted that handshaking as a salutation appears to have been an Ashanti custom before the advent of Europeans. In such cases hand must lock in hand – 'five must lie within five' was the Ashanti way of expressing the full grasp; to give the tips of the fingers only was discourteous (Rattray, 1916,

HAND JOINING

CLAPPING

p. 43; 1929, p. 103). Where the handclasp has been in vogue, it has been customary to use the right hand only; the left hand, especially in oriental countries, has often been associated with the toilet and is unclean. But a diversion may mark a special type of social relationship, as with the Ogboni of the Yoruba who, according to Ajisafe (1924, p. 91) use the left hand 'in a peculiar way known only to members of the cult' (cf. the handshake of boy scouts). But the handshake has been the traditional greeting of western countries par excellence. With the spread of western habits handshaking has now become very general, having been adopted in the course of the present century by many societies in which it was formerly unknown. But its introduction has sometimes been cautious, because of other possible ritual values involved. Junod has recorded how among the Thonga to shake hands with a chief was formerly taboo, the idea being that he was a person with ritual quality, with whose body contact was dangerous. But even forty years ago Junod noted that the ruler Muhlaba, on the adoption of Christianity, was somewhat reluctantly accepting the hands held out to him by the most modest of his subjects, even by children, on Christmas Day (Junod, 1927, vol. 1, p. 383). That the handshake as a formal greeting gesture is linked with status concepts can be seen from the circumstances in which it is omitted for some persons while given to others in greeting.

GENERAL OBSERVATIONS

Greeting and parting behaviour is often treated as if it were a spontaneous emotional reaction to the coming together or separation of people, carrying overtly its own social message. But sociological observation suggests, especially from cross-cultural study, that for the most part it is highly conventionalized, and that the conventions are apt to be culture-specific, not universals. In a broad sense greeting and parting behaviour may be termed *ritual* since it follows *patterned routines*; it is a system of *signs* that convey other than overt messages; it is *sanctioned* by strong expressions of moral approval; and it has *adaptive value* in facilitating social relations.

But though human societies show a wide range of variation in greeting and parting behaviour, everywhere they tend to use a comparatively small set of basic materials for the purpose. Ancillary cultural instruments are involved – articles of dress such as hats or gloves, gift articles such as scarves or greeting cards, noise producers such as guns for firing salutes, green branches or flags to provide visual signals. But for the most part these are extensions of the individual's physical apparatus, his body, organs, and limbs; to supplement his waving and shouting, the alteration of his features and his getting up and sitting down. This instrumental use of the human body, with its attachments, for social purposes emphasizes the way in which greeting and parting procedures fit into the establishment and maintenance of working social relationships. They help to insinuate new individuals into social situations, and fill the gap when known individuals depart. At the same time small differences in procedure, standardized, are made to serve as carriers of significant social features.

In greeting and parting behaviour I see three major social themes, each connected with the concept of personality. The first theme is that of *attention-producing*: a primary object of much greeting activity is often the attraction of the attention of another party – by directed glance or out-thrust hand if close by, or by oscillation of the hand (waving) if at a distance. Behaviour at parting is often also initially directed at attracting the attention of the person who is leaving. One object of greeting and parting ritual is that of focusing attention on the personality of each participant, of giving an appropriate sign that further communication is wanted. A second theme is that of *identification*. The people concerned want to be differentiated as persons individually entering into or continuing the social relationship. One function of much greeting and parting behaviour is in providing a framework within which individuals can identify each other as preliminary to further action. A third theme is that of *reduction of uncertainty*, or anxiety, in social contact. This operates particularly between persons not previously known to each other. Confrontation without communication is threatening, and even the most casual greeting gesture tends to remove an element of uncertainty from the encounter. To nod to or say a brief word to a stranger met on the road may not be just a token of friendliness; it puts him in a social context, and his reply establishes him as not primarily aggressive. Salutation at parting serves in parallel fashion to put a definite point to the departure, to establish the severance as a social fact and not to leave it hanging, so to speak, in the air as an unresolved issue.

Such human behaviour has clear analogy with ritualization behaviour in animals. With animals social identification is linked directly with personal security. The kind of contact that is made, often experimentally, has the function of establishing the freedom of the individual from immediate danger. By visual, aural, tactile, and olfactory means animals establish identity and social relationships. Human beings do not use the physical range of the senses so acutely or so widely – smell is rarely used in greeting behaviour, though sometimes it is discriminatory – but the use of bodily means of establishing relationship is common among humans. *Touching* – by hands, lips, noses – in such context is most marked, and is directly relatable to animal behaviour. (The significance of touching the other person by handshake would seem to lie not in immobilizing the other person's armament, as a popular interpretation would have it, but in indirectly creating a symbolic bond between the parties.)

But an important element in much greeting and parting ritual of human beings is that of status demonstration. Relative posture and gesture, especially as displayed in degree of bodily elevation, are used widely to indicate symbolically the relative status of the parties engaged. I would argue that a basic function of greeting and parting rituals is in creating occasion for establishment of relative status positions, or in providing a code (a 'vocabulary') in which status relations can be expressed. These rituals too may provide conditions for exploration or assertion of changing status. What is of special interest here is how certain simple physical actions involving the body as a whole are given symbolic significance. Forms of greeting or parting in which a person lowers himself, sets himself at a distance, or removes articles of clothing all indicate relative inferior status. The visible lowering, distancing, or stripping of the body, all acts that may leave the individual relatively unprotected, emphasize by contrast the other personality, which is protected by height, distance, and covering. So, social inferiority is expressed symbolically by a simulacrum of physical defencelessness. Analogies with animal behaviour in such status demonstration, which involves a repudiation of aggressive actions, are not hard to find.

However, the analogies between man and other animals must not be pushed too far in the greeting and parting field, as some anthropologists know (see Leach, 1966; Benedict, 1969). Apart from the immeasurably greater flexibility that human speech introduces into the operations generally, the specifications of identity by the use of personal names is absent with animals. Thus the possibility of manipulating these descriptive labels gives a totally different dimension to human greeting rituals. Again, the known aspects of human conceptualization of time period give a quality to parting ritual that animals apparently largely lack. The ability of an animal to differentiate the *length of time* during which another is absent seems fairly limited. Human parting conceptualizes a future with a time scale and the ritual is modified accordingly. Whereas animal greeting rituals are vital on personal security grounds, their parting rituals seem empirically scant and theoretically would appear less significant since, apart from care for the young, separation need not necessarily involve a threat to an animal's security. Human greeting and parting rituals seem to have developed other special features too: the use of intermediaries to provide introduction; the separation of formal from informal roles; the adoption of representative status, so that a person may be greeted or farewelled not for his own sake but as the symbol of a group of others not present.

Finally, a feature that marks off human greeting and parting rituals from animal behaviour patterns, in degree if not in kind, is the relative ease with which the former may change. There is something of a paradox here. Conventional forms of greeting and parting operate within fairly narrow limits in any one society at any given period, and are regarded as of high significance. Failure to give the 'correct' greeting or parting signals is usually regarded with strong disapproval, even as insulting to the party whose status has been apparently impugned. Lucy Mair has reported from her experience among the Ganda thirty years or so ago that children began to be taught phrases of greeting and farewell almost before they could speak and were drilled in the correct gestures – to kneel and put their hands between those of the stranger. 'Refusal to do this is one of the few reasons for which I have seen a child beaten' (Mair, 1934, p. 65).

Yet despite the moral sanctions in vogue for carrying out the 'correct' behaviour it is remarkable how easily these patterns can alter. The more elaborate formal procedures of many African and Asiatic societies have tended to be given up in modern times as familiarity with western patterns has permeated these societies; in particular the handshake between persons of all grades has been added to or superseded the traditional greeting gesture. The verbal forms of greeting or farewell have also been modified, as I have demonstrated for the Malays and the Tikopia. A significant point here is the seeming ease of change, for in most cases very little resentment of supersession of old forms seems to have developed. The primary element in facilitating such change appears to have been status considerations. As a rule adoption of the new forms of greeting has been credited with the prestige of association with a larger social universe, or alternatively has been stimulated by the wish to develop patterns of equal weight, such as Muslim

parallels to Christian forms. What stands out is that greeting
and farewell patterns tend to be modified or superseded by
others rather than just abandoned – it may not be important
what forms are used, but it is essential for social relationships
that *some* forms are used.

NOTES

1. I am indebted for facilities in the preparation of this essay to
the Department of Anthropology, University of Hawaii, where I
was visiting professor of Pacific Anthropology for 1968-9. Some of
the illustrative material is drawn from the Human Relations Area
Files in the Library of the University, to which I am indebted for
access.

2. An example of contrast in greeting custom is given by the
Maori of New Zealand. 'Where we sedately shake hands with a
party of guests on their arrival the Maori chanted rhythmic refrains
to them, accompanied by vigorous and equally rhythmic action;
this as a welcome. Women waved branches and garments; men
threw down a spear like a gauntlet and danced the warlike *haka*'
(Best, 1952, p. 144). The challenging aspect of Maori public greeting is such that 'it has been said of the Maori that his mode of
welcoming guests is to throw sticks at them and thrust out his
tongue' (Downs, 1929, p. 123). In modern times such formal greeting
challenges have persisted, as attested by many photographs.

3. The word *aue* is also used for giving thanks, but with different
intonation and stress.

4. Particularly puzzling to people of other countries is the English
convention of use of first name in a title of knighthood. 'Sir Brown'
seems to be regarded often as more appropriate than 'Sir John',
which seems too familiar.

5. Correspondence in *The Times* of March 1968 expressed some
of these difficulties. Some correspondents stressed the propriety of
use of surnames in administrative and professional circles, and found
Christian names and 'mistering' alike ill-bred, even between old
friends. Others, presumably a younger set, found surnames un-
adorned by either Mr or first name too familiar, even 'a relic of
serfdom', though they were divided as to what an acceptable form
of address should be.

6. Some analysis of the complexities of Javanese usage, even
between members of the same community, is given by Robert R.

Jay, in a section on 'Language as Gestures of Situational Rank' (Jay, 1969, pp. 240–6).

7. Work by Birdwhistell, Critchley, Efron, and Hall, for example, has established many of the general principles involved, but much investigation of the social aspects still remains to be done (cf. Benedict, 1969; Firth, 1969; Leach, 1966).

8. Instances are given in my discussion of postures and gestures of respect (Firth, 1969). An interesting description of body-lowering in greeting in Korea is provided by Osgood (1951, pp. 107–8).

9. Clasping to the breast is common as a greeting in many societies. Slapping one's own buttock or right thigh was formerly a greeting custom among the Yao of Central Africa (Stannus, 1910, p. 291). Patting the buttock of a man one is hugging in greeting has been a practice in parts of the New Guinea Highlands, as I have seen myself (in 1951).

10. The wink, a lowering of one eyelid, is a wordless gesture directed at a person to indicate a familiar relationship of complicity. It may be used in greeting, especially where a more formal action might disturb a gathering.

Charles Darwin studied such behaviour of nodding and face movement in terms of signs of affirmation or negation, and concluded that despite some cultural variation the forms were too general to be regarded 'as altogether conventional or artificial'. But he was looking for innate responses (Darwin, 1872, pp. 274–7).

11. Darwin's classic study of laughter and smiling is physiologically oriented and uses only random cultural illustration (1872, pp. 204–15).

12. It appears that in India censors have been required to cut kissing scenes from films for local distribution. A report from Bombay rather maliciously stated that the censors faced 'a monumental challenge' from a documentary film prepared to show the origin, practice, and social implications of kissing in various world communities, and 'being highly exploited for its so-called erotic values' (*Honolulu Star-Bulletin*, 19 October 1968).

13. In January 1969 Communist Party leader Leonid Brezhnev was reported to have 'greeted each of the [Russian] cosmonauts with a bear hug and a kiss' after their arrival from the space-centre on completion of their earth-orbit transfer feat.

14. At a Honolulu opera festival reception for the stars of *Turandot* the visiting Italian tenor, from La Scala, kissed the ladies' hands as he was introduced. Said one gratified lady 'Nobody's

kissed my hand in a long time' (*Honolulu Star-Bulletin*, 20 January 1969).

15. The familiarity of the gesture, ordinarily reserved in western society for people of close acquaintance, may also be a compliment, implying metaphorically that the recipient of the kiss is worthy of inclusion in the circle. When the kiss is administered by a young person publicly to an older one there may be an element of sex-vanity stirred in the recipient. In Hawaii the custom has developed of greeting visitors with a *lei* and a kiss. At a luncheon in Honolulu for wives of members attending an International Association of Police Chiefs conference, four police cadets were on duty distri-buting flower *lei*s. Each woman guest – about a thousand in all– received a kiss with her *lei* and the greeting '*aloha* Ma'am' (*aloha* – sympathy, affection, love). The kissing was treated in a joking way as part of the official greeting, but appeared to be very acceptable (*Honolulu Star-Bulletin*, 8 October 1968).

REFERENCES

AIYAPPAN, A. 1937. *Physical and Social Anthropology of the Nayadis of Malabar*. Madras Government Museum Bulletin (ns; gs) **2** (4).

AJISAFE, A. K. 1924. *The Laws and Customs of the Yoruba People*. London: George Routledge.

BENEDICT, B. 1969. Role Analysis in Animals and Men. *Man* **4**: 203–14.

BEST, E. 1952. *The Maori as He Was*. (1st edn. 1924.) Wellington, NZ: R. E. Owen, Government Printer.

BIRDWHISTELL, R. 1952. *Introduction to Kinesics*. Louisville: University of Louisville Press. London: Allen Lane, 1971.

CORMACK, J. G. 1935. *Everyday Customs in China*. Edinburgh: Moray Press.

CRITCHLEY, M. 1939. *The Language of Gesture*. London: Edward Arnold.

DANTON, G. H. 1938. *The Chinese People: New Problems and Old Backgrounds*. Boston: Marshall Hones.

DARWIN, C. 1872. *The Expression of the Emotions in Man and Animals*. London: John Murray.

DOWNS, T. W. 1929. Maori Etiquette. *Journal of the Polynesian Society* **38**: 148–68.

EFRON, D. 1941. *Gesture and Environment*. New York: King's Crown Press.

FIRTH, R. 1963. *Elements of Social Organization.* (1st edn. 1951.) London: Watts; Boston: Beacon Press.

FIRTH, R. 1969. Postures and Gestures of Respect. In Maranda, P. & Pouillon, J. (eds.), *Exchange and Communication: Mélanges Lévi-Strauss*, pp. 230–54. Hague: Mouton.

HALL, E. T. 1961. *The Silent Language.* (1st edn. 1951.) Greenwich, Conn.: Fawcett Publications.

HALLPIKE, C. R. 1969. Social Hair. *Man* **4**: 256–64.

JAY, R. R. 1969. *Javanese Villagers: Social Relations in Rural Modjokuto.* Cambridge, Mass.: MIT Press.

JENNESS, D. 1964. *The People of the Twilight.* (1st edn. 1928.) Chicago: University of Chicago Press.

JUNOD, H. A. 1927. *The Life of a South African Tribe.* 2 vols. London: Macmillan.

LEACH, E. R. 1958. Magical Hair. *Journal Royal Anthropological Institute* **88**: 147–64.

LEACH, E. R. 1966. Ritualization in man in relation to conceptual and social development. In Huxley, Sir Julian (ed.), A Discussion on Ritualization of Behaviour in Animals and Man. *Philosophical Transactions of the Royal Society*, Series B, **251**: 249–526.

MAIR, L. P. 1934. *An African People in the Twentieth Century.* London: Routledge.

MALLORY, W. H. 1926. *China: Land of Famine.* American Geographical Society Special Publication no. 6. New York.

MANGIN, E. 1921. *Les Mossi.* Paris: Augustin Challamel.

MERLEAU-PONTY, M. 1964. Indirect Language and the Voices of Silence. In *Signs* (trans. Richard C. McCleary). Evanston: Northwestern University Press.

NADEL, S. F. 1942. *A Black Byzantium: The Kingdom of Nupe in Nigeria.* London: Oxford University Press.

NEEDHAM, R. 1967. Percussion and Transition. *Man* **2**: 606–14.

OSGOOD, C. 1951. *The Koreans and Their Culture.* New York: Ronald Press.

PARSONS, E. C. 1916. Holding Back in Crisis Ceremonialism. *American Anthropologist* **18**: 41–52.

RADCLIFFE-BROWN, A. R. 1964. *The Andaman Islanders.* (1st edn. 1922.) N.Y.: Free Press of Glencoe; London: Collier-Macmillan.

RATTRAY, R. S. 1916. *Ashanti Proverbs (The Primitive Ethics of a Savage People).* Oxford: Clarendon Press.

RATTRAY, R. S. 1929. *Ashanti Law and Constitution.* Oxford: Clarendon Press.

SMITH, E. W. & DALE, A. M. 1920. *The Ila-Speaking Peoples of Northern Rhodesia*. 2 vols. London: Macmillan.

STANNUS, H. S. 1910. Notes on Some Tribes of British Central Africa. *Journal Royal Anthropological Institute* **40**: 285–335.

ZAINAL-'ABIDIN bin AHMAD. 1950. Malay Manners and Etiquette. *Journal Royal Asiatic Society Malayan Branch* **23**: 43–74.

'Greeting', 'begging', and the presentation of respect

ESTHER GOODY

Ritual has recently been described as that aspect of customary behaviour that makes statements about the hierarchical relations between people (Leach, 1968). This is vividly delineated in Audrey Richards's account of the *chisungu* ceremonies among the Bemba (1956). Her monograph is one of the very few that succeed in conveying the preoccupation with respect for authority that is so striking in the day-to-day life of certain African societies. Throughout, the *chisungu* rituals emphasize the importance of respecting chiefs, elders, the mistress-of-ceremonies, all those older than the initiates, and especially their betrothed husbands. This is done explicitly in the oft-repeated song which proclaims 'the arm-pit is not higher than the shoulder' (precedence is established at birth and not to be challenged). It is done through the miming of respect to seniors in the presenting of food and other offerings which occurs throughout the ceremonies. And one of the night-long rituals involves teasing the initiates until they weep, to make them show their respect for authority. Quite apart from those aspects of the rites themselves which focus concern on respect, there are many nuances of address, clothing, the manner in which food is proffered, greeting postures, and dance that implicitly re-affirm its importance.

This essay considers Dr Richards's theme of the ritual expression of respect, for another African society, and endeavours to show both the forms in which it occurs, and the ways in which prestations of respect can be utilized in order to emphasize or to manipulate status differences. As in our own society, to greet is to present one's respects.

In West Africa the English words 'greet' and 'beg' are among the commonest one hears and have a much wider range of meaning than they do among other English speakers. This reflects a usage embedded in the local languages and part of a total complex of communicative acts that include both verbal and kinesic behaviour.[1] For here as elsewhere the phrases of greeting are often accompanied by physical movements, such as offering the hand, kissing the cheek, or bending the knee.

Why is it that West Africans use the term 'greet' and 'beg' in such a wide range of contexts? To answer this question I want to examine the ethnography of greeting behaviour in a particular society, the Gonja of northern Gonja.

There are three general functions attached to 'greeting' in Gonja. First, it is used to open a sequence of communicative acts between two persons, irrespective of their positions. Second, it is a means of defining, and affirming, both identity and rank. And third, because the standardized forms of greeting contain an element of deference which is status enhancing, 'greeting' becomes a mode of entering upon or manipulating a relationship in order to achieve a specific result.

The second and third functions are enhanced by the fact that greeting behaviour indicates status in three main ways. First, there are the generalized aspects concerned with the initiation of communication, and the pose adopted. In Gonja it is the inferior who initiates and the superior who replies. As for the pose, it is the inferior who always places himself in a lower position (physical space thus reflecting differential status) or who removes an article of clothing (e.g. a hat). Moreover, in order to place himself in this pose it is the inferior who moves towards, or into the presence of, the superior. The tone of voice in which a greeting is made can also indicate the nature of the relationship and of the communicative act involved, as for instance when a supplicant adopts a wheedling tone.

Second, the verbal aspect of greeting often contains a designation of the person addressed: a role indicator of either a general or a specific kind. In English we may attach a variety of such words – 'father', 'sir', 'my lord'. In stratified societies such role indicators also reflect status in the hierarchical sense and may be very numerous. To know how to use them becomes in itself an accomplishment.

The manipulation of forms of greeting may lie in the crude use of an indicator to bring about the desired result. In patrilineal areas of Ghana one may find oneself addressed as 'mother's brother' to elicit bountiful behaviour. Or a man may be addressed by a rank superior to that he possesses (a common way in many areas of mollifying the police). Again, by repetition of the rank or title, one is praising the recipient.[2]

However, it is the central contention of this paper that in a society like that of Gonja, where greeting has been institutionalized as a way of affirming status, the proffering or withholding of greeting is in itself manipulative. Specifically, assiduous greeting exerts a coercive effect in circumstances where claims cannot be pressed on the basis of kinship. I suggest that it is for this reason that greeting and begging are so closely linked in West Africa.

In this paper I want to indicate how greeting in Gonja performs these various functions. In non-centralized societies, on the other hand, its functions are more restricted, and in conclusion I shall briefly consider patterns of greeting in acephalous LoDagaa society. Such a comparison suggests some of the conditions that may be generally associated with elaborate institutionalization of greeting.

The state of Gonja stretches across the width of northern Ghana immediately above the border with Ashanti. It is a large (15,000 square miles), sprawling, loosely federated collection of internally autonomous divisions, each of which is ruled by a hierarchy of chiefs belonging to two or three dynastic segments, which claim descent from the Mande conqueror, NdeWura Jakpa. There is a paramount chief, the YagbumWura, chosen

in turn from the heads of the eligible divisions, but his capital
is remote and his office has probably always been of relatively
minor importance. Despite this, the fact that the paramountcy
circulates among the divisions has maintained the idea of a
unitary ruling estate, the Ngbanya. According to the myth of
the founding of Gonja, NdeWura Jakpa was accompanied by a
wise and powerful Muslim, Fati Murukpe, whose descendants,
the Sakparebi, have important positions in the divisional
courts as advisers and religious officials. Many other Muslim
groups are also found within the state, some of whom were there
before the Ngbanya conquerors arrived, and some of whom have
come since, usually as traders. Collectively these Muslims are
referred to as Nkaramo, and they constitute the Muslim estate.
The commoner estate provides an even more heterogeneous
element of Gonja society. For included among the autochthonous groups are Akan, Guang, Gur, and Mole-Dagbane speakers,
as well as the Mper whose language is probably best assigned
to the class of Togo remnant languages designated by Wester-
man & Bryan (1952, p. 96). In all some thirteen dialect groups
are represented among these 'old commoners' (*Ngbanyamase*).
More recently the Lobi on the west and the Konkomba on the
east, as well as refugee Akan peoples have entered Gonjaland.
All these groups subsist by hunting, fishing, and farming, as
indeed do the Muslim and ruling estates also.[3]

THE FORMS OF GREETING

How to greet, when to greet, and whom to greet are among the
very first lessons the novice ethnographer must learn in Gonja.
Forms of address and salutation are fairly readily grasped, as is
the etiquette of taking a small gift when greeting an important
person, and of receiving chickens of all colours and sizes, and
innumerable eggs, in return. Less readily understood is the fact
that both gift and return gift are *katchoro* (*gbanyito* thanks,
greeting) as are the verbal formulae that accompany them. And
only gradually does one become aware of other contexts for,
and implications of, the greeting idiom.

The following paradigm is an attempt to set out systematically the wide variety of forms in which greeting behaviour occurs. The left-hand column lists the three broad categories of behaviour included by the Gonja as 'greeting': verbal salutations; physical gestures and movement; and prestations. The centre column differentiates each of these three categories of behaviour into the major types recognizable to both actors and observer. Essentially, however, this is a series of analytical distinctions. The final column lists the specific forms: actions, objects, and occasions appropriate to these analytic categories. At this stage the reader will probably find this last column a confusing welter of detail. It is to the discussion of such detail, however, that the body of the paper necessarily pertains, and consideration of the right-hand column of the paradigm may prove more rewarding once he has followed this discussion.

The paradigm also sets out the verbal, physical, and prestation aspects of begging as it occurs in Gonja. The same framework is then used for LoDagaa greeting and begging forms to allow for comparison in the concluding section of the analysis.

Paradigm for the analysis of greeting and begging behaviour: Gonja and LoDagaa

I GONJA (CENTRALIZED)
A Meanings of 'greet' (Gonja *choro,* noun form, *kachoro*)

Category	Type	Form
Verbal behaviour	(a) form of address	(i) kin terms
		(ii) greeting titles, *adilibi*; these vary with estate and status
	(b) topical salutations	(i) time of day
		(ii) activity
		(iii) weather
		(iv) health
		(v) special occasions
	(c) thanks	(i) 'thanks for service/gift', *ansa ni kushung* (lit. greetings for work)
		(ii) 'thank you', *me choro* (literally I greet) or *ansa ni kushung*
		(iii) 'thank you very much!' *me choro fo ga!* (literally I greet you very much!)

cont'd

Category	Type	Form
Physical behaviour	(a) abasement gestures	(i) removing hat (ii) crouching (iii) kneeling (iv) clapping hands (v) lying down: on left side (men) on right side (women)
	(b) approach pattern (visits within the community)	(i) morning and evening greetings: junior goes to senior kin (ii) twice weekly greeting of chief by minor chiefs and elders: subordinates to superior (iii) to convey information (iv) during *rites de passage* (v) on special occasions in ritual and political calendar (vi) to express thanks (vii) to seek favour(s)
	(c) visits (between communities)	as (b) (iii), (iv), (v), (vi), and (vii) apart from those depending on close proximity, that is, greeting visits occur on same occasions between as within communities
Prestations	(a) gift of object	(i) kola nuts (*kapushi*) (ii) millet beer, palm wine (iii) local gin (iv) bush meat (v) money (*kapushi*) (vi) gown, cloth, gun (vii) horse (rare)
	(b) gift of person	(i) wife (now rare)
	(c) gift of service	(i) token services, especially sweeping (*fege*) at Fire festival (ii) cooking, dancing, etc. at *rites de passage*
	(d) gift of respect	'greeting' in any of its forms
	(e) counter prestation (usually delayed) = thanks, *katchoro*	of form appropriate to the original prestation, but not necessarily in same medium; may be kola, beer, money, cloth, service, or in form of greetings; the last is particularly characteristic of concluding phase of *rites de passage*

B Meanings of 'beg' (Gonja *kule*)

Category	Type	Form
Verbal behaviour	prayer	opening phrase of public prayers is *an kul Ebori* (we beg God) repeated several times (to pray to God is *bu bori*)
	request for small favour	can use either verb for 'beg' (*kule*) or 'give' (*sa*); not formalized
	request for permission to leave a gathering, to go on trip	addressed to superior, or as courtesy to peers, *n kule ekpa*, 'I beg the path'
	request for services	e.g. reciprocal farm clearing, *ndɔ kule* 'farm (work) begging'
	entrust with commission	to send a message, ask that someone going on trip, visit, do a favour for one; verb 'beg' used with indirect object *n kule mu esako*; rendered literally by English speakers as 'I will message him to someone'
	request for major favour	never only verbal – must be in association with other forms of pressing claim (except for claims on kin of same or junior generation)
Physical behaviour	hand supplication	placing right hand, palm upwards, in open palm of left hand; accompanies verbal request among some sub-groups; used throughout Ghana in 'begging' (hitching) a lift from passing car or lorry; to proffer right hand is respectful, the left insulting
	repeated visits, or visits late at night	'greeting to beg' (*choro n' kule*) establishes respect debt against which to claim a favour of service; employed for major requests (implies other physical aspects of formal greeting; abasement gestures, approach pattern, etc.)
Prestations	small gifts	*kapushi* (kola nuts) or *kachoro* (greetings); may in fact be kola, beer, or bush meat; on occasion of morning or evening greeting, to seek small favour, to build up major respect debt over time

cont'd

Category	Type	Form
	gift preceding removal of bride	*kapushi kudu anyo* (12 kola nuts). 12 kola and 12 shillings: legitimates marriage and formally establishes in-law relationship.
	regular morning and evening greetings	*katchoro* (greeting) based on pattern of daily greeting of junior to senior kin; over time assimilates the relationship to a kin link; done in order to 'show respect' so that later claim will be honoured, i.e. establishes respect debt; typical of a would-be son-in-law or apprentice.
	large gift plus greeting	*choro n' kule* (greet and beg), done when seeking major favour from a senior man or a chief

II LODAGAA (ACEPHALOUS)

A Meanings of 'greet' (LoDagaa *puru*)

Category	Type	Form
Verbal behaviour	(a) form of address	(i) kin terms
	(b) topical salutations	(i) time of day (ii) activities (iii) weather
Physical behaviour	none	
Prestations	none	

B Meanings of 'beg' (LoDagaa *zele*)

Category	Type	Form
Verbal behaviour	none	
Physical behaviour	none	
Prestations	gift of service	'begging by farming', *kob zele* (literally farm begging), to gain right to remove bride to husband's house

J. R. Goody (1956) notes that begging is largely limited to *kob zele* because most requests are based on kinship obligations, and thus not considered *zele*.

VERBAL GREETINGS: SALUTATIONS AND THANKS

Malinowski described greetings and similar phrases as 'phatic communion'; as setting the tone for communication but having no cognitive content (1927, pp. 313–16). He was thinking, presumably, of the literal implications of the words contained in such phrases as 'so long' and 'how do you do?' The verbal salutations exchanged by Gonja on meeting are highly formalized and also carry primarily phatic content. Verbal salutations, apart from forms of address, fall into five classes. First there are specific forms appropriate to the time of day. These are the same throughout Gonja, and are the single most common greetings heard within the family and the village; they are strictly the equivalent of 'good morning', 'good afternoon', and 'good evening'. Next are three open sets of salutations that refer respectively to activities, to the weather, and to the health of friends and relations. Here, although there is slightly more content, the actual information that can pass is minimal, for the statement or question is standardized, as is the reply. Finally, there are a number of festivals during the year for which special salutations are exchanged. There is also a general form common to all such occasions, which says literally 'our year has come (round)' *amba kafe-a* (i.e. a year has passed since we last celebrated this festival).

As a group I refer to these as topical salutations because they reflect the particular circumstances relevant to the meeting being acknowledged.[4] All topical salutations are exchanged between those living in the same community and, except for inquiries about absent people, are used by those living in a single household. However, all these forms also make up elements of the prolonged, and highly formalized, verbal greetings required when someone arrives from some distance away.

Malinowski would not have been surprised to learn that in Gonja a single answer can suffice for all these salutations: *awo* 'it is cool'. This is the equivalent of 'all right', 'fine', 'ok'.[5] Some salutations can also be responded to by *alanfia* (literally 'healthy', 'health', meaning 'it is well', or 'we are well'). Clearly, if all these questions receive the same answer, the amount of information conveyed cannot be very great. The salutation is rather a declaration of sympathetic interest, and as such receives a friendly, but 'empty' reply.

The salutation 'greetings for your work!' (*ansa ni kushung*) has also the wider meaning of thanks for a service or for a gift. Although this form is available for the expression of gratitude, it is not often used. The Gonja are more likely to thank later with actions, either greeting by visits, as described below, or with prestations, both of which are included in the meaning of the word *choro*. It is in this context that one must view the alternative verbal formula for thanks, *me choro* (I greet/thank) or, to indicate effusive gratitude, *me choro fo ga!* (I greet/thank you very much!).

ABASEMENT GESTURES AND APPROACH PATTERN: THE
PHYSICAL DIMENSION OF GREETING AND THE RANKING
FUNCTION

Even the briefest discussion of topical salutations, however, immediately leads beyond the realm of phatic communion. The single most important duty of every child is to be respectful to his elders. This means many things, obedience above all, but also the inhibition of aggression in word and act, and respectful, deferential attendance on those senior in generation or office. Within the domestic family and close proximate kin the tendering of respect takes the form of obligatory morning and evening greetings that combine salutations and abasement gestures, and the approach of the junior to the senior.

Children must (even as adults) greet parents and grand-parents, wives must greet husband, his brothers, and his parents. In each case the junior goes to the senior, crouches by the open door of his room, offers the appropriate salutation, receives any instructions for the day, and slips quietly away. This greeting is not simply empty form; it conveys respect of junior to senior, and it expresses subordinate/superordinate status relations. The junior comes *to* his senior; *he* crouches, *he* initiates the greeting rite and may receive instructions, ask a favour, or report some occurrence. This is an example, in its simplest form, of the ranking function of greeting. That is, the institutionalization of greeting ritual in such a way that its participants act out their respective and unequal statuses. And the combination of obligation to greet with institutionalized deference re-enforces this ranking effect.

Daily greetings are only obligatory within the household and between close kin. But twice weekly, on Monday and Friday, the sub-chiefs and elders must greet the town chief in the morning and again in the evening. This is a formal occasion, the chiefs assemble outside, and then led by the spokesman, file into the council hall and sit down in order of precedence. When all are settled, they remove their hats and prostrate themselves before the chief, lying on their left sides, left arms extended, greeting with one voice. The chief responds through his spokesman (*dogte*) and the elders and sub-chiefs return to a sitting position. Now the business of the morning can begin. Here again, obligation to greet and institutionalized deference have the effect of expressing, of acting out, status differences between the town, divisional, or paramount chief and his sub-chiefs on the one hand, and among the sub-chiefs who are seated in order of precedence on the other. In greeting the town chief, the sub-chiefs literally present their respect(s), and thus express their subordination.

The ranking function of greeting is not, however, restricted to relations within the family and between officeholders. Daily life in the village constantly provides further examples. When two people meet on a path, the junior stoops, knees slightly bent, and offers a short greeting to which the other briefly replies before both pass on. A woman returning from the waterside with a heavy calabash on her head may make a verbal greeting only, if it is a young or unimportant man she passes. But should she meet her husband, or a chief, a woman will remove her burden and crouch beside it until he has gone on. Similarly, a young man passing an elder, even at a distance, bends low before continuing on his way. It is at first astonishing to see a man on a bicycle managing somehow to 'crouch' respectfully without dismounting. This he may do if he does not pass too close to the elder to whom he is deferring. If they are on the same path, then the cyclist dismounts and crouches beside his bicycle, still holding it upright by the handle bars. Two elders meeting will both bend slightly while exchanging the customary phrases. Only children are exempt from this reflex act, as though they were invisible to their seniors. And indeed this is just the point. For if the junior should fail to defer, the senior will ignore him entirely. But for an adult to refuse to acknowledge a fellow villager's presence in this way is a direct insult, equivalent to denying his social existence. It conveys the sort of intent we refer to in the phrase 'she cut him dead'. Therefore if a Gonja wishes to be included in the complex of significant social relations, he must be prepared to take the initiative in showing deferential behaviour to his seniors.

But it would be a mistake if, in emphasizing the importance of the ranking function of greeting behaviour, one were to imply that greetings convey no further information. Anyone coming from afar is subjected to a barrage of questions regarding his maternal and paternal kin, his wife and children, the people of his town, and of the towns he passed through on the way. The visitor answers 'all right' or 'in good health' after each query. But having made these required responses, when the greeting routine is over, real information is exchanged concerning common kin and friends. Both ranking and information are combined when the stranger is taken, as he must be, by his host or landlord into the presence of the town chief. Both by going *to* the chief and by the form of his initial greeting the stranger expresses deference. The chief responds with the same questions as did the host, and receives the appropriate answers.

GREETING TITLES: THE PLACING FUNCTION
OF GREETING

There is yet another way in which verbal greetings convey

information. For the form of address accompanying a greeting varies with the status of the person spoken to. The use of kin terms constitutes one form of the *placing* or identification function of greeting. The Gonja employ the terms for 'father', 'mother', and 'grandparent' when greeting a stranger about whom nothing at all is known, and among intimates kin terms may be used with morning and evening greetings. But for that vast area of social space lying between intimates and strangers, the placing function is fulfilled, not by assimilation to a kinship status, but by indentifying a person's estate affiliation, and often rank, local origin, and occupation. This information is conveyed by greeting titles (*adilibi*), which are appended to the first phrase of the salutation. Thus when a Gonja greets good morning, it is in the form of 'Good morning, child of the Jembito Earth priest's people' or 'Good morning, woman of the Court Muslims'. Every adult is placed by such a greeting title, first in terms of the estate he belongs to; second as to whether or not he holds office in that estate; and sometimes by occupation, and by what part of Gonja or elsewhere his people originally came from.

Given the scale of Gonja society and the high degree of internal differentiation, kin terms can be meaningfully applied to too few people to label effectively those with whom one comes in contact. And to use kin terms in as broadly classificatory a sense as would be required to compensate for this would be to denude them largely of meaning. Indeed, instead of making kin terms more generally applicable, the Gonja response has been to evolve a system of greeting titles which is highly specific.[6]

Both men and women are greeted by the titles appropriate to their paternal kin, and I have thus designated the groups that have a common greeting title as patronymic. Significantly, with few exceptions access to office is on the basis of paternal filiation. The following paragraphs summarize the different principles stressed by the greeting titles of each estate, for not only do the actual terms differ, but the way in which they are assigned within the estates varies as well.[7]

1. *Ruling estate*

  (i) *Hierarchy is a dominant principle in greeting titles of the ruling group*

  Only the ruling group is internally stratified beyond the designation of single officeholder and 'the rest'. In the ruling group, the hierarchical principle separates officeholders from those without office, both among men and women. Among officeholders, both men and women can be ranked for relative seniority. There are two entirely separate series of titles, one for men and one for women.

  (ii) *Spatial unity is the other dominant principle in greeting titles of the ruling estate*

  The greeting titles of the ruling group scarcely distinguish spatial origin at all. Non-officeholding men have different greetings in the centre, west, and east of the country, but these variations are not carefully observed, i.e. a member of the ruling group from eastern Gonja will be addressed by western terms for non-officeholding royal while he is in the west. It is essentially a dialect difference. Otherwise the same greeting and titles are used for members of the ruling estate throughout Gonja.

2. *Muslim estate*

  (i) *Equality is a basic principle among Muslim groups*

  With a single exception, Muslim patronymic groups do not recognize hierarchy. This exception is the holder of the office of Limam, that is, the official head of all Muslims in the community.

  (ii) *Spatial origin is another primary principle of Muslim greetings*

  Muslim greeting titles almost always lump men and women together, and refer not to the sex or status of the one greeted, but to the group of origin. Nearly all these groups have a spatial referent outside of Gonja (indeed outside of Ghana); Hausa, Bornu, the Ivory Coast, Haute Volta are all represented.

3. *Commoner estate*

  (i) *Commoner greeting titles allow weak distinctions by rank and sometimes by sex*

  Some commoner groups differentiate greeting titles by sex, but many do not. Many commoner greetings utilize the principle of hierarchy in designating a single officeholder and differentiating him from other members of the group. This officeholder may be a shrine priest, an earth priest, or a war captain. Occasionally assistants to shrine priests have special greetings, but when this happens, they are the single officeholders in their own kin group.

(ii) *Local reference is the major principle of commoner greeting titles, and this is often expressed by their association with earth-shrine parishes*
Most villages have members of two or even three commoner patronymic groups, and members of a single group are rarely confined to one village. Yet the distribution of a given commoner greeting title is usually limited to several adjacent communities, or to communities known to be linked by migration. People think of a given commoner greeting title as pertaining to 'the people of the earth-shrine of village "X" ' or to those who speak a single dialect, and they almost certainly represent autochthonous enclaves. There appear to be certain greetings which are Dumpo, certain ones which are Mper, Hanga, Tampluma, etc. This is clearer from the women's greetings than the men's. Even where men of two villages have different greetings, their women often share a single form. In any case the spatial referents of commoner greetings are interlocking, adjacent, and within Gonja. They are thus different as one moves across the country. Those of eastern Gonja are little known in the west, and vice versa.

(iii) *Some occupational groups have distinctive greeting titles, but they are not endogamous, and usually are not localized*
The exception to the emphasis on locality among commoners are those greeting titles that have an occupational rather than a spatial referent. Certain forms of divination are known and practised within families, each of which has greetings indicating their skill. In the same way, barbers are greeted as *ase*, as are some blacksmiths (others are *langsamo*) and ferrymen who have the speak, associated with the Mande conquerers, are *yitcha*. Ashanti who came to act as warriors for the Gonja are *anyaado*.

Thus greeting titles have placing functions and may also have ranking functions. But it must be remembered that, by placing a man or woman in the commoner estate, the greeting title also ranks them below members of the ruling estate in political contexts, though not necessarily in the day-to-day life of the village. And anyone addressed by a greeting title of the commoner or ruling estate is assumed not to be of the Muslim faith and, in the view of the Muslims, to be of a lower ritual condition. Placing in Gonja involves contextual ranking.

All aspects of Gonja greetings to which I have referred are included in the referents of the word *choro*, to greet or thank. Greeting titles, patronymically determined terms of address, are also considered a part of greetings, as indicated by the fact that a man can equally well ask a stranger, 'How do they greet you?' (*nsum ba choro fo?*) or 'How do they title you?' (*nsum ba dila fo?*). In either case the answer will be in terms of the appropriate greeting title (*kadilibi*).

Verbal greetings are compounded of greeting titles and topical salutations, and they are usually accompanied by physical gestures, and sometimes by gifts. It is by means of all these elements that greetings serve to open channels of communication and lay the basis for further interaction. While the words used in the salutation at first seem the most significant aspect of greeting, in fact they convey little information compared to that contained in the greeting title that accompanies them. And non-verbal behaviour, in the form of approach patterns and deferential gestures, and the giving of gifts, further define the status of both parties. These are the building blocks of Gonja greeting idiom. They lay the basis for interaction between members of a heterogeneous society. But they also serve as the means by which changes of status are recognized (as in *rites de passage*) and as one of the primary means by which political influence is affirmed and manipulated. Finally, by making possible the initiation of relationships between non-kin, formalized greeting is a way of obtaining favours that are paid for in a currency of respect and deference.

THE MANIPULATIVE ASPECTS OF GREETING

Rites de passage: reciprocal greeting and non-hierarchical placement

The definition of status conveyed by a greeting title is determined at birth by the patronymic group of the father, and remains fixed throughout a person's life-time, unless a man should succeed to office. Relative changes of status do occur, however, with the major *rites de passage* of birth, marriage, and death, and these are the occasion for reciprocal *acts* of greeting. As a class, these acts of greeting associated with *rites de passage* serve to place individuals in new roles. Apart from the content of the role itself, they do not imply or enforce status differences. Shifts in domestic and kinship roles have no important effects on the hierarchy of the political domain,[8] and greetings in the course of associated *rites de passage* tend to be reciprocated, so that in the end the account is even. First others greet the novice, then the novice returns their greetings. Obligations to kin and neighbours are acknowledged and thanks given. These latter observances, although called 'greetings' by Gonja, could equally well be termed 'thanks for greetings'. And as already noted, there is a sense in which *choro* means 'thanks'. Neither party has deferred to the other, and no status imbalance exists.

While both the greeting of a new baby and of a new bride are institutionalized, the most highly elaborated of the *rites de passage* greetings is that required at death, for one of the main obligations of both kinship and affinal roles is to greet funerals. The minimal definition of 'greet' in this context is to go and offer the formal phrase of condolence, *ada nakana*. Distance is not an excuse for failing to condole. Thus to honour this obligation, kin or in-laws may have to travel from distant villages, or from jobs in the south. If the relationship is a close one, mourning obligations include monetary contributions, gifts of animals for slaughter, and labour in dancing and catering. All these forms of participation are covered by the phrase *ba choro kali*, 'they greet the funeral'. As an index of the importance with which such obligations are treated, greeting a funeral may be postponed for weeks, or even months, in order that a suitable contribution can finally be made. For sons-in-law in western Gonja, the proper funeral greeting is to bring a party of dancers and a band, in order to hold an additional wake in honour of the deceased. In eastern Gonja, a gift of a sheep is specified instead.

At the conclusion of a funeral, the women of the bereaved household go around the town and greet, using a simple verbal formula, at each house that contributed to the work and cost of entertaining the mourners. The men of the household also go around the village separately and greet each household whose menfolk joined in the dancing and associated expenses. This serves both as an expression of gratitude for the help rendered, and as formal indication that the funeral observances have ended.

Gifts as greetings

The greeting behaviour I have so far discussed consists of verbal forms, conventions of who shall approach whom, gestures which convey deference in various ways, and, finally, in the context of *rites de passage*, visits and gifts. Prestations are a pervasive element in the complex of greeting behaviour. There are, for instance, situations in which a visit or a gift are equivalent; if it is not convenient to make a visit, the sending of a gift, which is also referred to as *katchoro*, will do equally well. Even when the two are combined, when for example a man brings a gift on coming to greet, the gift is often referred to as the greeting: *fo ba katchoro nde*, 'here is your greeting', is the verbal formula which accompanies the handing over of kola nuts or bottle of gin.[9]

Greeting and the affirmation of hierarchy

In the political sphere, regular greeting has two main functions which follow from the reaffirmation of status differences, that is, from ranking. In the first place, by regularly greeting the town, divisional, or paramount chief on Fridays and Mondays, elders and sub-chiefs demonstrate their acceptance of his authority, and do so in a way which publicly provides him with a following. This is obvious at the higher levels of the state hierarchy, when the paramount's council hall is crowded with richly robed men who prostrate themselves before the elevated platform on which the YagbumWura sits on his skins of office. But it is equally, indeed perhaps more, important, for the lowly village chief whose daily life is so close to that of his subjects, and who is often linked to them by ties of kinship and marriage, as well as of neighbourhood. For him the public performance of greeting ritual on Mondays and Fridays is an occasion when he is clearly set apart from his followers as the recipient of their respect and deference. And on this day the whole village sees the homage of their elders to the chief. He is seen to be respected and to have a following.

The most emphatic expression of this public homage occurs at the annual Damba ceremony when all the chiefs assemble in the capital of each division of the Gonja state. On the final day the whole population of the town, as well as those who have come from outlying villages, gathers outside the chief's palace. The skins of office are brought from their usual place inside the council hall and arranged outside, under a silk cotton tree, and Muslim elders, commoner elders, the royal women, and finally the divisional chief, take their places in a huge crescent of seated dignitaries. The high point of the ceremony follows, with the slow entry of all the sub-chiefs in strict order of precedence. Directed by the spokesman (*dogte*), they prostrate themselves three times in the customary greeting ritual, except that on this occasion the *dogte* strolls up and down the ranks, calling to one and then another to get his head down onto the earth. And on this occasion too, it is not the chief and his attendants alone who are present, but everyone who cares to come, and particularly the subjects of these sub-chiefs lying in the dust. All can see the size, splendour, and humbleness of the chief's following. Yet for all their humility, the sub-chiefs are within the circle, the subjects outside it. And the greeting over, the sub-chiefs take their seats among the dignitaries, and one by one on the invitation of the divisional chief, come out into the circle and dance *damba*, the dance of the conquering Mande horsemen.

Greeting and the manipulation of political influence
Given the central importance of greeting in defining the relations between superior and subordinates in the political realm,

it is not surprising to find that 'greeting', and more specifically, 'greeting to beg', has a prominent place in the suit for a vacant chiefship. When a man who is eligible wishes to compete for office, he must first of all secure the support of the elders of his own dynastic segment. Having done this, his next move is to greet the divisional chief and announce his interest in the post.

The Gonja insist that they do not 'buy chiefship' like some other Ghanaian peoples, and they despise this practice. There is considerable evidence to suggest that formerly this was true in the sense that 'greeting to beg for chiefship' was not done with money but with bush meat, kola nuts and drink, and perhaps an embroidered gown or a horse. Nowadays an erstwhile candidate will bring with him a substantial sum of money which is presented to the divisional chief. Although the amounts involved are small in comparison with those which apparently pass in the suit for office in Dagomba and Mamprusi, I was for some time puzzled by the fact that money gifts were made at all, and also by the failure of the divisional chief to return the greeting gifts of the unsuccessful candidates. For if the money is a payment for the award of office, then those who don't get the office ought at least to have their money back.

An alternative view is that of the Gonja themselves who say that a would-be chief must greet with money so that his superior will listen to him, and in order to show respect. In this sense, a money gift is more like an entrance fee to a competition that is decided on quite different grounds. A man who refuses to 'greet and beg' is unlikely to be considered a serious candidate. If he were really interested in the office, he would show his respect for the divisional chief in whose gift it lay, and to whom he would be subordinate in a new sense, should he be successful in his suit. And if he will not respect the divisional chief as a candidate, why should he do so as a sub-chief? So 'greet' he must.

Having greeted and not gained his object, what is he to do then? Demand that his greeting, his money, be returned? In Gonja eyes this is not possible, for the divisional chief remains his political superior. To alienate him would be unwise, and in any case, he has in his control other offices and the granting of other favours. Rather, what seems to be happening is that cash greetings are left with the recipient to 'gather interest' in the form of an unredeemed debt.

We saw that greetings are made, and reciprocated, within the set of observances that marks a *rite de passage*, and that in this context greeting did not imply any difference in status between the parties concerned. 'Greeting to beg' for chiefship does affirm a status imbalance and this is further emphasized by the delay in and unequal nature of the reciprocity. For the greeting is never returned, as a greeting, or in kind, by the divisional chief. Instead there is an outstanding debt in the supplicant's favour which binds the two men in the pursuit of mutual self-interest. The office-seeker has shown his loyalty, and hopes to be rewarded eventually. It is to his advantage to support the present divisional chief thus in his debt. The chief has received tangible proof of the willingness of a subject to recognize and defer to his authority, and stands to benefit from retaining this loyalty by some form of reward. Thus, where a return of money gifts to the unsuccessful candidate would leave both candidate and divisional chief free of obligation, and very possibly set the stage for a state of hostility between them, the retention of the greeting gift has the opposite effect. The request for preferment has been properly made and ought to be honoured, if not now then later. It is an investment in the future benevolence of the divisional chief. Next time he may be more obliging – but only if he is persuaded of the loyalty of his supplicant, that is if the respect debt stands in his favour.

Greeting rituals, then, are institutionalized at every level of the political system. The following two examples illustrate how they enter into the by-play of political life. Both turn on the implications of withholding greetings from a political superior. In the first instance, the two gates of Kanyasi and Leppo were disputing the succession to the Kpembe divisional skin towards the end of the last century. The incumbent Kpembe chief, of the Leppo family, summoned the Kanyasi elders to come and greet him. But instead of receiving them in his council hall, he arranged his skins under a tree surrounded by an expanse of mud. The peculiar quality of village mud in the rainy season derives from its being well churned by goats, chickens, ducks, cows, and children. When the Kanyasi elders arrived, there was nowhere they could lie down to greet (*dese n'choro*) except in this very rich mud. On this occasion they did so. But the success of the Leppo chief in humiliating them added to their resolution to rebel, and this they later did.[10]

The second instance occurred when we were living in Busunu, capital of a virtually autonomous sub-division in central Gonja. The chief was very old, and the issue of who would succeed him preoccupied the elders. The NamaWura was a strong candidate but he had recently opposed the giving of a minor office to the chief's son.[11] Not surprisingly, the chief of Busunu was furious and, determined to prevent the Nama-Wura from succeeding him, sent gifts and messages to the paramount chief asking that the NamaWura should not be given the Busunu chiefship, whoever else should get it, and in fact suggesting an alternative choice.

The NamaWura first sought to prevail on the Busunu chief to change his mind, and again he did so in the idiom of greeting. For, taking some money (a few pounds I believe, but I was unable to discover the exact amount) he went in the dead of night to beg the BusunuWura to support his candidacy. *E choro n'kule*, 'he greeted and begged', I was told. The use of *choro*, greeting, here implies that the NamaWura declared his loyalty and willingness to follow his chief, and at the same time it conveys the giving of a prestation, here money. In return, the NamaWura hoped that the BusunuWura would withdraw his opposition to his succession. In the event, the Busunu chief remained adamant. From that time on, the NamaWura refused to greet him by day *or* by night, and was conspicuously absent from the Monday and Friday assembly. In short, he not only refused to support the BusunuWura on public occasions, but did so in a way that was an open declaration of insubordination, for it is every chief's duty to attend at these times. Here there was a complete breakdown of reciprocity: the Busunu chief refused to support the NamaWura in his legitimate aspirations and the NamaWura refused to act as a loyal follower, and openly challenged the Busunu chief to do anything about it.

These two instances taken together illustrate the dual nature of greeting between political unequals: on the one hand, there is the element of force, difficult to assess in the post-contact period but of undoubted relevance. The Kanyasi elders would not have lain down in the mud had they known how to avoid it, but they were forced to, and it was only by demonstrating superior force of arms that they later reversed the situation. On the other hand, reciprocity is an equally important element in the relationship.

Greetings as gifts: reciprocity and respect debts

I noted earlier that in the greetings that accompany *rites de passage* there is institutionalized balance which leaves no basis for inequality, for ranking the participants. And this is entirely appropriate where every family in turn is involved in the same basic situations of birth, marriage, and death. But greeting in the political sphere moves all one way. For the subordinate always greets, goes to the senior, and may also bring with him a small gift. It is the subordinate who lies or kneels in the dust while the chief sits on his official skins. How can we speak of reciprocity in such a situation? I take my cue here from Mauss's assertion that a prestation always implies a return. And greeting is, even in its non-material forms a gift, a gift of respect and deference. Once put this way, it is no longer confusing that the Gonja use the verb 'to greet' to cover not only visiting and verbal exchanges, but also the offering of gifts. Indeed without additional information it is often impossible to know which sense is meant (see also n. 9).

Such greetings establish, in the view of both donor and re-cipient, a debt based on the proffering of respect. The obligation

involved is diffuse, and covers rights and privileges of citizen-
ship, the right to protection and to justice at the chief's court.
But quite specific claims can also be made against this respect
debt; claims for assistance, support, preferment and clemency.
Such seeking for favours is covered by the Gonja word *kule*,
to beg. But beg (*kule*) and greet (*choro*) are not infrequently used
together or interchangeably.

'Greeting to beg': establishing a respect debt

The usual *gbanyito* word for 'beg' is *kule*. This has a number of
related usages which are outlined in the paradigm on pages
45 and 46. Of particular interest here is the explicit employment
of greeting in seeking a favour which the Gonja term *choro n' kule*,
literally 'greet and beg'.

While one may go and *kule* a piece of burning charcoal with
which to light a fire, and readily receive it, requests for major
favours are rarely made directly on the first occasion of meeting
between the supplicant and the bestower. Not only would it
be bad form to ask for something the first time you meet a
person, but you almost certainly would not get it, unless you
occupied a position of power which left the bestower no choice.
For to ask for a favour/gift/knowledge/money, etc. is to assume
some basis for the reciprocities which this initiates.

It is characteristic of Gonja society that outside the market
place the scope of purely monetary transactions is limited. In
transactions concerning services there is either equivalent
reciprocity – perhaps delayed, as in farm clearing *ndɔ kule*,
that is, farm (work) begging – or there is a mixture of prestations
of items and deference which serves as payment. One who
wishes to learn a skill, such as drumming or divining, does not
seek out an expert and ask him how much lessons will cost.
Rather such a would-be apprentice sets up a pattern of greeting
his selected teacher, morning and evening, and on some of his
greeting visits he may bring with him a few kola or some local
gin, or if he is a hunter some bush meat is appropriate. Only
after some time, during which these greetings have been

regularly made (the length of time varies with the importance
of the favour or skill sought), will the supplicant venture to
state his request. In order to beg successfully a man must greet
assiduously, for favours cannot be expected of strangers.

Such a begging-greeting relationship can persist over a long
period of time, and can also exist in institutionalized form. An
example of the latter, in which the prayer aspect of *kule* is also
present, is the Friday greeting of the KpembeWura by the
senior Muslim woman, the *kasowatche*. Her arrival is incon-
spicuous, for she slips into the council hall as the sub-chiefs file
out. She kneels and mutters barely audible prayers, lasting
but a few moments, in front of the KpembeWura's skins.
As she finishes the divisional chief motions to one of his
retainers to give her a few coins, and she then quickly with-
draws. This Friday greeting by the *kasowatche* is a jealously
guarded prerogative, for old women are of necessity alert to
any regular source of income. It is the right of the eldest
Sakpare woman to say prayers on Friday in return for coins –
called by all *kusɔjiso* 'a thing (something) to eat'.

It might seem to be stretching the analogy to class the *kasowatche's* Friday prayer for the chief with other forms of greeting
and requests for favours. However, this is how the *kasowatche*
herself sees it. She always spoke of her right to receive *kusɔjiso*
from the KpembeWura when she greeted (*choro*) on Fridays.
To her, *her* prayers were the appropriate form of *her* greeting
(as the representative of Muslim women) to take.

Another situation in which begging and greeting are jointly
concerned is marriage. On different samples between 60 per cent
and 90 per cent of first marriages follow on a successful courtship by the husband (*katcholte*) and it is often with shy pride
that a woman explains that she was wooed in this way.[12] Other
marriages are arranged by parents or other relatives, though
in these too the girl is given a chance to refuse the match.
But a marriage based on courtship must still gain the consent of
the girl's parents, and the wise suitor is almost as attentive to
her parents, especially to the girl's mother, as to the girl herself.

In Gonja idiom, he greets her parents. These greetings will probably include gifts of small sums of money or kola nuts, and from a careful suitor the morning and evening verbal greeting ritual. In acting in this way he is anticipating the respect relationship due to in-laws and, as in the case of the followers of the chief, is establishing a respect debt against which to lodge his claim for their daughter's hand. It may even happen that a young man regularly greets an elder known to have many dependents in the hope that he will be given one or other of the girls in whose marriage arrangements the elder has a say. This too is institutionalized in the custom of greeting a mother's brother during the Muslim festival of *Jentigi* (*Ashura*), at which time he has an obligation to repay a token service (sweeping) with a sizeable gift, a wife being particularly appropriate. However, as with the man seeking to learn a craft and skill, such a favour is only likely to be forthcoming to one who has in fact established a respect debt on the basis of greetings and small services.

CONCLUSIONS: COMPARISON OF GONJA AND LODAGAA GREETING PATTERNS

In order to raise, however tentatively, the question of the distribution of elaborate forms of greeting, and in particular of the linkage between greeting and begging, I want to consider very briefly the role of greeting among the acephalous LoDagaa. Although little weight can be attached to a comparison of only two societies, there is the advantage that the LoDagaa are near neighbours of the Gonja and, while differing in political organization, share a number of economic and cultural features with them.[13]

Reference to the paradigm of greeting and begging forms on pages 43–6 shows that in both cases the entries for the Gonja far outweigh the LoDagaa equivalents. But there is a difference not only in the number of references, but also in the type represented in each society. While the Gonja can, and occasionally do, use kin terms as the form of address in verbal greetings, this is rare. For the LoDagaa, kin terms are the *only* form of address used with salutations, though again infrequently. They completely lack the greeting titles that fulfil such important placing and ranking functions for the Gonja.

While both Gonja and LoDagaa make use of what I have called topical salutations – greetings related to weather, activities, or the time of day – again the Gonja have elaborated this usage greatly in comparison with their northern neighbours. Further, the morning and evening greetings are obligatory for close kin among the Gonja, and on Mondays and Fridays to the chief, as is not the case among the LoDagaa.

Turning from purely verbal greetings to those involving a physical dimension, the abasement gestures and approach patterns which reflect hierarchical ranking so explicitly among the Gonja are entirely lacking in LoDagaa culture. Indeed, the LoDagaa deny that they would lie down in the dust for anyone. Nor does the prestation aspect of greeting appear to be present among the LoDagaa. This is true both of objects and of the counter-prestations (which serve as thanks), and also of the use of greetings themselves as valuables to be bestowed in return for favours or services. Begging (*zele*) is limited to the context of bride service. In the absence of an accepted political hierarchy, the LoDagaa are unwilling publicly to defer to one of their number. The Gonja, on the other hand, appear to have made a virtue of necessity, and manipulate the offering and withholding of respect as a part of political life.

Conditions associated with elaborate institutionalized greeting

At the beginning of this essay I suggested three general functions that greeting behaviour appears to fulfil among the Gonja: the opening of a channel for communication and interaction; the defining of role and status; and acting as a means of manipulating relationships to secure a specific result. We have seen that all these aspects of greeting are highly elaborated among the Gonja, but while the LoDagaa make limited use of greeting to open communication, they virtually ignore the remaining functions. Why should such an extreme difference occur between these two neighbouring groups?

Obviously a large part of the answer lies in the difference between the political systems of the two societies. The Gonja state is defined in terms of a hierarchy of offices; officeholders and their followers constantly employ the idiom to affirm and manipulate political relations. However, if the only basis for these extensive differences between a centralized and an acephalous society lay in their respective political structures, we would expect to find that the differences themselves were largely confined to the political realm. That this is not the case can be seen from the examples cited. Obligatory greeting within the kin group is in part related to the extreme deference required of sub-chiefs and the compulsory nature of the Monday and Friday greeting. But the widespread use of greeting as a means of creating respect debts against which to claim wives, tuition in a variety of skills from drumming to witchcraft,[14] and even 'something to eat' indicates that the greeting idiom reaches far beyond the political sphere.

In seeking an underlying factor that might help to explain both the political and the more general emphasis on greeting behaviour, it might be as well to return to the description of the Gonja state with which we began. We saw that Gonja was large, and contained many different ethnic and linguistic elements. Yet a single language is understood throughout the country, and there is a single ruling estate which provides the chiefs who administer the country with the help of Muslim officials. There is both great ethnic complexity and constant assimilation, for only two marriages in five are between members of the same estate. Despite the propinquity rule[15] of marriage, half of all unions are between spouses from different villages and of these, half come from villages more than 30 miles apart.

In such a heterogeneous and spatially mobile society, the extent to which kin ties can effectively serve as a basis for instrumental relationships must be severely limited. At the same time, internal functional differentiation is greater than in a simple acephalous community. There is a greater level of interdependence, and those concerned are less often kin. I suggest that it is due to the necessity for making claims on non-relatives as well as to the pervasiveness of hierarchical relations deriving from politics that greeting behaviour has such prominence in Gonja. Indeed, given the great emphasis on respect for seniors within the kin group, one function of regular greeting is to assimilate outsiders to a quasi-kinship status.

It seems not unlikely that the recurrent tendency for bureaucratic officials, throughout the world, to succumb to bribery is related to attempts by their clients to find a way of enhancing claims that otherwise must be made without any basis in reciprocity. In Gonja greeting is closely associated with begging, and acts to establish claims both in the political sphere and in everyday affairs. Greeting behaviour is a means of initiating and pressing such claims because the one who comes to present his respects, presents something that is of great value in this society. In doing so he creates an implicit obligation on the one greeted to honour this respect debt at some later date. The analysis of these debts of respect and their manipulation in wider social contexts has an important part to play in the understanding of indigenous African states. A major problem for the nation states that are superseding them is the fact that 'greeting' in traditional life is 'bribery' in a bureaucratic context.

NOTES

1. See Birdwhistell (1952, 1968) for discussion of kinesics.

2. See M. G. Smith (1957) for an analysis of institutionalized praise-singing among the Hausa.

3. See J. R. Goody (1966, 1967) for a description of Gonja political organization.

4. The words used in salutations are either completely standardized, as with the time-of-day salutations and those for the various festivals, or they take one of two set forms: (1) 'greetings for . . .' *ansa ni* . . . (work, the heat, your tiredness, the farm, the market, etc.) and (2) 'How is . . .?' . . . *duniso*? (work, the heat, your tiredness, the farm, the market, etc.). It is the latter form that is employed when inquiring after the health or welfare of friends and relatives, but otherwise the two forms are used interchangeably. The one important exception is the use of 'greetings' *ansa*, or 'greetings for work' *ansa ni kushung* as 'thank you'.

5. The association of coolness and well-being in both idiom and ritual is a general one and widespread in Africa. For example, when one's anger fades, the Gonja say that one's chest has cooled. But so automatic is the *awo* response that this association is probably of little importance. Some informants denied it, while others asserted that *awo* in response to a salutation did indeed mean cool (also *awo*). See also Richards's discussion of danger of a 'hot' condition (1956, pp. 30ff.).

6. The Ashanti of southern Ghana are similar to the Gonja in having a federal form of centralized state, but resemble the acephalous LoDagaa in that unilineal descent groups (matrilineal) and complementary descent groups (agnatic) play an important part in community life. In Ashanti salutations are responded to differently by members of each agnatic *ntoro* (Rattray, 1929, p. 103 and 1923, Ch. II; Nketia, 1955, p. 106). While this might be seen as a kind of classificatory use of kin terms, I would argue that this view would be incorrect, because instead of establishing the relationships between ego and the one addressed, the *ntoro* responses, like the Gonja greeting titles, place the alter in one of a finite number of categories which form segments of the total society and are independent of egocentric relationships.

7. These principles were derived from an analysis of the greeting titles of fourteen Muslim and twenty commoner patronymic groups in addition to the *adilibi* of the ruling estate.

8. A partial exception to the independence of domestic and political domains in this respect occurs in eastern Gonja. There a son of the divisional chief may not succeed to any chiefship while his father is still alive. Thus his father's death marks his eligibility for, though not necessarily his receipt of, office.

9. The *gbanyito* word for kola nut is *kapushi* and it is entirely consistent with the composite nature of the greeting idiom that in

daily parlance *kapushi* is often used to mean 'money'. Thus if a man says he greeted the chief or an elder with *kapushi*, it is impossible to know whether he actually gave kola nuts, or whether he is obliquely referring to a money gift. Similarly when a person says he 'greeted' someone (*choro*), it is impossible to tell whether a visit and verbal greeting is meant, or whether he is referring to the sending of a gift (of whatever sort) or to both together. Uchendu's analysis (1964) of 'kola hospitality' among the Igbo suggests that in this acephalous system such a dual meaning is not assigned to the giving of kola nuts.

10. This incident and the Kpembe civil war that followed are described in Briamah & Goody, 1968.

11. This situation was further complicated by the fact that the original site of the capital of Busunu was several miles away. About 40 years before it had been moved to the road and joined with a town called Damba Yiri. The BusunuWura as sub-divisional chief became chief of the amalgamated settlement. The minor chiefship which the BusunuWura gave his son was the chiefship of Damba Yiri, and the elders feared that after his father's death he would insist that as DambaYiriWura he was the rightful chief of the community that had come to be called Busunu. It was, in short, a highly sophisticated take-over bid.

12. There are variations by estate and by region in the relative frequency of arranged and courtship marriage. A higher proportion of first marriages is arranged in western Gonja than in the east. This pattern appears both in a survey of men's marriages and in a quite separate study of women's marriages. Commoner men are least likely to have had an arranged first marriage, Muslim most likely. For a fuller treatment of Gonja marriage see E. N. Goody, 1962.

13. See J. R. Goody (1956) for an account of LoDagaa social structure.

14. See my analysis of Gonja witchcraft (1970) for a discussion of this.

15. Bossard's original paper on 'Residential propinquity as a factor in marriage selection' (1932) led to a number of studies. These tend not only to confirm his original generalization that the proportion of marriages in a sample decreases as the distance between the two partners increases, but they also indicate that the relationship holds under a variety of different conditions. The figures for propinquity in Gonja are based on data from Buipe, central Gonja, and on a sample of 175 men from all estates in communities

in east, central, and western Gonja. The data from the Buipe survey (1956) and the men's survey (1966) show the same pattern to within 4 per cent. Data on estate endogamy is based on these two surveys (Buipe, 35 per cent marriages estate endogamous; men's survey, 45 per cent) plus a stratified random sample of women in two communities (western and northern Gonja) where endogamy was 41 per cent.

REFERENCES

BIRDWHISTELL, R. L. 1952. *Introduction to Kinesics*. Louisville: University of Louisville Press. London: Allen Lane, 1971.

BIRDWHISTELL, R. L. 1968. Kinesics. *International Encyclopedia of the Social Sciences* **8**.

BOSSARD, J. H. S. 1932. Residential propinquity as a factor in marriage selection. *American Journal of Sociology* **38**.

BRAIMAH, J. A. & GOODY, J. R. 1968. *Salaga: The Struggle for Power*. London: Longmans.

GOODY, E. N. 1962. Conjugal separation and divorce among the Gonja of Northern Ghana. In M. Fortes (ed.), *Marriage in Tribal Societies*. Cambridge: Cambridge University Press.

GOODY, E. N. 1970. Legitimate and Illegitimate Aggression in a West African State. In M. Douglas (ed.), *Witchcraft Confessions and Accusations*. ASA Monograph 9. London: Tavistock.

GOODY, J. R. 1956. *The Social Organization of the LoWiili*. London: Oxford University Press for International African Institute.

GOODY, J. R. 1966. Circulating succession among the Gonja. In J. R. Goody (ed.), *Succession to High Office*. Cambridge: Cambridge University Press. Cambridge Papers in Social Anthropology **4**.

GOODY, J. R. 1967. The Over-kingdom of Gonja, in D. Forde, P. Kaberry (eds.), *West African Kingdoms in the Nineteenth Century*. London: Oxford University Press for IAI.

LEACH, E. R. 1968. Ritual. *International Encyclopedia of the Social Sciences* **13**.

MALINOWSKI, B. 1927. The problem of meaning in primitive languages. In C. K. Ogden and I. A. Richards, *The Meaning of Meaning*. London: Routledge.

MAUSS, M. 1954. *The Gift*. Glencoe, Ill.: The Free Press; London: Cohen & West (Trans. I. Cunnison).

NKETIA, J. H. 1955. *Funeral Dirges of the Akan People*. Achimota.

RATTRAY, R. S. 1923. *Ashanti.* Oxford: Clarendon.

RATTRAY, R. S. 1929. *Ashanti Law and Constitution.* Oxford: Clarendon.

RICHARDS, A. I. 1956. *Chisungu: A girls' initiation ceremony among the Bemba of Northern Rhodesia,* London: Faber & Faber.

SMITH, M. G. 1957. The social functions and meaning of Hausa praise-singing. *Africa* **27**.

WESTERMANN, D. & BRYAN, M. A. 1952. *Handbook of African Languages.* Part 2. Languages of West Africa. London: Oxford University Press.

UCHENDU, V. C. 1964. Kola hospitality and Igbo lineage structure. *Man* **54**.

Twinship and symbolic structure

AIDAN SOUTHALL

'Plus troublant est le cas de diverses tribus africaines . . . Dans des cas de ce genre, on ne sait plus très bien à quel type de société on a affaire.' Lévi-Strauss (1962, p. 149)

In her review of the Anglo-French dialogue on African systems of thought, Audrey Richards (1967) drew attention to a number of important issues in the study of myth, ritual, symbol, and cosmology. Have the Bantu no cosmologies, only symbols (1967, p. 278)? Turner found that 'the Ndembu have a paucity of myths and cosmological or cosmogonic narratives. It is therefore *necessary* to begin at the other end, with the basic building blocks, the "molecules" of ritual' (1969, p. 14). Do elaborate cosmologies go with elaborate social structures, fragmentary sets of symbols with segmentary structures? Are consistent systems of ideas universal, and have we already enough material to start mapping those areas of Africa in which elaborate cosmologies exist and to study the social mechanisms for transmitting them (Richards, 1969)?

It is therefore appropriate that an essay in her honour should continue the exploration of questions which she raised. Symbols are the basis of both myth and ritual (Turner, 1968, pp. 576–578) and the re-enactment of myth in living (usually ritual) experience has constantly been stressed. For Turner, both partake of the pure potency of liminality. The key to understanding one is often found in the other. Turner cracks the code of myth through ritual and Lévi-Strauss draws from ritual supplementary evidence on the structure of myth. These are influential and characteristic British and French approaches though the extensive comparative work of Lévi-Strauss diverges somewhat from the unparalleled depth of intensive concentration by Griaule and his associates in West Africa. Lévi-Strauss pays little attention to ritual for its own sake, Turner little to myth for its own sake; the former is more interested in the underlying logical structure (not to be confused with the overt logic of conscious individual rational thought), the latter in the underlying sources of psychosomatic experience and life-generating power.

Richards suggests that French Africanist anthropologists are prone to 'cosmological determinism' (1969, p. 290) as when A. Lebeuf claims that the idea system of the Fali and their acceptance of a dual and quadruple division of the world is the basis of their clan division, whereas British anthropologists until recently assumed that ritual exists to do something for man and his societies, apart from solving his cognitive difficulties. Few would dispute the general contrast. However, Lévi-Strauss himself has pointed out that both assumptions are found in Durkheim, on the one hand the primacy of the social over the intellectual and on the other a greater autonomy of intellect (1963, pp. 96–7). The former predominates in Durkheim and has done so in British anthropology, whereas the latter is certainly preferred by Lévi-Strauss[1] and has recently come into more general vogue. 'The empirical hackles of the British ethnographer tend to rise when the autonomy, consistency and logic of primitive systems of belief are stressed' (Richards, 1967, p. 295), but 'this does not of course apply to the thought systems postulated by Lévi-Strauss, which are at least three degrees removed from the ethnographic data . . .' (op. cit., p. 297).

The issue is not only a question of radically different views of the nature of culture, society, and human behaviour, as to how far systems of action reflect systems of ideas or the other way about, but also of misleadingly different understandings of what is meant by systems of thought, of knowledge, or of cosmology. Evidently, from one point of view, such systems are not considered to be present unless at least some members of the culture in question can give a coherent account of them *as systems*. But the likelihood of this must surely depend in large part on the degree of specialization of roles and institutions. The most crucial debate turns upon whether it is legitimate for the anthropologist to discover such systems in the speech, symbols, myths, and rituals of cultures none of whose members give an explicit verbal account of them as such. The analogy of language (and more recently of music) is constantly brought in here. If we do not necessarily expect any member of a speech community to be able to give a comprehensive analytical account of its language, why should we expect it in the case of ritual or mythology? The Dogon might at first sight seem to constitute an exception, but it is rightly pointed out that the comprehensive knowledge of a Dogon informant cannot be considered in isolation from the joint experience and inquiry of informant and interviewer over long periods of time and cannot be immune from influence by the systematic frame of reference developed with him by the interviewer over a period of many years. However, the remarkable cosmological system expounded by Ogotemmeli on behalf of the Dogon elders is evidence that cannot be explained away (Griaule, 1948).

No doubt the question of esoteric knowledge is also relevant, but cannot be the general explanation. The *biru* dignitaries of Ruanda (Maquet, 1961, pp. 126–7) were 'concerned with the preservation of ritual knowledge and the accomplishment of ceremonies essential to the existence of Ruanda and its government. This knowledge and activities were kept secret from everybody' (other than the *biru*). However, no single dignitary knew the entire body of customs. This knowledge was divided among the dignitaries of various descent groups, which in this sense owned it. 'The present day *biru* are still very reluctant to provide information and still less to let it be published, in spite of the encouragement to do so that they receive from the king' (ibid.). The Bemba *bakabilo* also 'own' and guard secret rituals and objects, and Richards notes some of the many African parallels (1960, pp. 183–8). It is surely symptomatic of the secondary emphasis, at best, that social anthropologists used to put upon just those bodies of data most calculated to reveal the symbolic and cosmological core of a culture, that Richards stresses the 'exceedingly intricate accession ceremony' of the Bemba Citimukulu, 'the most elaborate piece of King-making I have read of', involving thirty to forty separate ritual acts, only to express the pious but unfulfilled hope of describing it in its entirety (1960, p. 184). She has recently (in 1969) added a further fascinating account of the Bemba Kingship and segmentary state, but was not able to analyse the symbolism or describe the ritual in full. On the other hand, her 'superb study of Bemba girls' puberty rites' (Turner, 1967, p. 101), recorded in 1931 and published in 1956, was certainly a pioneer in its field. Dedicated to the memory of Malinowski, it is meticulously detailed and empirical. We know the exact nature of all the evidence: observed action; simultaneous comment by involved experts and participants; subsequent reflective interpretation by educated Bemba. It is true to this scientific spirit that the ethnographer is perhaps over-cautious in her reluctance to hazard further interpretation or analysis – the actors speak for themselves. Yet in their action was structured sequence, repetition of symbols and themes from other rituals and myths – all this meaning was immanent for the actors and obviously required no verbalization, but it is lost to the reader unless the whole immanent structure is pieced together and analysed (Turner, 1964, pp. 27–8).

This cautious conclusion is given by Firth in his assessment of the systematic analysis of his own material by Lévi-Strauss: 'though it might be possible to find in myths transformations which would allow one to construct a more symmetrical arrangement, this would be a highly selective process . . . the picking and choosing of details in the interests of a symmetrical arrangement would mean doing violence to the perspective and framework of events in the myths and ignoring a great range of apparently more significant relationships' (Firth, 1966,

p. 12). Firth does not deny the presence of system, but insists that it is incomplete and that considerable irregularities remain. As far as Africa is concerned, the same general impression is conveyed by the debate on Nyoro symbolism by Needham (1967) and Beattie (1968). One scholar finds many elements of systematic symbolic classification never previously rendered explicit, the other accepts the presence of such a system but points to inaccuracies in the data and to questionable inter-pretations that go far beyond reliable proof. A synthesis of the two points of view is easy enough, though not particularly exciting. The symmetrical elements may be perfectly genuine, while the irregularities equally properly represent various phases of transformation and metamorphosis, over space as well as time, together with expressions of faction, status dif-ference, and idiosyncratic points of view. As in so many an-thropological arguments it is mainly a difference of interest. Those who enjoy a particular frame of reference are inclined to push it too far; those whose major interest lies elsewhere criticize deficiencies and exaggerations. The process is salutary and illuminating, particularly when conducted on the basis of empirical data. Indeed, the same kind of error is involved as in earlier forms of functional theory: total integration and con-sistency is ultimately stultifying, an implicit denial of the possibility of the system in question ever having come into being. If symbolic structures have any link with social life they must be subject to change and for this to be possible they must harbour elements of irregularity, asymmetry, and ambiguity. Diachronic studies present formidable difficulties in this field, but comparative studies of concomitant variation are more feasible. This is one of the most interesting possibilities broached by 'The Story of Asdiwal' (Lévi-Strauss, 1958, 1967).

'The Story of Asdiwal', with the later *Le Cru et le cuit*, has been regarded as the most successful structural analysis of myth (Leach, 1967, p. 1). It is at the end of the account that particu-lar attention is paid to interpreting the differences between the form the myth takes among the Tsimshian and among the

Nisqa to the north. Unfortunately, the latter version is very poor, none the less it is said to exhibit 'permutations which, without any doubt, form a system' and also to include 'genuine inversions' (op. cit., pp. 34–5). It is natural to work from the known to the unknown, therefore the poor Nisqa version is studied in the light of the better Tsimshian ones, but it seems somewhat surprising that Lévi-Strauss speaks of the 'weakening' and 'impoverishment' of the Nisqa version. Leach concludes with the principle that 'when a mythical schema is transmitted from one population to another, and there exist differences of language, social organization and way of life which make the myth difficult to communicate, it begins to become impoverished and confused. But one can find a limiting situation in which instead of being finally obliterated by losing all its outlines the myth is inverted and regains part of its precision' (op. cit., p. 42). Perhaps there are valid reasons for treating the Nisqa as marginal to the Tsimshian and Tlingit, but, knowing the dubious origins of tribal identities in ethnographic writing (Tsimshian simply means 'inside the Skeena river'), the attribution of borrowing seems risky. What evidence is there that the myth was transmitted from Tsimshian to Nisqa? The optical analogy that follows (op. cit., pp. 42–3) would imply that a mythical schema is transmitted from point A to C through B. At A it is clear and 'rich', at B it is obscure and 'impoverished', but at C it is clear and reversed. Such a model may well apply to many elements of mythical structure, but very often group B will be marginal or peripheral with respect to one element and original or central with respect to another. There may be no reason for considering C a reversal of A any more than A is a reversal of C. At least we should require empirical evidence for taking one view rather than the other.

In the exposition of the South–North series of transformations in Australia, from Arabanna through Aranda, Kaitish, and Umatjera to Warramunga (or vice versa) there is no suggestion of impoverishment, dominance, or transmission in the one direction or the other (Lévi-Strauss, 1966a, pp. 81–8).

But – apart from a veiled hint (op. cit., p. 90) – nor is there any suggestion of how, or whether, such transformations relate in any meaningful fashion to the societal interaction of groups of human beings or to the process of establishment, differentiation, and modification of ethnic and cultural identities. Indeed, in the preceding discussion (op. cit., pp. 79–80) of the systems of Ulawa, Malaita, and Lifu on the one hand, and Motlav, Mota, and Aurora on the other, as symmetrical reversals of one another, ideas of unidirectional derivation or chronological priority are rejected, but the fact that these islands are scattered over some 800 miles of ocean in no consistent order, with many other islands in between, is also conveniently ignored. If we designate the first group A1, 2, 3, and the second group, B1, 2, 3, with intervening islands N1, we arrive at the following spatial sequence approximately: A1, N10, B1, N2, B2, B3, N7, A2, A3. Such a distribution may have meaning but it is certainly not apparent; small comfort, that 'the greater our knowledge, the more obscure the overall scheme' (Lévi-Strauss, 1966a, p. 89).

I shall discuss and illustrate these issues with reference to the particular focus of symbolic ideas about twinship among some East African peoples. The subject is hackneyed, but despite the number of articles on it, there is very little comparative perspective. Comparison is virtuous not merely for its own sake, but in the old sense of studies of concomitant variation, which illuminate both the presence and the absence of particular items of meaning. Beattie (1962, p. 1) compares the Nyoro euphemism that a dead twin has 'flown away as a bird does' to the now celebrated account of the Nuer association of twins with birds (Evans-Pritchard, 1956, p. 129). That the neighbouring Ganda make use of the same euphemism as the Nyoro is attested apparently independently, by both foreign and indigenous scholarly observation (Roscoe, 1911, pp. 124–5, and Nsimbi, 1956, p. 32). The Nilotic Alur immediately to the north of Bunyoro across Lake Albert bury the umbilical cords of twins under a tree called *atyendowinyo* ('I am the feet of a bird'). Are such echoes to be interpreted as elements of a common cultural tradition (for which there is some evidence) or as logical parts of analogous cognitive structures, or simply ignored? The ethnographic record is far too incomplete, even in relation to rather well-studied cultures, to permit a reliable answer. There are many other neighbouring cultures for which this theme is not reported. It is easy to point to the profound ambivalence generally characteristic of attitudes to twins, requiring but a slight change of emphasis to tip the balance for or against. It is much too simple merely to distinguish positive and negative attitudes, but we can for the sake of brevity note that in some cultures twinship is so close to the ideas of fertility and divinity that twins must in principle be welcomed, however much the particular parents and families concerned fear the danger, expense, and inconvenience involved, whereas in other cultures twinship receives much less conceptual and ritual elaboration and the attempt is made to evade the implications of the dread phenomenon by putting twins to death, reducing them to the normality of a single birth by expecting or inducing the death of one of them, or testing them by exposure or other trials.

Thus, to the north of the Alur and Nyoro, the Kakwa exposed the last-born or the female twin, the Bari kept twins born to twinprone families but otherwise only kept mixed pairs of twins and, in the case of male or female pairs, only one was allowed to survive. The Pojulu exposed twins for one night and kept them if they survived. Among the Lotuko it is reported that twins usually died but were not actually put to death. The Logoli neglected one twin so that usually only one survived, but if both lived no special rites were required. The Kikuyu are said to have put twins to death or to have given them away, especially if they were first-born children. Among the matrilineal peoples of eastern Tanzania, twins were usually put to death by the Kaguru, Kutu, Kwere, Ngulu, and Zaramo. Among the Luguru, one or both were killed by their *watani* (cross-cousins, or joking partners) and among the Zigua, *watani* could sell them as slaves. While among the Ndembu of Zambia an explicit connection is made between the joking of the twinship ritual *Wubwang'u* and the customary joking of cross-cousins (Turner, 1969, p. 81). In Ndembu the ritual emphasis is upon the mother, and in Nyakyusa on both parents, rather than on the twins themselves.

Schapera (1927) long ago noted similar contrasts in southern Africa. It is striking that, as in eastern Africa, similar reactions to twins accompany marked differences in language and culture. Only the Herero are noted as generally welcoming all twins. The Venda of Transvaal and Kalanga of Rhodesia used to put both to death, but in general the commonest pattern was to kill one twin, thus returning to a semblance of normal single birth. The Tswana Hurutse and the Hottentots always buried alive the female of a mixed pair. But the Hottentots rejoiced greatly at two male twins, less so at two females. The Kung Bushmen and the Bergdama likewise buried one twin alive, but always the male of a mixed pair. The Pedi, Pondo, Xosa, Zulu, and Thonga all killed one twin, the weaker in the case of the Thonga, the younger in that of the Pedi (Shapera, 1927). However, these variations as so far interpreted bear no consistent relationship to the structural significance of kinship, as suggested by Schapera and by Turner (1969, p. 45).

The Nilotic–Bantu borderland, as represented by the Alur, Nyoro, and their neighbours, seems to be a marked area of elaboration in twinship concepts and rituals. Ganda and Nyoro twinship has been dealt with in some detail by Roscoe (1911, 1923) and Beattie (1962). My aim is to carry somewhat further the examination of twinship in relation both to divinity and kingship.[2] My own data for the Alur is reasonably detailed, but is not matched by comparable details for their immediate Nilotic neighbours (Junam, Palwo, Acholi). There is reasonably full detail on Nyoro and Ganda also, but a comparison of these three bodies of data immediately emphasizes their woeful inadequacy, and drives home the fact that only the most careful study of neighbouring and cognate systems can make the fieldworker aware of the full range of information, negative as well as positive, which this kind of study requires.

This very fact is perhaps worth documenting by an attempt at comparative analysis. The association of twinship with divinity is much more familiar than that with kingship, and can therefore be more easily dealt with first. In Bunyoro *Rubanga* is 'one of the most powerful of the traditional Cwezi spirits and especially concerned with twin birth' (Beattie, 1962, p. 2). *Ruhanga* is the supreme creator deity in Bunyoro. It can be shown that the roots *-banga* and *-hanga* in Bunyoro and *-wanga* and *-banga* in Luganda, together with their respective verbal and nominal forms, are cognate and include identical meanings.[3] Thus the divinities *Muwanga* and *Wanga* in Buganda are cognate with and carry the same etymological significance as *Rubanga* in Bunyoro. In Alur, Rubanga is the supreme manifestation of *Jok*, which is the most general term for spirit and divinity. The root *jok* appears among all the Lwoo-speaking Nilotes and among the Dinka, Nuer, and Lotuko.[4] It thus appears obvious that the Alur (and also the Junam, Palwo, and Acholi) have effected a union of Bantu and Nilotic sounds and meanings. However, the matter becomes a little less straightforward when we note that Rubanga appears among the Sudanic-speaking Madi also as God and as the Earth (Williams, 1949, p. 203) and among the Sudanic Lugbara as an ancestor shrine (Middleton, 1960, p. 69), while among the Acholi *bang'i* means twins and among the Teso *ibangin* has the same meaning (Lawrance, 1957, p. 89).

The oral tradition of the Ukuru Alur (Southall, 1954, 1956) links kingship with twinship from its inception, and, at the same time, with the division and separate organization of the human and animal kingdoms. The present dynasty of rulers purports to go back in the male line to *Ucak* ('The Beginner') also sometimes called *Upodho* ('He who fell', presumably from the sky).[5] *Ucak* found *Nyilak*, the daughter of *Kwong'a* (also meaning 'the beginning'), herding the cattle and impregnated her. *Kwong'a's* people captured him and tried to kill him. He showed them how to do so by pointing a spear at his forehead and at his liver, and foretold the birth of twin boys by *Nyilak* and the rainmaking powers of the stones that would be found in his heart and in his breastbone. The twins were called *Upiyo Lavur* and *Udongo Atira*. The elder and younger twins are always so named *Upiyo* (the quick one) and *Udongo* (he who lingers) in Lwoo. *Lavur* means lion and *Atira* could be taken to refer to straight, upright posture. Their grandfather *Kwong'a* condemns them to death, but they are hidden and preserved. *Kwong'a* later accepts them as his heirs in place of his own sons. He intends to confer the kingdom on the elder, *Upiyo*, as is usual in Alur custom, but in a Jacob-and-Esau-like episode *Udongo* deceives him into conferring it on him. The result is that the people eventually accept *Udongo* as king and drive out *Upiyo* the lion into the bush, where he becomes the King of the Beasts. The animal-human twin theme is of course parallel to the foundation myths of so many Dinka clans reported by Lienhardt (1961, p. 119) and Seligman (1932, 1950). The theme occurs only sporadically among the Alur, and this is the most celebrated instance. Ukuru chiefs thus derive from a younger twin and their rainmaking powers from his father. The shrines of Alur chiefship are *Jok Rubanga*, but, as noted, *Rubanga* is a vague supreme divinity to the Alur, not specifically the divinity of twins as in Bunyoro. However, the material manifestation of the *Jok Rubanga* shrine of Ukuru chiefship is a pot with two necks (*adhogariyo*) containing earth from their original homeland. Such pots of beer must always be exchanged between the lineages of the father and mother of twins in the succession of rituals required to control and canalize the blessing of twinship. The sacred spear (*tong' jok*) of Ukuru is a spear with two heads.

There appears to be a complementary inversion here between the Ukuru Alur and Bunyoro. The Alur dynasty is founded by a younger twin whereas eldest sons usually succeed. The Bito dynasty of Bunyoro is founded by an elder twin, whereas in Bunyoro an eldest son cannot succeed.[6] The Alur founder is the son of a native mother by a stranger father. The

Nyoro founder is the son of a native father by a stranger mother.

The Alur ritual numbers relevant to birth, including that of twins, are three for males and four for females. The Nyoro not only reverse these ritual numbers to four for males and three for females, but they also reverse the accompanying symbolic objects in associating a knife with a female twin and a needle with a male twin (Roscoe, 1923, p. 163) whereas the Alur cut the umbilicus of a male with a cock's feather and that of a female with a hen's feather.

Extensive interchange of lexical items accompanies the exchange of symbols between the Alur and Nyoro. The Nyoro creator deity Ruhanga is cognate with Rubanga, the supreme *Jok* (spirit) of the Alur (Southall, 1970, *passim*). In Alur Rubanga is twinship, as we shall see, though not regarded anthropomorphically as a twin. In Nyoro Rubanga is the particular Cwezi deity concerned with twins, while Ruhanga appears to be a twin, since he constitutes an indivisible unity with his brother *Nkya* (dawn) and is referred to in combination with him as *Ruhanga Nkya Kankya* (Roscoe, 1923, p. 120).

The Alur *Kwong'a* (Beginning) is father of Nyilak, bride of *Ucak* (Beginner) and mother of the twin founders of the ruling Alur dynasty. In Nyoro the Kwong'a clan (a section of the ruling Bito clan) is repeatedly represented in myth and ritual as 'mother' of Nyoro kings. Nyatworo is mother of the Nyoro twins Isingoma Mpuga Rukidi Nyabong'o and Kato Kimera, who founded the Nyoro and Ganda dynasties respectively. She was a member of Kwong'a clan and congruent with the Alur Nyilak. It was Mukaikuru of Kwong'a clan, wife of the departed Cwezi, who remained to instruct Isingoma in the arts of kingship. She was thus also 'mother' or source of kingship and her part is re-enacted in every Nyoro succession ceremony by a woman of Kwong'a clan called Mukaikuru. It is Kwong'a women who present all Nyoro royal children to their mothers to nurse, who perform at royal twin births, who were buried with every Nyoro king, and who were actual mothers of several of the Nyoro Bito Kings, in addition to the first. As Kwong'a tries to kill his daughter's twins in Alur, so in Nyoro Bukuku tries to kill his daughter's son, who though not a twin is actually claimed by his foster-father to be one, in order to get more cattle to provide him with sustenance (Roscoe, 1923, p. 87). This feigned twin was born by Nyinamuiru to Isimbwa, who came up from the underworld to seduce her, whereas it was his own mother Nyamata who came up from the underworld to seduce his father Isaza. On the other hand, in Alur, Ucak (Beginner) came down from the overworld (sky) to seduce Nyilak the mother of kings. Lost cattle led the Nyoro Isaza temporarily down to the underworld; lost cattle led the Alur permanently up into the highlands. In Alur, Rubanga and the potency of twinship is represented by a pot with two mouths, whereas in Nyoro two bags with one mouth were used by Ruhanga to release Hunger and Disease upon the Earth while in another pair of bags (or baskets) with one mouth he took twin virtues to Heaven (Fisher, 1911, p. 75). In Alur myth, the twin brothers who founded Alur and Nyoro dynasties fell out with one another over a bead, which the son of one swallowed and the other recovered by cutting a fatal incision in the child's stomach and pouring in milk to make the bead visible in the blood (Crazzolara, 1950, p. 65); in Nyoro myth the King of the Dead and the King of the Living fall out over the twin seeds of a coffee bean, which was to make them blood brothers through being exchanged between them after dipping into milk and into the blood of incisions in the stomachs of each of them (Fisher, 1911, p. 80; Roscoe, 1923, p. 45), because the latter administered it to his slave instead of to himself. We thus have: Alur bead extracted from blood and milk inside stomach incision spoils intrinsic (twin) brotherhood; Nyoro (twin) bean inserted in blood and milk outside stomach incision spoils extrinsic brotherhood. These formulations are distilled from ethnographic data most of which has already been published by Crazzolara (1950, 1951, 1954), Fisher (1911), Roscoe (1923), and many others (see *Table 1*).

TABLE I   *Alur-Nyoro tranformations*

These oppositions within correspondences can be summarized as follows

Alur	Nyoro
1. 3M–4F	4M–3F
2. cock–hen	needle–knife
3. *Kwong'a* – father of kings	*Kwong'a* – mother of Kings
4. *Kwong'a* tries to kill D's twin sons	*Bukuku* tries to kill D's 'twin' son.
5. F of twin up from underworld	F of twins down from overworld
6. cattle lead Alur permanently up to Highlands	cattle lead Nyoro *Isaza* temporarily down to underworld
7. one pot with 2 mouths = twinship in concrete (natural human) mode	2 bags with 1 mouth = twinship in abstract (supernatural) mode
8. brothers break 'natural' brotherhood over bead extracted from blood and milk	brothers fail to make 'cultural' brotherhood over twin coffee beans immersed in blood and milk

For certain purposes we may distinguish two points in these oral traditions, point A referring to the beginnings of human society and point B referring to the establishment of the present dynasty in the country. In the Ukuru Alur version the founding of the dynasty is taken back to point A, referring both to the initial ordering of human society and the separation of men and animals, although there is another body of myth at point B, referring to the establishment of the dynasty in its present territory. In Bunyoro the dynastic foundation is at point B. Thus in Alur the twin theme refers to point A, but in Bunyoro to point B, while the theme of distribution between brothers occurs at point A in Bunyoro and point B in Alur. In Bunyoro the three brothers are sometimes called sons of Kintu 'the created thing' (Beattie, 1960, p. 11) and stand for the three orders of traditional Nyoro society: *Bairu* (agricultural serfs); *Bahima* or *Bahuma* (pastoralists); and *Bakama* (rulers). But the order of social precedence is reversed in the age-order of the brothers: Kairu being the eldest, Kahuma next, and Kakama the youngest. The brothers who figure in the Alur distribution theme at point B are Nyabong'o, Nyipir, and Thiful. The last is said to have disappeared to the west, Nyipir established the Ukuru Alur in their present country, and Nyabong'o founded the ruling dynasty in Bunyoro. Nyoro tradition is in agreement on this position, of Nyabong'o, although Nyabong'o is also known there by the other names of Isingoma Mpuga Rukidi. For Bunyoro Nyabong'o is a twin. For Alur he is not, but the major shrine of Jok Rubanga in Alur is also called Rukidi.

Rubanga appears in Buganda in the linguistically cognate forms Muwanga and Wanga. Wanga is referred to as the oldest of the Ganda spirit pantheon, though not the most important in degree of attention. Neither are specifically concerned with twins, which are the gift of Mukasa, the most important of the spirits. However, Mukasa is regarded as the son of Musisi, the son of Wanga. All these beings are *Balubale*, corresponding to the Nyoro *Bacwezi* and including several of the same named beings. Balubale are generally linked with Lake Victoria, the Sese Islands, and their people. Lake Victoria itself was traditionally known as Nalubale. These interrelationships are tabulated in *Table 2*.

Twinship is equally closely connected with kingship in Buganda, but in a different way. The king's umbilical cord, and indeed that of commoners also, was preserved, decorated, and referred to as the king's twin. On accession the king took a special name for himself and for this twin. It is interesting, however, that these twin names are not recorded for the first king, Kintu, nor for the second, Cwa Nabaka, but for the third, Kimera, who came from Bunyoro and all subsequent kings down to Mutesa I (Edel, 1934).

While the Ganda Kings took separate Kingship and twinship names, both in Luganda, the Bito Kings of Bunyoro took Nilotic drum names as well as Bantu names, and some early Alur kings took Bantu (Nyoro) names. Furthermore, the Nyoro were given special Nilotic *mpako* names in addition to their Bantu names. These names mean nothing in Bantu but are easily recognizable as Nilotic names. The term *mpako* is also derived from the Nilotic root *pak* meaning to praise. Thus the

TABLE 2   *Rubanga and Cognate Forms*

Nyoro 'h' = Ganda 'w'; e.g. Nyoro *hano*, Ganda *wano*, = here
Nyoro: -HANGA, *v. tr.*, create, fix in handle, mortise, dig deep, plough
Ganda: -WANGA, *v. tr.*, injure, fix in handle, mortise, treat badly
Nyoro: -BANGA, *v. tr.*, cut notch in, mortise
Ganda: -BANGA, *v. tr.*, found (city), cut notch in, mortise, begin at
Nyoro: -HANGAHANGA, *v. tr.*, invent
Nyoro: -HANGA, *v. i.*, to shine at midday (sun)
Ganda: -WANGA, *v. i.*, to be sharp
Acholi: -BANG'I, *n.*, twins
Teso: -IBANGIN, *n.*, twins
Nyoro: RU-HANGA (class I), God
Nyoro: RU-HANGA (class VI), a skull
Ganda: LU-WANGA, a skull (especially of dead notable)
Ganda: EKI-WANGA, a skull (ordinary)
Nyoro: NYA-MU-HANGA = RU-HANGA
Ganda: MU-WANGA, *n.*, a god (LUBAALE)
Ganda: -WANGA, *n.*, the oldest of the gods
Nyoro: RU-BANGA, *n.*, god ((CWEZI) of twins
Ganda: LU-BANGA, *n.*, a god (LUBAALE), thwart or seat of canoe (which
      is *mortised* in)
Ganda: LUBAALE (pl. Balubaale), *n.*, god, deity, spirit
Nyoro: RUBAALE, *n.*, red bull with white spots (apparently not in Ru-
      class just as LUBAALE is not in Lu- class)
Nyoro: OMU-IRU RUBAALE, *n.*, bondslave
Ganda: KA-DDU LUBAALE, *n.*, 'little slave of god,' -chief wife of King
      -DDU (Ganda = -IRU (Nyoro)
Ganda: NA-LUBAALE, *n.*, Lake Victoria (implies female, mother or
      source of gods)
Nyoro: KI-BAALE, *n.*, spirit shrine
Ganda: M-BAALE, *n.*, name of a number of sites associated with important
      shrines of deities

Alur call praise names *nying' pak*. The drum names and *mpako* are listed by Pellegrini (1949, pp. 48–9). In Crazzolara's recording of the oral tradition of the Patiko Acholi (1951, p. 223) there were again three sons, their father being Labong'o (= Nyabong'o), here said to be the son of Lwoo. The sons were Kijook, Tere, and Tika. Their relative fitness to rule was tried out by their father in various tests involving the twinship motif such as who could cause a cow to give birth to a 'black bull calf having a tail with two tips', or who could strike two spades (hoes) together and cause them to unite. Tika who was apparently the youngest of the three, as in the Nyoro version, won all the tests and succeeded to the kingship of his father. In much more recent Nyoro tradition the explorer Sir Samuel Baker himself tested the Mukama of Bunyoro with a two-hoe puzzle (Southall, 1951), and the same theme appears among the Kinga.[7]

From the Bunyoro point of view, *Kimera* is the younger twin brother (Kato = the little one) to Isingoma Mpuga Rukidi Nyabong'o, founder of the Bito dynasty in Bunyoro and brother of Nyipir, who established the Alur in their present country. For the Baganda, Kimera is not a twin, but the son of Kalemera, son of the Ganda King Cwa Nabaka, by Wanyana, wife of the King of Bunyoro whom Kalemera seduced. As Nyabong'o is a twin in the Nyoro version but not in that of the Alur, so Kimera is a twin in the Nyoro version but not in that of the Ganda. Thus the Alur, Nyoro, and Ganda stress kingship as twinship in three different ways (see *Table 3*).

TABLE 3   *Twinship*

	Alur	Nyoro	Ganda
Nyabong'o	−	+	o
Kimera	o	+	−

TWINSHIP present (+)   absent (−)
Character not represented (o)

We have seen that Alur numerical symbolism for male and female is reversed in Bunyoro. Such permutations appear among a number of neighbouring peoples, but unfortunately the ethnographic data supply no interpretation. There are some surprises. The Acholi neighbours of the Alur to the east, who are culturally very close to them, have the reversed numerical symbolism of the Nyoro. So also do the Lang'o further east, who speak Lwoo like the Acholi and Alur, but in other respects are culturally linked with the Nilo-Hamites. Among the northern Nilo-Hamites, the Lotuko have the Alur version and the Bari and Kuku that of the Nyoro and Lang'o. The Nyoro share two different patterns of numerical symbolism, for while expressing sex differences in the ritual numbers three and four, nine is the most important in the rest of the ritual system. The Ganda likewise stress nine in their ritual practices, including those for birth and for both males and females, while no ritual importance attaches to the numbers three and four. It would appear that two systems of numerical symbolism are combined in Bunyoro, which appear separately in Buganda and Alur respectively. However, the Nilo-Hamitic Kipsigis, neighbours of the Luyia and Kenya Luo, also stress the number nine in ritual, together with four symbolizing male and three symbolizing females as in Bunyoro. Not only does the 4–3 symbolism appear in major rituals of birth, circumcision, and death, but on various social occasions men are formally grouped in fours and women in threes. On the other hand, certain aspects of Kipsigis religion are associated with the ritual value of nine, as in the case of the supreme deity Asis, associated with the Sun. Chepkelyen Sogol ('nine feet') refers to the sun's rays and also has the sense of 'infinity'.[8] We may recall that the Dinka always group subordinate segments into threes, as eldest, middle, and youngest brother, even if the genealogy generates segments descended from, say, five brothers (Lienhardt, 1958, pp. 120–4), while the Bedouin of the Western Desert in Egypt always group subordinate segments into fours, symbolized in descending order of seniority as chest, neck, stomach, and head of an animal.[9] On the other hand, the Arusha group all segments in pairs, whether based on descent, age, or locality (Gulliver, 1961; 1963, p. 31, pp. 116–18, pp. 144–6).

This somewhat fragmentary information on numerical sex symbolism is presented in the following table as a stimulus to further inquiry (*Table 4*).

However, Alur and Lugbara were hardly in contact before the colonial period, and the status of the Palwo is somewhat anomalous.

Such an incomplete selection of data certainly seems to confirm the fact that ethnography is very poor in this respect and

TABLE 4

3M 4F	4M 3F	9	
N Alur	CB Nyoro	Nyoro	5M 4F
N Jo-Luo (Wau)[1]	NH Kipsigis	Kipsigis	
N Dinka	N Acholi[2]	SB Kikuyu	Kikuyu
NH Lotuko[10]	N Lang'o[3]	CB Ganda	
N Palwo[12]	N Kenya Luo[4]		4M 5F
N Padhola [12]	NH Bari (Kuku)[11]		
	S Lugbara[5]		N Nuer[6]
			4M 2F
3M 2F	3		NH Sebei[9]
SB Luyia[7]	NH Nandi		
	NH Teso[8]		

CB = centralized Bantu
SB = stateless Bantu
N = Nilotic (Western Nilotes)
S = Sudanic
NH = Nilo-Hamitic (Eastern Nilotes)

Thus, if we relate political or cultural identity or opposition to symbolic identity or opposition, among adjacent peoples, we have a majority of cases where identity on the one dimension is associated with opposition in the other:

Adjacent peoples.	Identity: political or cultural	–	symbolic
Alur/Acholi	—	+	—
Palwo/Acholi	—	+	—
Palwo/Nyoro	+	—	—
Padhola/Luo	—	+	—
Acholi/Lang'o	—	—	+
Luo/Kipsigis	—	—	+
Kipsigis/Nandi	—	+	—
A few pairs are dubious, such as			
Alur/Nyoro Bito	—	+	—
And a few run contrary			
Alur/Palwo	—	+	+
Alur/Lugbara	—	—	—

[1] Butt (1964, p. 173)
[2] Butt (1964, p. 91)
[3] Driberg (1923, p. 139)
[4] Mboya (1945, p. 77)
[5] Middleton and Winter (1963, p. 265) Middleton (1961, p. 34)
[6] Evans-Pritchard (1956, p. 145)
[7] Wagner (1949, p. 304)
[8] Lawrance (1957, pp. 87–8)
[9] Weatherby (1967, p. 248)
[10] Huntingford (1953a, p. 83)
[11] Huntingford (1953a, p. 47)
[12] Southall, unpublished field notes.

reflects a lack of interest and awareness. It throws into yet sharper relief the volume, complexity, and coherence of the

Dogon data. This was referred to at some length by Richards (1967, p. 288) but it is still necessary to draw attention to some other aspects, most obviously the symbolic representation of both sex differences and twinship. Among both the Dogon and the Bambara (Dieterlen, 1951, pp. 26–7, p. 150, p. 352 fn.) three represents masculinity and four feminity. Twinship is also at the heart of things. The male number forms the basis for a sexagesimal system of numbers through the *doubling* of three to six and reproducing it in multiples of ten. The same process of *doubling* and reproduction in the case of the female number leads to the ultimate figure of 800, signifying infinity. The sexagesimal system is called the counting 'of the Mande' and the octogesimal system the counting 'of the East'. But on the other hand the Bambara system is vigesimal, representing the twenty digits of hands and feet and again the multiplication of this sum by the male number to produce 60 and by the female number to produce 80 (Dieterlen, 1951, p. 27). Furthermore, the male and female numbers are explicitly related to 'la verge et les deux testicules' and 'les quatres levres', respectively (op. cit., p. 17).

Nothing approaching such multifold elaboration has ever been reported from East Africa. Nor is it likely that this is solely due to sloppy fieldwork. It is easy to point to the historical links of the Dogon, Bambara, and other peoples of the Western Sudan with the great medieval empires, such as Ghana and Mali, and with literate civilizations extending beyond the borders of Africa. This does not detract from the cultural achievement of the Dogon or Bambara, since no precise replica of their symbolic system has ever been reported from the Mali Empire or from Islamic peoples. It does, however, leave the question unanswered as to what degree of symbolic elaboration and coherence was achieved by other African cultures in other regions. Nor do the Sudanese studies offer any answer to the question as to whether seemingly complementary symbolic features *between* cultures are to be interpreted as fortuitous or meaningful. The Dogon-Bambara interpretation of their male and female numerical symbols seems so fundamental that it is almost surprising not to find it universal. However, it is much easier to accept the fact that in certain cultures this potential source of symbolism is simply not selected for emphasis than to comprehend how it actually comes to be reversed. In fact, none of the East African peoples who share the Bambara numerical sex symbols are reported as having the same interpretation of it (nor indeed any other). It is perhaps reassuring that there are other West African peoples, studied by French scholars, who are admitted not to possess any very elaborate, multifaceted structure of symbolism. Thus, it is recognized that the cosmology of the Diola of Senegal shows a certain lack of epistemological structure and many inaccuracies and contradictions of detail (Thomas, 1966, p. 377). Although there is reference to bipolarity, dichotomy, and complementarity, these features do not seem very marked.

The symbolic structure associated with Peul initiation (Dieterlen, 1966) shares the same numerical sex symbols as Dogon and Bambara, but in other respects is elaborated quite differently, although Peul and Bambara are in close contact and Bambara marry Peul women. No inverse or complementary aspects of their symbolic systems are reported.

It is implied that the same general system is widespread in the Western Sudan.[10] The only hints of complementarity are superficial: while the Dogon and Bambara, as cultivators, have eight grains of cereal in their clavicles, the Bozo fishermen have eight fish (Dieterlen, 1950, pp. 360, 363) and that for the Dogon double ears of millet and for the Bozo two fish in congress – called twins (les poissons accolés – ils son dits jumeaux) – symbolize the twinship that pervades their cosmology. When a Dogon finds in his field a head of small millet with two ears[11] (un épi de mil *yu* a deux panicules), it is cut, taken to the domestic shrine and used at the next sowing, when one grain is thrown in the direction of the Bozo. However, since the Bozo are actually quite far from the Dogon, this reciprocal relation is transferred within Dogon society and carried out between regions, such as Sanga and Bamba, which are in a joking partnership, each group being considered to have *sixteen* grains in its clavicles in relation to the other group (Dieterlen, p. 364). Correspondingly if a Bozo finds two fish in congress he must find a Dogon and eat them together with him.

The Ifa divination of the Yoruba is at least as complex numerically as the Dogon and Bambara symbolism, but although it is also based essentially on the concept of twinship (McClelland, 1966, p. 424) and on units of eight and sixteen, its numerical development is completely different. Its sixteen columns of signs are said to be identical with those of an ancient Near Eastern system adopted in medieval Europe and also by the Arabs (Morton-Williams, 1966, p. 407). But it has been 'thoroughly integrated into Yoruba cosmological conceptions' (ibid.) and appears to be the focus of systems used over a wide area by Yoruba, Benin, Fon of Dahomey, Ewe of Togo and Ghana, Idoma, Igala, Ibo, and peoples of Yoruba descent in Cuba and Brazil. A similar inspiration is frequently suggested for the Sikidy divination in Madagascar (ibid., cf. Bloch, 1969), but all these systems are so completely different from one another when taken as wholes that only the general idea can have been borrowed and as systems they have to be regarded as independent.

In the interactions of neighbouring peoples (*Table 4*) on the Nilotic–Bantu borderland Alur-Acholi represents likeness of language and general culture combined with reversal of numerical symbolism, Acholi-Lang'o represents likeness of language, but unlikeness of general culture and social organization with identity of numerical symbolism. With Kenya Luo-Kipsigis we have unlikeness of language and culture with strong traditional hostility combined with identity of numerical symbolism. With Alur-Nyoro there is a stratum of cultural likeness, with reversal of numerical symbolism linked in Nyoro to another (Bantu) stratum of cultural unlikeness with its own distinct numerical symbolism. Obviously many further questions are raised and these cannot be answered fully here.

Neither Alur nor Acholi are wholly meaningful units of comparison. There may be subsidiary transformations between chiefdoms or clusters of chiefdoms within them, or with Junam as intercalary to Alur and Acholi, or Palwo as intercalary between Nyoro on the one side and Acholi on the other. The connection between interlocality symbolic transformations and joking relationships, suggested by the Bambara account, certainly needs further study.

Most accounts of the articulation between symbolic ideas and social groupings refer to descent groups. However, in eastern Africa there is a striking elaboration of symbolism in relation to age-groups. The study of this aspect has been badly neglected, in spite of its obvious importance, for example, among the Masai-speaking peoples, and it is paradoxical that the cosmological referents of age organization should only have been recorded for the Teso, where the system has long been abolished. 'The whole sphere of natural existence was methodically divided between the eight age-sets, so that each set had religious or ritual powers over a series of associated objects or activities' (Lawrance, 1957, pp. 78–8). Thus, the Floods had control over water and heavenly bodies, the Buffaloes over the seasons, the Elephants over things of strength like fire, iron, and wood, the Warthogs over fertility, the Hawks over wealth and especially cattle, the Leopards over plunder and theft. There are many apparent inconsistencies or obscurities, but no fieldwork was done on the subject while the system still flourished.

The analysis of Fipa myth by Willis (1964, 1967) is perhaps the most interesting to date by an Africanist in the tradition of British social anthropology, because it presents an elaborate symbolic structure at many interlocking levels, which is not the product of esoteric knowledge by specialists within the culture, but of relating together different aspects of Fipa culture that carry these latent implications. It is not essential for them all to be integrated or comprehensively formulated by any one mind within the culture. Their logic, consistency, and integration is to be found in the ongoing collective activity of the culture as a whole. 'The relative explicitness or otherwise of all these ideas in Fipa thinking' is recognized as variable (Willis, 1967, p. 529) and the myths are not only generally restricted to a formally consistent logical structure, but are also particular in relating to the 'one or more organisational aspects of the society that produced them' (op. cit., p. 531). Willis is concerned to bridge the gulf between social thought and social action represented by the synoptic approach of Lévi-Strauss in *Le Cru et le cuit*, which 'achieves astonishing coherence and complexity – but at the price of severing virtually all links with the solid ground of ethnography' (op. cit., p. 529).

Willis's own work also suggests another important middle road, in which ethnographic touch would not be lost by ranging too widely over whole continents, but the structure of myth in one society would be set in a limited but meaningful comparative context, by analysing the permutations and transformations in similar mythical structures in closely cognate or interacting cultures. Such a development was implied in *La Geste d'Asdiwal*. Willis's ethnography of the Fipa and their neighbours (1966) provides data that suggest the metamorphosis of mythical themes in relation to the differing organizational aspects of neighbouring societies. For example, whereas in the Fipa myth it is the middle or elder of the sisters who overcomes the King because he is embarrassed at his underarm hair, in Lungwa to the northeast it is the younger sister who prevails over the older because of the latter's embarrassment at underarm hair and also because the younger had slept on the ground she claimed, not on a bed like the elder. For the Pimbwe neighbours west of Lungwa and northwest of Fipa, it is the younger brother who prevails by sleeping on the ground. Through further permutations these themes are transformed into the mythical charters of Ngonde-Nyakyusa-Kinga peoples (*Figure 1*).

These cannot be set out with any adequacy, but strongly suggest again that a variety of themes are played in counterpoint by a number of neighbouring peoples. Thus in the religious systems of the Ngonde–Nyakyusa–Kinga cluster there was 'no single supreme power' (Wilson, 1959, p. 156). 'The evidence suggests that Kyala, Lwembe or Mbasi, Kyungu, and Ngulube were used in the same way in different areas, Kyala being the hero of the northeast shore of the Lake, Kyungu of the northwest, Lwembe of the central Nyakyusa valley, and Ngulube of the scarp edge of the Livingstones' (ibid.). Ngulube (Nguluwe, Ngulwe, Nguluvi) appears again as supreme divinity of the Kuulwe (Willis, 1966, p. 66) and also among the Safwa (op. cit., p. 71) where he is often associated with sun, although in many Bantu languages the root means 'pig' (cf. Beidelman, 1964). It may, however, be the root *gulu* (= sky, above) rather than the root *guluwe* (= pig).

Figure 1

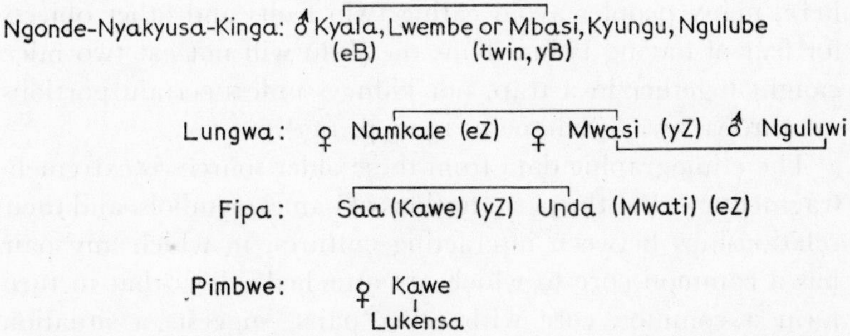

Ngonde-Nyakyusa-Kinga: ♂ Kyala, Lwembe or Mbasi, Kyungu, Ngulube
(eB)   (twin, yB)

Lungwa: ♀ Namkale (eZ) ♀ Mwasi (yZ) ♂ Nguluwi

Fipa: Saa (Kawe) (yZ) Unda (Mwati) (eZ)

Pimbwe: ♀ Kawe
          |
        Lukensa

Among the Nyakyusa 'there were hints of some special connection between the hero Mbasi and twins (*amapasa*), the elder of whom is *Mbasa*' (Wilson, 1957, p. 167, fn. 1). Indeed, the hints are many. *Mbasa*, like Rubanga in Bunyoro, is constantly involved in the prolonged and elaborate rituals for twins and other abnormal births classed with them. The parent of twins is 'the child of Mbasi' (ibid.). There are the following suggestive derivatives and cognates: Nyakyusa *amapasa* = twins – also in Fipa and Pimbwe (Willis, 1966, pp. 31, 58), *ampasa* in Ndembu (Turner, 1969, p. 58), and *ubasa* in Zaramo (Beidelman, 1967, p. 20), *ipasa* or *ilipasa* = twin or abnormal birth, *abipasya* = parents of twins, 'the fearful ones', *ukupasya* = to be afraid, *ukupasa* = to beget twins, or abnormal children,

ukupasana = to branch from one root (Wilson, 1957, p. 152).
In Runyoro we have *mahasa* = twins (Davis, 1952, p. 89), which
Beattie says denotes 'a concept rather than a thing' (1962, p. 1).
Despite the distance of seven or eight hundred miles between
the Nyakyusa and the Ganda–Nyoro–Ankole cluster, and the
relative remoteness of any possible cultural or historical connection between them, the idea of twin bananas and human
twins is closely linked in both cases. In Runyoro -*hasana* means
'grow together (e.g. twin plantains), be superfluous' (Davis,
1962, p. 41), and in Runyankole -*hasanura* means 'divide (e.g.
twin plaintains)' (ibid). In Luganda (*y*) *asa* means 'chop, split;
asamu, chop in two' (Kitching and Blackledge, 1925, p. 2). In
Nyakyusa pagans do not eat twin bananas because they are
twins (Wilson, 1957, p. 167). Though this is not made explicit
here, many peoples avoid eating twin fruits and other objects
for fear of having twins. Thus the Zulu will not eat two mice
caught together in a trap, nor kidneys unless certain portions
are thrown away (Schapera, 1927, p. 127).

The ethnographic data from these older sources is extremely
fragmentary, but the permutations of names, symbols, and their
relationships between interacting cultures, in which any pair
has a common core to which are attached others that in turn
form a common core with other pairs, suggests a situation
analogous to the one we have explored among the cluster of
interlacustrine Bantu and Nilotic peoples.

It is clear that East African peoples were not without cosmology and quite elaborately articulated symbolic structures. But
so far these structures are built up by the anthropologist from
the whole body of data, not explicitly presented by experts
within the culture concerned. The comparative data are not
good enough to tell us whether the fragmentary appearance of
the cosmologies of some cultures is due to poor fieldwork, to
loss in the course of recent rapid change, to the relatively
shallow time depth of most East African compared with West
African cultures, or to the intrinsic conditions of segmentary
societies. It would be possible to argue that cosmologies based

upon or incorporating a fixed symbolic pattern of social groups are incompatible with the diachronic mechanism of segmentary lineage systems. There is plenty of room for symbolic and cosmological expression and development apart from this, but perhaps not in such intricate contrapuntal articulation. However, East African age organizations have a built-in tendency to elaborate and pervasive dualism, both in their symbolism and their structure (Gulliver, 1961; 1963, p. 31, 116–18, 144–146; Huntingford, 1953c, pp. 117–21). Another interesting form of reversal here is that, while the Arusha speak the Masai language and share their age organization and much common culture, the dualism of the agricultural Arusha is expressed in the dichotomous division of the corporate social groupings, but not in their symbolism; on the other hand, the dualism of the pastoral Masai is expressed in their symbolism and not in their corporate social groupings.

Eastern and western Africa contain within them such wide variations in the sheer size of social systems and their degree of specialization, that any simple contrast between them must be crude. However, the evidence strongly suggests that cosmologies are less elaborate in East Africa, though this is compounded by the fact that they have been poorly studied. No British studies in the East come near to matching the long-term devotion and commitment of the best French studies in West Africa.

But it is well to remember that the most impressive analysis of the symbolic structure of myths has been done for South America (Lévi-Strauss, 1964, 1969) whose ethnographic record would not usually be considered better than that of East Africa were it not for the rather narrow focus of much work by social anthropologists in the latter region, which leaves a sense of inadequacy when theoretical fashions change.

What has been attempted here is much more limited in range of available data and depth of analysis than the treatment of the South American myths, but it raises some different questions, as well as bringing in some new ethnographic material, or new emphases upon the old. While Lévi-Strauss chose his ethnographic starting-point by intuition if not arbitrarily (1962, p. 2) and recognizes that he could have started anywhere within the group of myths, he keeps insisting that all the myths he deals with constitute a single set; that although his analysis spreads like a nebula and cannot be contained within any territorial limits or single system of classification, yet the nebula condenses as it spreads, and the central parts disclose a structure, while uncertainty and confusion continue to prevail along the periphery (Lévi-Strauss, 1969, p. 3).

In the East African context, and with regard to other types of ethnographic analysis as well, I should wish to stress that no centre is to be assumed other than that arbitrarily chosen by the anthropologist according to the distribution of his knowledge. In view of its manifest political pre-eminence and ritual elaboration, it would be easy to assume that Bunyoro was the centre of a ramifying set of symbols. But while for certain aspects, such as the Cwezi, this is probably true, for others it is not, and such an assumption is a temptation to which we have succumbed far too much and by which our understanding of ethnic identities and interconnections has been extensively vitiated. Lévi-Strauss implies that if his project could be accomplished it would spread throughout the Americas. Would this also still constitute a 'single set'? My fleeting vision, derived from work in East Africa, is certainly not of a single set of mythical themes gradually ramifying across Africa as understanding spreads, but of a very large number of interlocking sets, to which there is no beginning and no end. And, of course, this is true in time as well as space. The immense time depth and the endlessly repetitive quality of symbolic items through time has been vividly conveyed by Thomas Mann (1963, pp. 1–10).

Recourse to distributional analysis of myth and symbol by computer as envisaged by Lévi-Strauss (1966a, pp. 89, 151), must call to mind the older style distribution studies of culture by Boas, Kroeber, Klimek, and their colleagues and disciples. For these were the most sophisticated ever made, and many of the same problems of definitions will be encountered again, although the objectives would be very different. Boas at least recognized that the distribution areas of technology, social organization, ritual, art, music, or myth do not coincide, but such an admission was rejected by Kroeber as 'contrary to the overwhelming run of the facts' (1939, p. 4). Kroeber did see that two peoples classified in separate areas yet adjoining one another might have more in common than either had with peoples at the focal points of their respective areas, but he claimed that this was no worse a twisting of empirical reality than that involved in faunal and floral classifications. Boundaries would be better represented by shaded areas than by clear-cut lines, but this was inhibited by mechanical difficulties (Kroeber, 1939, pp. 5–6). The aspects of data in which we are interested here are strictly speaking antithetical to those of Kroeber, since we are particularly exploring the ways in which adjoining peoples who are most unlike identify themselves symbolically. Such facts are of an entirely different order from those that served Kroeber's primarily historical interests.

Historians endeavour to distinguish the historically relevant parts of oral tradition from the rest in a way which is not necessary in the structural study of myth. Lévi-Strauss deliberately refrains from precise definitions of myth. Symbolic structure may be traced in recounted or enacted myths, in ritual performances, stated belief, royal genealogies, clan traditions, and in so-called animal stories.

Different parts of the body of evidence relate differently to graded levels of generality, from possibly universal archetypes,[12] to less than universal but very widespread themes; large regional and possibly multilingual communications systems; neighbouring or cognate languages and cultural groups; single cultures somewhat arbitrarily defined; ritual and symbolic items belonging to particular groups and institutions within a society; and, finally, the variations in ritual and symbolic performances between individuals and of a single individual over extended periods of time. As Lévi-Strauss recognized (1969, p. 7), the evidence when seen in this way, as it must be, can never possibly be complete.

The unicultural analysis of 'The Head and the Loins' (Willis, 1967) intentionally presents us with the opposite procedural pole to that of *The Raw and the Cooked*. The transformations wrought from myth to myth by Lévi-Strauss usually between societies, sometimes quite far-flung, are wrought by Willis within Fipa culture between different conceptual and affective fields of activity. Admirable as is this restoration of sociological correlates and relation of symbolic structure to empirically established social institutions, it would seem that a synthesis to this antithesis is still required, for in what sense can we conscientiously regard these structures as produced by the Fipa alone? Certainly much of the content is particularly Fipa, yet the comparative ethnographic work of Willis himself (1966), as well as that of Monica Wilson nearby (1957, 1959), makes it quite clear that the Fipa are participating in a much wider communication system over time and space. The full meaning of the particular cast that the Fipa have put upon this structure will not be apparent until we know how it relates and reacts with that of their neighbours who share so much of it, especially since the designation Fipa, like so many ethnic names, is itself both highly ambiguous and far from indicating a neatly bounded entity. It is perfectly legitimate for one scholar to prefer an intensive intracultural interpretation like Willis, while another is drawn to intracultural analysis like Lévi-Strauss. But it is hard to see how the one can be more valuable or complete than the other, or even wholly intelligible without it. The work of Griaule, Dieterlen, and their colleagues seems mainly of the intracultural variety, although it relates to Dogon, Bambara, Bozo, and other local groups and is traced back in part to a central focus in the medieval Mali empire (Dieterlen, 1957). Although there are many hints of possible transformation and complementarity in the distribution of cultural items and languages among these various groups, such aspects have not been systematically analysed.

In my preliminary exploration of the Nilotic–Bantu border-land I have drawn attention to one further dimension of analysis, the sharing and transmission of symbolic elements across major linguistic and cultural boundaries, and the transformations and reversals that occur between neighbouring peoples of similar language and culture. Etymology here reveals a vital part of the orchestration. Inevitably the problem of varying levels of socio-cultural complexity, deliberately excluded by Lévi-Strauss, is also involved. Bunyoro and Buganda were among the most centralized kingdoms in Africa. The chiefdoms of the Alur and Acholi were segmentary states. The Lang'o, Kenya Luo, Kipsigis, Lugbara, and other neighbouring peoples were stateless societies with variable emphasis on segmentary lineages, age organization, and cross-cutting cult groups. There was no boundary between the Alur, Acholi, and Palwo; they were interpenetrating and each shaded imperceptibly into the other. How then can we speak of transformations and complementarities between units that we cannot precisely define and that indeed appear to have been quite indistinct? The much smaller political units of chiefdoms, or localized lineages and cult areas were somewhat more distinct, but even here the perception of inter-group identities was highly egocentric, depending upon the position of the person or group whose particular vantage point we adopt. This brings us to the fundamental issue that the mystery of relating symbolic transformations and reversals to fluid cultural and group boundaries cannot be solved unless we can study individual and local variability in symbolic heritage and perception in and across supposed transition zones. In the study of structure, process, and change in the context of general social behaviour this is now commonplace, and even in relation to ritual is becoming so. The symbolic structure of myth so often regarded as deep structure, supposedly immune from such tiresome vagaries, has to be brought into the same discourse after all.

The approaches of Turner and Lévi-Strauss illustrate most of the main differences of emphasis between British and French interpretations of symbolism.[13] In Turner's analysis of *nkula, isoma, mukanda,* or *wubwang'u* (1967, 1969) we get a profound insight into meaning and sequence in symbolism as the ordered phases of a ritual unfold. In Lévi-Strauss's South American studies we are stunned by the recurring logical properties of myths over a wide area. From Turner's work we have no idea yet whether the logical properties and structural principles enunciated by Lévi-Strauss can be found to underlie either the relation between successive phases of a ritual or the relation between the different dimensions, codes, modalities, or planes of symbols, within a culture, let alone between the differing meanings attached to colour codes or psychosomatic codes in the symbolism of neighbouring or related cultures. We see the rich significance of red, white, and black in Ndembu; we note similar echoes and then divergent echoes scattered about Africa and elsewhere. Is this order or chaos, harmony or discord? Why is black sterility here, rain-fertility there? Fire blackens and destroys everywhere (as well as cooking and so encultur- ing); rainclouds are black everywhere and bring fertility to the soil (as well as lightning and flood). If the seeming contra- dictions are resolved by situations and contextual distinctions, do the latter follow discernible rules? Is it not reasonable to suppose that colour symbolism operates at a more general level than that of a particular botanical species of limited dis- tribution, such as the *mudyi* (milk) tree (Turner, 1967, p. 20), or do such vagaries occur 'outside the mind' as Lévi-Strauss would say (1966a, p. 65)? These echoes of harmony and discord are left without rhyme or reason. It is the diverse richness of possible meanings flowing from a single symbol, which is emphasized, rather than any intelligible order or principle underlying the diversities.

With Lévi-Strauss we do not know why correspondences and transformations can be extracted from the myths of groups A, C, and E, rather than B, D, and F, or why within group A or D they appear in some myths and not in others, or whether they are echoed and confirmed in the sequential phases of ritual. Thus one set of data yields structure in myth, the other yields process in ritual (itself diachronic structure in this case), though both sets of data are plausibly assumed to be composed of the same symbolic elements.

Paradoxically, it is the vast spatial range of correspondences and transformations unearthed by Lévi-Strauss that is impressive, yet the spatial distribution itself makes no sense. Myth is presented as essentially primeval and 'synchronic' with social factors as negative restrictions rather than positive stimuli to symbolic process. The perfect logic of the primeval structure is twisted and destroyed by them rather than giving them positive expression. The practice and process of Ndembu ritual expresses deep meaning both at universal human and particular social levels. But how is the relative invariability of the universals and the infinite variety of the particulars reconciled as between different times and places? It is conceivable that the particulars represent reactions to situations that are unique, in the sense that the same combination of elements in the same proportion or strength is never and nowhere repeated, yet at the same time the reactions reflect the same limited corpus of logical properties and principles everywhere. It still remains to be demonstrated that such principles operate in Africa and that their distribution in South America makes sense.

There is a striking contrast between Turner's emphasis on the many meanings of a single symbol in ritual and that of Lévi-Strauss on the many different symbols equated in a single meaning in myth. All conceivable phenomena of human experience can be brought into play by the mythical imagination, and all things are possible to the mythical actors, so that a limited number of themes can be illustrated in innumerable different ways. On the other hand, in ritual the actors and their materials are definitely limited, but they can represent a very wide variety of meanings within these limitations. This, also, was foreshadowed in Richards's analysis of Chisungu (1956, pp. 165, 169). Lévi-Strauss reduces the complex action of myth to a limited number of recurring themes; Turner expands the limited action of ritual to a complex variety of themes. Myth uses all five senses, whereas ritual can make distinctive use of only two or three. It is not easy to see how even dominant symbols can 'possess a high degree of constancy and consistency throughout the total symbolic system', when at both sensory and ideological poles are clustered 'disparate and even contradictory *significata*' (Turner, 1967, pp. 31, 33). It is natural enough that red should stand for a number of things, both good and evil, but it does not appear that the different *significata* correspond consistently to the different substances used for redness. Whereas, in the South American myths, jaguar, alligator, and opossum are interchangeable (Lévi-Strauss, 1969, p. 195), having the same symbolic value as one another among a number of different peoples. There is at present no demonstrable consistency, integration, or complementarity – whether through equivalence or transformation – between the ritual structures of different people comparable to that demonstrated for the mythical structure of various South American peoples. We conclude that while myth and ritual are of the same stuff and have a considerable common core where myth charters ritual and ritual re-enacts myth, and both obey a grammar that is paralleled through the social structure, beyond this the elaboration of symbols and meanings proceeds along rather divergent lines in the one case as compared to the other. Perhaps further work will show this divergence to be due more to interpretation than to data. Data that are as little subject to ambiguity and equivocation as the ritual numbers of the sexes on the Nilotic–Bantu borderland may provide convincing clues to the existence and extent of the rules of symbolic transformation in both myth and ritual between neighbouring cognate and interacting cultures.

Somewhat strangely, in *The Savage Mind* we were kept hovering on the brink of these issues, from which the narrower mythological focus of the later works has veered away (Lévi-Strauss, 1966a). We are treated to the whole gamut of inter-related conceptual systems in non-literate cultures; not myths

merely, but numerology, personal and clan naming, the classification of plants and animals and the detailed parts of their
anatomy; colours, smells, and hairstyles; the cardinal directions, seasons, and heavenly bodies, not to mention the basic
features of social structure. The irresistible implication is that
all these systems fall into an integrated, grand design, not only
within a single culture but from one to another. But two in-
surmountable obstacles dash our hopes. When the data are
available they are too numerous, and must be 'reserved for the
ethnology of a future century' (1966a, p. 151). But often the
traditional data are hopelessly inadequate and unreliable, collected 'when the traditional institutions no longer existed
except in old informants' memories' and 'partly made up of
old wives tales' (1966a, p. 119). Yet when we come to contemporary societies with working institutions it is no better, for
vulnerable synchronic structures are shattered by diachrony
and ways of thinking degenerate into ways of remembering
(op. cit., p. 67), for 'history and demographic development
always upset the plans conceived by the wise' (op. cit., p. 155)
and 'the nearer we get to concrete groups the more we must
expect to find arbitrary distinctions and denominations which
are explicable primarily in terms of occurrences and events and
defy any logical arrangement'. Such an extreme commitment
to the homeostatic model of society, rejected by most people
along with the excesses of functionalism, is alarming, and
seemingly nonsensical, since it is impossible rationally to conceive how cognitive structures could ever have arisen in cultures free of occurrences and events. Indeed, bricolage is
history.

Despite Lévi-Strauss's claims of universal application for his
version of structural anthropology, his attempts to bring contemporary western culture into its framework have been feeble.
His admiration for Kroeber's study of feminine dress fashions,
his analysis of French and Chinese cuisine – 'this somewhat
flimsy example' (1963, p. 87) – or his analogies with French
intellectual debates (1966a, p. 70), intriguing as they are, lead

nowhere. Despite the undoubted stimulus brought to the world of intellect so dramatically from the reconsideration of non-literate cultures, and despite the universal claims, the scientific attitude towards the contemporary world and social change is essentially negative – a courageous stance when so many anthropologists are scurrying to put on modern dress and claim contemporary relevance.

The new vista opened with such vast documentary erudition is quite foreign to the genius of social anthropology in one essential respect – the negligible contribution of the data or experience of field research. By contrast, Turner's profound immersion in field experience led not only to a new view of ritual but inspired particular interest and conceptual development in the study of socio-political processes. However, as we have seen, neither Turner's mainly intracultural concentration on Ndembu (or that of the Griaule School on Dogon), nor the vast intercultural panorama ranged over by Lévi-Strauss, have so far thrown effective light on the essential problem of the cross-cultural dynamics of symbolic structures. One of the most obvious but untried lines of attack would be to extend the classical field experience to a contiguous cluster of cultures, the relationships between which are in part those of interacting neighbours and in part those of genetic cognates. This would offer the possibility of tackling together the definition of the socio-cultural and linguistic units of analysis and comparison, often to be seen as ego-centric fields rather than bounded entities, the symbolic structures associated with them, and their transformations in both space and time, so leading on to consideration of the relation between intercultural symbolic structure and the processes of social change in contemporary societies. If indeed there is a constant battle between synchrony and diachrony (Lévi-Strauss, 1966a, p. 155) in which the latter must always emerge victorious, how can we specify the significant modalities in the transformation of synchronous cognitive structures into viable diachronic substitutes? If synchrony and diachrony are different levels of abstraction no meaning can attach to battle between them, since they occur in the mind of the observer, not in the society observed. If they refer to changes in cultural conditions they are matters of degree and phase into one another. Synchrony is a timeless fantasy involving the same unreality as the 'ethnographic present'.

NOTES

1. Despite a rather elliptical disclaimer (1966a, p. 130).

2. In the oral tradition of the origin of the Lunda Empire 'the country was governed by Mwaakw, a male twin born from a long line of twins, descendants from the first men' (Vansina, 1968, p. 78). The dynastic foundation myths of the Pharaonic Egyptians, the Yoruba, etc. also emphasize the theme of twinship.

3. I have set this out at some length in 'Cross-cultural meanings and Multilingualism' in W. H. Whiteley, 1970.

4. The concept of *eng'ok* in Kipsigis and Masai is also probably cognate.

5. In some versions, *Ucak* descends in a cloud (*afuru*).

6. Indeed, there are widespread reports indicating ambivalence towards the relative age and seniority of twins, the one that emerges from the womb last sometimes being accounted the elder (the last shall be first).

7. Dr G. K. Park, personal communication.

8. I am indebted for this information to Mr Richard Koech, of Syracuse University, himself a Kipsigis.

9. Dr Abdulhamid Zein, personal communication.

10. Dieterlen (1950, p. 351, fn. 2): 'il va sans dire que de nombreux indices permettent d'affirmer des à présent que d'autres populations soudanaises offrent les memes représentations'.

11. Cf. avoidance of twin objects and association with them (Nyakyusa, Nyoro, Zulu), p. 98.

12. The concept of archetype seems to have been misconstrued by Lévi-Strauss who rejects it by remarking that 'only forms and not contents' can be common (1966a, p. 65). However, Jung, who was well aware of the extent of popular misunderstanding, himself stressed the absurdity of supposing that the variable representations of mythological images could themselves be archetypical, and

precisely stated that archetypes are *mental forms*, 'a tendency to form such representations of a motif – representations that can vary a great deal in detail without losing their basic pattern' (Jung *et al.*, 1964, p. 67).

   13. Cf. M. Douglas (1970).

REFERENCES

BEATTIE, J. H. M. 1960. *Bunyoro, An African Kingdom.* New York: Holt, Rinehart and Winston.

BEATTIE, J. H. M. 1962. Twin Ceremonies in Bunyoro. *Journal of the Royal Anthropological Institute* **92** (1): 1.

BEATTIE, J. H. M. 1968. Aspects of Nyoro Symbolism. *Africa* **38** (4): 413.

BEIDELMAN, T. O. 1964. Pig (*Guluwe*): An Essay on Ngulu Sexual Symbolism and Ceremony. *Southwestern Journal of Anthropology* **20**: 359–92.

BEIDELMAN, T. O. 1967. *The Matrilineal Peoples of Eastern Tanzania.* Ethnographic Survey of Africa. London: Oxford University Press for International African Institute.

BLOCH, M. E. F. 1969. Astrology and Writing in Madagascar. In Jack Goody (ed.), *Literacy in Traditional Societies.* Cambridge: Cambridge University Press.

BUTT, A. 1952. *The Nilotes of the Sudan and Uganda.* Ethnographic Survey of Africa. London: OUP for IAI.

CRAZZOLARA, J. P. 1950, 1951, 1954. *The Lwoo.* Part I: Lwoo Migrations. Part II: Lwoo Traditions. Part III: Clans. Verona: Editrice Nigrizia.

DAVIS, M. B. 1952. *A Lunyoro-Lunyankole-English and English-Lunyoro-Lunyankole Dictionary.* Kampala: Uganda Bookshop; London: Macmillan.

DIETERLEN, G. 1950. Les Correspondances cosmo-biologiques chez les soudanais. *Journal de Psychologie Normale et Pathologique* Juillet–Septembre, 350.

DIETERLEN, G. 1951. *Essai sur la religion Bambara.* Paris: Presses Universitaires de France.

DIETERLEN, G. 1957. The Mande Creation Myth. *Africa* **27** (2): 124.

DIETERLEN, G. 1966. L'Initiation chez les pasteurs peul. In M. Fortes & G. Dieterlen (eds.), *African Systems of Thought.* London: Oxford University Press for International African Institute.

DOUGLAS, MARY 1968. Dogon Culture – Profane and Arcane. *Africa* **38** (1): 16.

DOUGLAS, M. 1970. The Healing Rite. *Man* 5 (2): 302–08.

DRIBERG, J. H. (1923) *The Lango, A Nilotic Tribe of Uganda.* London: T. Fisher Unwin.

EDEL, MAY MANDELBAUM (ed.) 1934. The Customs of the Baganda Sir Apolo Kagwa (trans. E. B. Kalibala). New York: Columbia University Press.

EVANS-PRITCHARD, E. E. 1956. *Nuer Religion.* Oxford: Clarendon Press.

FIRTH, R. 1966. Twins, Birds and Vegetables: problems of identification in primitive religious thought. *Man* (ns) 1 (1): 1.

FISHER, A. B. 1911. *Twilight Tales of the Black Baganda.* London: Marshall.

GRIAULE, M. 1948. *Dieu d'eau, entretiens avec Ogotemmeli.* Paris: Éd. du chêne.

GULLIVER, P. H. 1961. Structural Dichotomy and Jural Processes among the Arusha of Northern Tanganyika. *Africa* 31: 19.

GULLIVER, P. H. 1963. *Social Control in an African Society.* London: Routledge & Kegan Paul.

HUNTINGFORD, G. W. B. 1953a. *The Northern Nilo-Hamites.* ESA. London: IAI.

HUNTINGFORD, G. W. B. 1953b. *The Nandi of Kenya.* London: Routledge & Kegan Paul.

HUNTINGFORD, G. W. B. 1953c. *The Southern Nilo-Hamites.* ESA. London: IAI.

JUNG, C. G., *et al.* 1964. *Man and His Symbols.* New York: Doubleday.

KITCHING, A. L. & BLACKLEDGE, G. R. 1925. *A Luganda-English and English-Luganda Dictionary.* Kampala: Uganda Bookshop; London: SPCK.

KROEBER, A. L. 1939. Cultural and Natural Areas of Native North America. University of California Publications in American Archaeology and Ethnology, Vol. 38. Stanford, Calif.: University of California Press.

LAWRANCE, J. C. D. 1957. *The Iteso.* London: Oxford University Press.

LEACH, E. R. (ed.) 1967. *The Structural Study of Myth and Totemism.* ASA Monograph 5. London: Tavistock.

LÉVI-STRAUSS, C. 1958. La Geste d'Asdiwal. École Pratique des Hautes Études, Section des Sciences Religieuses. Extr. Annuaire. 1958–59: 3–43.

LÉVI-STRAUSS, C. 1962. *La Pensée sauvage.* Paris: Plon.

LÉVI-STRAUSS, C. 1963a. *Totemism* (trans. Rodney Needham). Boston: Beacon Press.

LÉVI-STRAUSS, C. 1963b. *Structural Anthropology*. New York: Basic Books; London: Merlin.

LÉVI-STRAUSS, C. 1964. *Mythologiques: Le Cru et le cuit*. Paris: Plon.

LÉVI-STRAUSS, C. 1966a. *The Savage Mind*. London: Weidenfeld and Nicolson.

LÉVI-STRAUSS, C. 1966b. *Mythologiques: Du Miel au cendres*. Paris: Plon.

LÉVI-STRAUSS, C. 1967. The Story of Asdiwal (trans. N. Mann). In E. R. Leach, (ed.), *The Structural Study of Myth and Totemism*. London: Tavistock.

LÉVI-STRAUSS, C. 1969. *The Raw and the Cooked*. New York: Harper & Row.

LIENHARDT, G. 1958. The Western Dinka. In J. Middleton, and D. Tait (eds.), *Tribes without Rulers*. London: Routledge.

LIENHARDT, G. 1961. *Divinity and Experience, the Religion of the Dinka*. Oxford: Clarendon Press.

MANN, THOMAS 1963. *Joseph and his Brothers* (trans. H. T. Lowe-Porter). London: Secker & Warburg.

MAQUET, J. J. 1961. *The Premise of Inequality in Ruanda*. London: Oxford University Press for International African Institute.

MBOYA, PAUL 1945. Luo Kitgi gi Timbegi. *East African Standard*. Nairobi.

MCCLELLAND, E. M. 1966. The Significance of Number in the Odu of Ifa. *Africa* **36** (4): 421.

MIDDLETON, JOHN 1960. *Lugbara Religion*. London: OUP for IAI.

MIDDLETON, JOHN 1961. The Social Significance of Lugbara Personal Names. *Uganda Journal* **25** (1).

MIDDLETON, JOHN and WINTER, E. H. (eds.) 1963. *Witchcraft & Sorcery in E. Africa*. London: Routledge and Kegan Paul.

MIDDLETON, JOHN and KERSHAW, G. 1965. *The Kikuyu and the Kamba of Kenya*. ESA. London: IAI.

MORTON-WILLIAMS, P. 1966. Two Studies of the Ifa divination. *Africa* **36** (4): 406.

NEEDHAM, R. 1967. Right and Left in Nyoro Symbolic Classification. *Africa* **37** (4): 425.

NSIMBI, M. 1956. Village Life and Customs in Buganda. *Uganda Journal* **20** (1): 27.

PELLEGRINI, V. 1949. *Acoli Macon*. Kitgum, Uganda: Catholic Mission.

RICHARDS, A. I. 1956. *Chisungu: A girls' initiation ceremony among the Bemba of Northern Rhodesia*. London: Faber & Faber.

RICHARDS, A. I. 1960. Social Mechanisms for the transfer of Political Rights in Some African Tribes. *JRAI* **90** (2): 175.

RICHARDS, A. I. 1967. African Systems of Thought: an Anglo-French Dialogue (review article). *Man* (ns) **2** (2): 268.

RICHARDS, A. I. 1969. Keeping the King Divine. Henry Myers Lecture 1968. *Proceedings of the Royal Anthropological Institute*. London, 1969.

ROSCOE, J. 1911. *The Baganda*. Cambridge: Cambridge University Press.

ROSCOE, J. 1923. *The Bakitara of Banyoro*. Cambridge: Cambridge University Press.

SCHAPERA, I. 1927. Customs relating to Twins in South Africa. *Journal of the African Society* **26**: 117-37.

SELIGMAN, C. G. 1932, 1950. *Pagan Tribes of the Nilotic Sudan*. New York: Humanities Press; London: Routledge.

SOUTHALL, A. W. 1951. The Alur Legend of Sir Samuel Baker and the Mukama Kabarega. *Uganda Journal* **15** (2): 187.

SOUTHALL, A. W. 1954. Alur Tradition and its Historical Significance, *Uganda Journal* **18** (2): 137.

SOUTHALL, A. W. 1956. *Alur Society, a Study in Processes and Types of Domination*. Cambridge: Heffer.

SOUTHALL, A. W. 1970. Cross-cultural meanings and Multilingualism. In W. H. Whitely (ed.), *Language Use and Social Change*. London: OUP for IAI.

THOMAS, L. V. 1966. Brève esquisse sur la pensée cosmologique du Diola. In M. Fortes & G. Dieterlen (eds.), *African Systems of Thought*. London: OUP for IAI.

TURNER, V. W. 1964. Symbols in Ndembu Ritual. In M. Gluckman (ed.), *Closed Systems and Open Minds*. Edinburgh: Oliver & Boyd.

TURNER, V. W. 1967. *The Forest of Symbols*. Ithaca, NY: Cornell University Press.

TURNER, V. W. 1968. Myth and Symbol. *International Encyclopedia of the Social Sciences*. London: Macmillan; New York: Free Press.

TURNER, V. W. 1969. *The Ritual Process*. London: Routledge and Kegan Paul.

VANSINA, J. 1968. *Kingdoms of the Savanna*. Madison: University of Wisconsin Press.

WAGNER, G. 1949. *The Bantu of North Kavirondo*. London: OUP for IAI.

WEATHERBY, J. M. 1967. Aspects of the Ethnography and Oral Tradition of the Sebei of Mount Elgon. Unpublished MA thesis, University of East Africa.

WHITELEY, W. H. (ed.) 1970. *Language Use and Social Change*. London: Oxford University Press for IAI.

WILLIAMS, F. R. J. 1949. The Pagan Religion of the Madi. *Uganda Journal* **13** (2).

WILLIS, R. G. 1964. Traditional History and Social Structure in Ufipa. *Africa* **34** (4): 340.

WILLIS, R. G. 1966, *The Fipa and related peoples of South-west Tanzania and North-east Zambia*. ESA. London: IAI.

WILLIS, R. G. 1967. The Head and the Loins: Lêvi-Strauss and beyond. *Man* (ns) **2** (4): 519.

WILSON, MONICA. 1957. *Rituals of Kinship among the Nyakyusa*. London: Oxford University Press for IAI.

WILSON, MONICA. 1959. *Communal Rituals of the Nyakyusa*. London: Oxford University Press for IAI.

Spirit, twins, and ashes in Labwor, Northern Uganda[1]

R. G. ABRAHAMS

I

The Labwor people, who call themselves Jo Abwor, number about 9,000 and live in a well-watered hilly area, known as the Labwor Hills, in the far west of Karamoja District in north-eastern Uganda. In contrast to the Nilo-Hamitic speaking Jie and Karimojong pastoralists to the east, and rather more like the Acholi and the Lang'o to the west, the Labwor are a Luo-speaking group whose main economic activities are agriculture and iron-working – although some cattle and other livestock are kept. However, a number of important links exist between the Labwor and the pastoral tribes, especially the Jie: Labwor has for a long time been the pastoralists' main source of spears and other iron goods, and in times of food shortage the pastoralists may seek grain and even long-term refuge in the area; in addition, the Labwor have apparently incorporated into their social organization a system of age and generation groupings borrowed from these pastoral neighbours.

This system of age and generation groupings has for long formed one of three main frameworks of social organization in Labwor. The others are, today, the system of local government administration under a County Chief, which has superseded a traditional and relatively poorly developed form of chiefship (*ker*) in the area, and the system of kinship and marriage in which the basic units are a series of exogamous patriclans (*kaka* or *ateker*) and their constituent segments.

With the main exception of the rituals associated with the age
and generation system, Labwor religion is most closely linked
to that of other Nilotic and especially Luo-speaking peoples.
This applies both to the form of fundamental, almost all-
pervading concepts such as that of *juok,* which may be roughly
translated as 'spirit', and also to the more special details of
particular ritual complexes such as the twin cult, which I shall
consider in this paper. Because of its central position in Labwor
religious thought, a brief examination of the people's view of
juok will form a useful background to my main discussion.[2]

II

Among the Labwor, as among the Lang'o and other Luo-speaking peoples, one quickly learns that the idea of *juok* (plural,
juogi) is a crucial one in their religious system.[3] People say that
many hills, big trees, and rivers are occupied by *juogi* that may
seize those who approach too near or otherwise arouse them. In
various homesteads one may see small table-like stone shrines[4]
erected for some *juok* that has attacked one of their members.
Witchcraft may also sometimes be referred to as *juok* and witches
are described by the related term *ajuok.* Diviners are known by
another related word, *ajuoga,* and a twin (*rut,* plural, *rudi*) and
certain other special children are referred to as *atin juojuok* or
atin juok, i.e. a *juok*-like or *juok* child. Lastly, the idea of a high
God was, it appears, also traditionally expressed by the term
juok, sometimes with the qualification *malo,* above, or *i polu,* in
the sky. Nowadays, however, the term *Rubang'a,* which appears
to be of Bantu origin, or a more strongly Luo form of it,
Obang'a, are in general use for this.[5]

It is, however, easier to establish the importance of the concept of *juok* than to define and translate it accurately.[6] One
problem here is that the people themselves do not feel compe-
tent as mere humans to provide a set of detailed, systematically
coherent statements on the subject. This, of course, is in itself
significant as a reflection of the superhuman character of *juok*

which is said, as in related areas, to be invisible, *pe nen*, and like the wind, *calo yamo*. I have suggested above that 'spirit' might be a satisfactory rough translation of the term but some writers seem to feel that even this vague word may have misleading connotations. Thus Hayley describes *juok* as the 'Mana principle of the Lang'o and as a 'natural power permeating the Universe' and Wright, with reference to the Acholi, treats it similarly and compares it to a store of electrical power.[7] Such approaches, however, seem to pay too little attention to the apparently purposive aspects of the behaviour of *juok*. Thus, at least in Labwor, *juok* is held to have created the world and *juok* communicates to man through the medium of an *ajuoga* who may speak with *juok*'s voice or may read *juok*'s word in the intestines of a sacrificial animal. *Juok* is also said to drink, *mato*, the blood of such animals. Some hill *juogi* are even said to keep cattle that are, like themselves, invisible, but whose bells may occasionally be heard faintly tinkling.

Juok then in its singular and plural forms seems to have a variety of references ranging from something like a high God on the one hand, to an indefinite number of terrestial spirit powers on the other. I was unable to obtain any clear picture of the relationship between these different forms of *juok* and I gathered that this question was considered by the people to be both insoluble and, in itself, of relatively small importance. What was important – and to this extent, at least, the emphasis of Wright and Hayley upon 'power' is well placed – was to be able to recognize, interpret, and exercise as much control as might be possible over situations in which the direct influence of *juok* was present in the world of men and their affairs.

As I have implied, the *ajuoga* or diviner is a most important medium for such interpretation and control of man-*juok* relationships, and the process of becoming an *ajuoga* illustrates what seems to be the intrinsically ambivalent nature of the power of *juok* and of man's interest in it. The *ajuoga*'s powers are seen as resulting typically from some direct contact with *juok*, such as a visitation in dreams coupled with possession while out herding livestock. The immediate result of such contact is sickness, but this can be ritually brought under control by someone who is already an *ajuoga*. Once this has been achieved, the new *ajuoga* can himself begin to serve as an intermediary between *juok* and his fellow men. Potentially then, in this and other contexts, a visitation by *juok* is extremely dangerous to man, but by approaching it with the right help in the right way man can hope to mitigate the dangers involved and perhaps even obtain some benefit from the situation.

III

The cult of twins, whose birth is looked upon as an important manifestation of *juok*'s presence and power, is a major element in Labwor religion.[9] The shrines, which are erected for the twins and customarily maintained and passed on from one generation to another, are by logical extension held to be of particular importance for the fertility of the human population and the land, and it is not surprising that these are matters of recurrent and more than ordinary concern to the people. A person who does not possess such a shrine can usually make use of one when necessary in the home of one of his agnates, but many homesteads in fact have their own shrines. Often these are for twins of the past and have been inherited or, in a few cases, remembered and resuscitated on the advice of a diviner, after having for some reason been allowed to lapse for a time. In addition, some shrines, though called by the same term *rudi* (like the twins themselves) and constructed in the same fashion, are not strictly for twin births but for the occasional birth of triplets or, more commonly, for breach-born children, *odoc*, who are also incorporated into the cult.

This inclusion of the birth of breech-born children in the cult deserves some comment.[9] The people themselves claim that a breech delivery presages the birth of twins, and they also consider that *juok* is particularly evident in both kinds of birth. I was also told by one informant that breech presentations were relatively rare and much more difficult to deliver, because of the position of the legs, than a face-down presentation, for example, which is not included in the cult.[10] In these circumstances, while it is true that the people appear to associate the cult primarily with twins – both by their use of the term *rudi* to cover *odoc* shrines and, indeed, in general discussion of the subject – it would not seem to be justified to place exclusive emphasis upon the idea of *twin*-ness in itself in an attempt to understand all aspects of the cult. For the more general idea of a problematic abnormal birth, which would include a twin delivery, would also seem to be significant.

It may be worth while in this context to try to draw a distinction between such aspects of the cult as the erection of shrines and the performance of ceremonies at them on the one hand, and the character of social relationships with and concomitant attitudes towards actual living twins, and especially young ones, on the other. For it is, I think, particularly in this latter area of relationships and attitudes to living twins that their peculiar combination of unity and duality, or at least plurality, is most clearly relevant. Although a breech-born child, or any *juok*-child for that matter, is almost by definition a source of some anxiety to its parents and others, twin children are held to be especially troublesome and dangerous. People stress that they must always be treated alike. If one is punished the other should be punished also. If one is given a piece of cloth, the other should be given a piece of the same colour and pattern. A failure to treat them equally can lead to mystical retribution against the offending party and can also endanger the well-being of the twins themselves and subsequently that of others close to them.[11] It appears, moreover, that this very oneness of twins, which the people thus respect and foster, is itself a major source of danger. For it is felt that twins are extremely likely to conspire against one or both of their parents if they are offended by them in some way.[12] In one case I recorded, a pair of young twins were said to have made their mother seriously ill when she neglected her domestic duties, and they then began to make their father ill when he attempted to intercede on their mother's behalf. In another case, twins were said to have caused their father's beehive to dry up because he regularly gave honey only to their mother's co-wife. In a third case, some twins were said actually to have killed their mother when she maltreated them. In such cases the twins are usually described as first secretly discussing together and then plotting the trouble in question, and I gathered that they must agree before they can effectively cause serious harm. It seems reasonable to suggest that this fear of conspiracy against the parents of twins is, at least partially, a function of the common identity of twins whose unity, unlike that of ordinary siblings, is not counterbalanced by important inequalities of relative seniority.[13]

The unity of twins, I have suggested, is both recognized and even fostered by the people, but it should perhaps also be noted that there are clear limits to this recognition. No one, for example, ever went so far as to describe twins to me as 'one person', and people reacted critically to my suggestion that they might be considered as such.[14] Apart from the obvious fact that there are two of them, people pointed out that twins have separate names, Opio (female, Apio) and Ocen (female, Acen), and these names mark the fact that one twin's birth precedes that of the other. Thus Opio, the name for the first-born twin, seems literally to mean 'the quick one', and Ocen comparably means 'the one behind'. It may be added also that there is no preference, as among the Nuer, for twin girls to marry at the same time as each other, and this is consonant with the fact that people are in general more concerned with treating twins alike when they are children.[15]

Shrines for twins are usually erected a few months after their birth, though they may be set up sooner than this if one or both babies die. The shrines themselves vary a little in form, but almost all of them consist of one or two forked branches of a tree set upright in the ground, with a small conical thatched roof covering the upper part. They stand some two to three feet high, and a photograph of one is to be seen accompanying

Wayland's early account of the area.[16] Very occasionally a Lang'o-style *peru* shrine is found.[17] Sometimes a separate shrine is made for each twin but more usually a single shrine serves for both of them. A pot is normally kept in the fork under the thatch and this will contain the bones of chickens or goats killed at ceremonies for the shrine. The remains of dead young twins are also said to be kept in such pots. It may be mentioned in this context that it does not appear to have been customary in Labwor deliberately to kill one or both of twin children.

I have never witnessed the erection of a shrine, though I did attend part of a ceremony (*kwer*) for this following the death at birth of triplets very early in my fieldwork. By the time of my arrival at the homestead concerned, the shrine itself had already been set up and people were mostly indulging in dancing to drums, beer drinking, and horseplay. This last mainly consisted of men and women chasing and smearing members of the opposite sex with ashes to the accompaniment of banter and much laughter.[18] There was also some mutual smearing between participants of the same sex, and this was of a quieter nature. I was told the ceremony was necessary to ensure the future fertility of the dead triplets' mother, whose upper body was particularly thickly covered in ash. It was also said that the fertility of crops would be increased. The ash was taken from the cooled parts of the dying remains of a wood fire in the compound, and it appears that a goat that had been killed for the occasion had been cooked upon this fire, though I am not completely certain of this. Some ash had been placed at the base of the shrine.

Some further data on the setting up of shrines was collected from informants. I was told that the ceremony was the counterpart of the second shaving for ordinary children which takes place about two months after their birth. A baby's head is first shaved three or four days after birth, according to its sex. In the case of the ceremony for twins, as many as five months may elapse before the shrine is erected, owing to the need to collect extra large quantities of food for the occasion. As with the ordinary second shaving, the main participants are said to be the clansfolk of both parents, and much of the food is brought to the ceremony by the mother's people. The erection of the shrine is supervised by a local female ritual expert who should herself have given birth to twins. The shrine is set up at the back or side of the mother's hut. A local student who worked for me for a time pointed out that the shrines seemed generally to be sited on the north side of the huts, but people denied that there was any significance to this. At the ceremony a goat is killed and its skin is used to make a carrying harness, *abeno*, for the twins. The ritual expert ties necklets, wristlets, and anklets, made from a special creeper grass, *modho*, upon the mother and the children and she also provides necklets of white sea-shells for them. Ostrich-egg necklets may be worn sometimes instead of these. The ritual expert is paid with various types of foodstuffs. Dancing to drums and smearing with ashes are a normal part of the ceremony, but according to one informant some people nowadays restrict the smearing to the parents of the twins themselves. A failure to carry out the ceremony properly could, I was told, lead to the death of the parents or the children. It is also said to be important for the parents of twins not to resume sexual relations until the shrine has been erected.[19]

Once a shrine has been set up, a variety of ceremonies may be performed at it. Some of these are annual, taking place before the start of cultivation and at harvest-time. Others take place monthly, and others again take place from time to time as need arises.

At the annual pre-cultivation ceremony, the father of the twins – or whoever has inherited the shrine if it is old – sacrifices a goat, or if a goat is not available, a chicken for the shrine. In either case the colour of the sacrificial animal must be white. It may be mentioned here in passing that a further white chicken is also kept permanently dedicated to the shrine and this bird must not normally be killed for any reason. The goat is jointed for cooking but the chicken should be cooked unjointed. Whether the sacrifice is a goat or a chicken, neither the whole nor part of the creature should be allowed to come in direct contact with the cooking fire, even in order to help remove the chicken's feathers. In both cases the meat must be boiled. The intestines of the sacrificial animal are read to see if all will be well for the coming season. A further sacrifice should be made if the omens are bad. Chyme (*wei*) from a 'good' animal is smeared on the parents of the twins, upon the twins themselves, and on the local ritual expert who should supervise the ceremony. Any repairs to the shrine that may be necessary should be carried out at this ceremony. There should also be a dance to drums and those present should smear each other with ashes. Smearing with white clay also sometimes occurs.

Smaller rituals are performed after harvesting the main crops. Paste made with new simsim is dabbed (*gwelo*) on the shrine, and so too are porridge and beer made from new millet. In addition some beer may be poured at the foot of the shrine or spat in blessing upon it by the ritual expert.

Monthly rituals are carried out during the childhood of the twins and tend to lapse after this. The ceremonies take place early on the first evening when the new moon can be seen. No ritual expert was present at monthly ceremonies I have attended or have had described to me, and participation is mainly confined to the twins and their parents. A description of a ceremony I saw, in which the twins concerned were girls about five years old, will serve as an example of what happens. The new moon in this case was first seen on a Friday evening, but the sky was cloudy and the mother of the twins said that they would wait till Sunday. At about 6 pm on the Sunday evening, the father of the twins brought some ash in a calabash out of their mother's hut and placed the vessel beside the two shrines that had been erected for these particular children. He then sent one of the twins to fetch her mother from nearby, and when the mother came he began to pour ash at the foot of each shrine starting with that of the 'elder' twin, Apio. He then caught a white chicken, which was dedicated to the shrines, and knelt down holding it beside the shrines. The mother moved to join him and also knelt down. The two twins stood close by her, one on either side. The father then made the chicken flap its wings (*buko*) about and over them and, having done this, sat it down upon the top of his wife's head where it remained, apparently quite used to the procedure, for most of the ensuing ceremony. Next all four of the main participants smeared ash liberally over each other, and finally the father and mother danced a little to two small drums beaten by two children who, apart from my own small party, were the only others present. One of these children was an elder sister of the twins and the other was a young boy from a neighbouring and related homestead.

As I have said, a variety of other rituals take place before such shrines as need arises. Typically, their performance depends on the advice of an *ajuoga*. In most cases, questions of human fertility seem to be involved, and this is reasonable in view of its non-seasonal nature. Sacrifices at such a shrine are felt to be particularly useful to procure conception of a child, though the people readily admit that some cases cannot be helped by any amount or form of ritual since, as one old woman put it, *Obang'a* has absolutely refused them (*Obang'a opyemgi*). The shrines may also be of use in other troubles such as sickness. Thus a sick person, especially a child, may be taken to the shrine and washed there in the early morning with water that has been left out before it overnight.

Finally, I should like to say a little about procedure at the death of twins: if they are still young, their bones, as I have mentioned, are said to be placed in the pot that forms part of their shrine; if they are older and too large for this, I was told that they are buried and that later, when the corpse has rotted, the grave is opened up and the skull removed. This skull is then kept in the shrine pot. It is perhaps worth while to mention that a comparable removal of the skull from the grave of an *ajuoga* takes place, though in this case it is said to be taken to a secluded place in the hills and is particularly important for obtaining good rainfall. As in Acholi and elsewhere, the ordinary word 'to die' (*to*) is not used of twins. Instead they are described as having 'escaped' (*olo oko*), a term occasionally also used about the deaths of ordinary children.[21]

IV

I turn now to consider some problems of interpreting the ceremonial of the cult and I want to pay particular attention to the use of ashes which forms one of its most regular and characteristic features. The people themselves have little to say in exegesis of this. As I have noted earlier with relation to the concept of *juok*, they are not much inclined to speculate about their religion and the details of its constituent beliefs and rituals, though I should mention that such lack of speculative interest is not typical of all their thought. They are for instance very much at home in the discussion of economic questions, and I have had very sophisticated analyses presented to me of such matters as the distributive and broader social implications of the substitution of cattle and money for goats and iron goods in bridewealth payments. But on religious issues, their attitude is typically that they are largely ignorant and cannot expect to be otherwise. Thus when asked, for example, why such a particular form of ritual act as smearing or pouring of ash takes place, they say, like many other peoples, that it has long since been like that, that perhaps people in the past tried it and found that it was successful, and that they cannot really hope to know what was going on in the minds of people of that time when they made their decisions about such matters.[21] For them the performance of the ritual is basically directed towards a specific end, to procure some good and/or avert some evil, and the form of the ritual is accepted by them and is not of special interest in its own right.

Thus the social anthropologist is left to interpret for himself, as best he can, the significance of the various ritual forms that he encounters, and I shall presently attempt to do this in this case. It is perhaps worth while, however, to bear in mind the possibility that the 'positivist' arguments that the people advance about speculation of this sort may deserve more serious consideration than one might at first be tempted to give. For it may be that the points they make are relevant for all, including anthropologists, who might wish to investigate such questions, and their contention that one cannot seriously hope to penetrate the thoughts of those long dead is possibly quite apposite, since I suspect that this is sometimes what we unwittingly attempt in such studies. However, this may be, they clearly seem to be correct when they suggest that such a feature of the twin cult as the use of ash has a long history. For ash is also used in the twin ceremonies of such peoples as the Lang'o, the Acholi, the Jopaluo, and the Nuer, as well as in those of the Nyoro among whom one also finds such other similarities as the keeping of a white fowl for the cult.[22] Such a wide distribution across the spectrum of Nilotic-speaking peoples and beyond into connected Bantu-speaking areas betokens both a long and complicated history, since it can scarcely be due to coincidence, and this has implications for interpreting such elements of the cult. Certainly it raises problems for any interpretation heavily based upon one or more special features of one of the areas concerned, for example the great importance of ironworking in Labwor and the crucial role of fire in this. Although the discussion that follows is based mainly on my knowledge of Labwor, the variables considered are I trust of general enough relevance to avoid at least some of the difficulties entailed here.

One interesting feature of ash (*buru*) in Labwor is that it seems to be considered by the people as the opposite of fire in some contexts. I say that it *seems* to be so considered since my inquiries failed to reveal a Labwor term or phrase for 'opposite' in this sort of sense. The people do, however, speak of ash as cool, in contrast to the heat of fire, and there is a proverbial saying, also found among the Lang'o, that 'fire begets ashes' (*mac nywolo buru*).[23] I was told that this saying is typically used to describe a situation in which a fiery aggressive father has a quiet weak child. Such opposition between fire and ash seems relevant to the twin cult in at least two ways. One is that the concept of coolness is in general associated by Labwor, as by many other peoples, with the ideas of tranquillity and ritual well-being, and the idea of ash as something that has been 'born' cool may make it specially suitable for a cult of dangerous births.[24] Second and less obvious, it appears to relate to the prohibition on bringing sacrificial victims for twin shrine rituals into direct contact with fire. Here some aspects of colour symbolism also seem to be involved.

It will be recalled that the sacrificial victims I have just referred to are customarily white goats or chickens. The people themselves also describe ash as white (*tar*), and whiteness appears in a mass of other contexts in the cult.[25] Thus we find cowrie or ostrich eggshell necklaces – which are of course white – worn by the twins and their mother, and there are also the white chickens dedicated to the shrines. White clay is sometimes smeared on the participants at annual pre-cultivation ceremonies. The association of ash with whiteness is, moreover, not apparently restricted simply to its light colour. There is a Labwor expression that someone who is very poor 'lives (or sits) in ashes' (*bedo i buru*) and I was told that this refers to the fact that he lives in a 'white' place (*kany matar*). It was further explained that the word *tar* was used here to express the idea of 'emptiness and cleanness', somewhat as in our own colloquialism that a person is 'cleaned out' when he has nothing left. Some informants also said that white is a cool colour. It would be tempting to oppose it in this context to red as the colour of fire, but the people themselves do not seem consciously to do this.

So far I have tentatively outlined a very simple scheme of linked oppositions and associations that appear to be relevant to the cult and to the place of ash within it. However, too rigid a picture of the nature of such oppositions and associations should be avoided. The colour white, for example, is associated in iron-working contexts, as among ourselves, with intense heat rather than coolness, and there are other situations in which ash and whiteness seem to represent the warmth and brightness of hot sunshine. Thus a person who wishes for the rain to hold off while he dries his first millet crop often places some ash or a 'white' (*tar*), shiny object such as a shilling or a metal spoon upon the roof of his hut. Again, people sometimes throw ash from inside their huts if there is a very heavy rainstorm that they wish to stop. I may also add here that a person who quarrels and fights with someone, for example his wife, in the rainy season is believed to be likely to stop the rains by his actions and is said to have 'done ash' (*timo buru*). His neighbours will force him to make a sacrifice in order to undo the damage and this is described as to 'kill ash' (*neko buru*). In contexts of this sort ash seems to be more closely linked to the ideas of heat and fire than directly opposed to them, and there are other situations where its use in ritual appears to represent the very antithesis of coolness, peace, and calm. Thus a person who feels that he has been wronged, for instance by a witchcraft accusation, may take up ash from the hearth at his home and throw it on the ground in his accuser's compound. As he does so he announces that the ash will return to kill him if he is a witch, but if he is not a witch the ash will kill his accuser. This also is called 'to do ash' (*timo buru*) and it is felt to be a very dangerous and powerful form of oath.[26] The fact that the ash is from the accused's homestead, and is thus closely associated with him personally, is also probably important here. For I was told that in an alternative form of the oath, which is still none the less spoken of as 'doing ash', the wronged person may lay his spear or a piece of his clothing on the ground and step over it while proclaiming his innocence.

I have mentioned that the positive association between ash and fire appears to be more important in such contexts than the contrasts between them. It also seems likely that this aspect of ash is relevant for understanding its position in the twin cult. First, and most simply, it gives to ash, when combined with its other qualities, an overall ambivalent status; and I have noted earlier that such ambivalence is of the very essence of the power of *juok* and of man-*juok* relations with which the cult is in its special way concerned. In addition, it may lead us to consider a further implication of the people's view of ash as fire's off-spring and to see ash as essentially a product of a transformation and reduction process in which fire forms a necessary previous stage. From this point of view, which stresses genesis as much as form, ash, even when thought of as cool, becomes not merely the antithesis of fire but also a modified, controlled form of it, which can literally and metaphorically be handled.[27] This quality of descent and change from fire perhaps contributes to ash's suitability for use in the ceremonial of the cult. It seems to symbolize not only the desired ritual end but also the kind of process needed to achieve it, and it also possibly represents a recognition of the need for man to show himself to be anal-ogously subdued and tamed before the power of *juok*.

Such considerations fit quite well with certain other char-acteristic features of Labwor and related ritual. Thus the Labwor typically sacrifice castrated beasts, the victims of a somewhat comparable reduction process, some aspects of which have been analysed in detail for the Nuer.[28] Again, the chyme (*wei*) of sacrificial animals – another product of a pro-cess of reduction – is very often smeared or dabbed on the participants at a variety of Labwor rituals as a form of blessing. Last, I may mention that, for Labwor at least, old age especi-ally in men is of itself a source of ritual power, and the curses and blessings of the very old are said to be heard most clearly by *Rubang'a*. In this context also, ritual efficacy can perhaps be seen to lie where the fires of life and manhood have begun to cool.

V

I have attempted in this paper to present some ethnographic data on the twin cult in Labwor and to discuss the significance of the use of ash as a central and recurrent feature of the ritual of the cult. I have outlined the nature of the concept of *juok* in the area, and I have gone on to describe the rituals consequent upon twin births and comparable deliveries held to be a special manifestation of *juok*'s presence and power. I have noted that the shrines erected for such births are maintained and passed on from one generation to another, and that rituals are regularly performed at them long after the events they celebrate. I have also pointed out that too much emphasis upon the idea of *twin*-ness would be misplaced in an attempt to understand the cult, notwithstanding the people's tendency, and my own, to designate it simply as a *twin* cult. I have suggested that the characteristic use of ashes in the cult appears most likely to be understandable, if at all, in terms of their qualities of coolness and whiteness, and also their genesis from fire. I have noted that the transformation process involved here seems analogous to that which characterizes a variety of ritually powerful media such as sacrificial animals, chyme, and old men. In framing these tentative arguments, I have tried to bear in mind the fact that many features of the cult, including the use of ash, are very widely spread among Nilotic-speaking peoples and their neighbours. While this creates its own particular problems, it also offers special opportunities for the comparative investigation of such cults and ritual forms, and it is hoped that the present paper may be of some value for such future study.

The need for such comparative studies of widely distributed ritual complexes has been clearly recognized by Audrey Richard in her study of *chisungu* (1956, pp. 170–86 and *passim*). There is also a further point which she has stressed there which closely relates to the material presented in this paper. I refer here to her insistence, with which the people of Labwor would most strongly agree, that 'rites are invariably . . . an effort to "do" – to change the undesirable, or to maintain the desirable' (1956, p. 113). This is a point that may be all too easily forgotten as we follow new directions of study that have often first been clearly surveyed and signposted by Audrey Richards herself.

NOTES

1. The fieldwork upon which this paper is based was carried out during the greater part of 1967. A return visit to the area is planned. I am extremely grateful to the British Academy, the Makerere Institute of Social Research, and the University of Cambridge for generous financial and other help in support of this work.

2. For a general discussion of this concept and its distribution see Ogot (1961).

3. Cf. Ogot (1961), and also the accounts in Driberg (1923, pp. 216–25), Hayley (1947, pp. 2–22 and *passim*), Lienhardt (1954, p. 145 and *passim*), and Wright (1940).

4. These shrines are made with three stones, two of which are used to support a third flat one, which lies across them.

5. On the complex issue of the spread of the name Rubanga see especially Southall (1971, pp. 379–90 and *passim*) who also discusses the connection of the name with twins in Bunyoro and Alur. See also his contribution to this volume.

6. For similar difficulties among the Lang'o see also Driberg (1923, p. 216).

7. Hayley (1947, p. 2) and Wright (1940, p. 130).

8. The same is true of the Lang'o and possibly the Acholi. Cf. Hayley (1947, p. 97) and Seligman (1932, pp. 120–1).

9. Such an association of twin births and breech deliveries is not uncommon. It is found among the Lang'o (Hayley, 1947, p. 99) and in Bunyoro (Beattie, 1962, p. 2), as well as further afield, e.g. in Unyamwezi (Abrahams, 1967, p. 72) and even in parts of West Africa (cf. Ottenberg, 1968, p. 67).

10. Western gynaecology apparently shares this view. It also seems that one of a pair of twins is often born by breech delivery. Cf. Myles (1959, pp. 353, 358–9, 347–8).

11. It is of interest that if one twin dies, the other is believed to be liable to follow.

12. Cf. Evans-Pritchard (1936, p. 230) and Seligman (1932, pp. 165–6) on this for the Nuer and Dinka. In contrast to these two areas, the sex of twins appears to be irrelevant in this context in

Labwor and this also seems to be the case in Acholi; cf. Crazzolara in Seligman (1932, p. 120).

13. The logical implications of the contrast between twins and ordinary siblings are discussed in detail by Schapera (1926, pp. 134–7 and *passim*). In the light of Schapera's paper and my discussion here, it seems worthy of consideration on a comparative level whether the form and intensity of special attitudes to twins is linked to more general patterns of intergenerational and intersibling conflict.

14. This is, of course, in contrast to the Nuer, cf. Evans-Pritchard (1936, p. 231).

15. Evans-Pritchard, (1936, p. 233). The preference is also said to exist among the Dinka, cf. Seligman (1932, p. 166).

16. Wayland (1931, p. 230, plate xxiii). Note the ashes at the base of the shrine.

17. Cf. Driberg (1923, p. 142) and Hayley (1947, p. 98).

18. Opposition between affines, which Beattie describes for Bunyoro, does not seem to be an important element in this horseplay.

19. There is no long period of post-partum sexual abstinence in this area. In ordinary circumstances, parents will resume sexual relations at the second shaving of their child or even earlier.

20. Cf. Crazzolara (1954, p. 291, sub *loo*). Unlike Acholi, Nyoro, and Nuer, Labwor do not appear to describe dead twins as having 'flown away', nor do they associate twins otherwise with birds. Cf. Crazzolara (1954, p. 291), Evans-Pritchard (1936, p. 235), and Beattie (1962, p. 1).

21. This is not to say that Labwor religion is completely fixed and mechanistic. New cults come into the area from outside from time to time and there is potential, in the persons of 'inspired' diviners, for some internal innovation. The diviner may also be a source of ritual failure through faulty or only partial diagnosis of the forces at work in a situation that calls for ritual action.

22. Cf. Driberg (1923, p. 143), Hayley (1947, p. 99), Seligman (1932, p. 121), Evans-Pritchard (1936, p. 232), and Roscoe (1923, pp. 251, 255). The information on the Acholi is my own. A white fowl is also kept among the Ganda and the Lang'o; cf. Roscoe (1911, p. 73) and Driberg (1923, p. 143). The use of two drums in the cult is also very widely spread (cf. Roscoe, 1911, p. 65; Driberg, 1923, p. 145; Hayley, 1947, p. 98; and Beattie, 1962, p. 2). A feature found in Lang'o and Alur and possibly elsewhere, but only very

rarely in Labwor, is the use of a two-mouthed pot in the cult (cf. Hayley, 1947, p. 99 and 187; and Southall, 1956, p. 372).

23. Cf. Driberg (1923, p. 136).

24. The Nyoro belief that twins may 'burn' those whom with they come in contact is interesting in this context. Cf. Beattie (1962, p. 2).

25. This is true of other areas. In addition to the references about white fowls in note 22, cf. Seligman (1932, p. 121) for the Acholi, Driberg (1923, pp. 64, 144), and Hayley (1947, pp. 98, 100) for the Lang'o, and Beattie (1962, pp. 3–6) for the Nyoro.

26. The use of ash for oaths is also found among the Dinka (Mackrell, 1942).

27. For a comparable view of ash in a West African society see Goody (1962, pp. 69, 89).

28. Beidelman (1966). There is also an interesting reference to the varied use of ash in Nuer ritual in footnote 18 to this paper.

REFERENCES

ABRAHAMS, R. G. 1967. The Peoples of Greater Unyamwezi, Tanzania. *Ethnographic Survey of Africa*. London: International African Institute.

BEATTIE, J. H. M. 1962. Twin Ceremonies in Bunyoro, *JRAI* **92**. Part 1: 1–12.

BEIDELMAN, T. O. 1966. The Ox and Nuer Sacrifice: Some Freudian Hypotheses About Nuer Symbolism. *Man* (ns) **1** (4): 453–67.

CRAZZOLARA, J. P. 1954. *A Study of the Acooli Language*. London: Oxford University Press for IAI.

DRIBERG, J. H. 1923. *The Lango, A Nilotic Tribe of Uganda*. London: T. Fisher Unwin Ltd.

EVANS-PRITCHARD, E. E. 1936. Customs and Beliefs Relating to Twins Among the Nilotic Nuer. *Uganda Journal* **3**: 230–8.

GOODY, J. R. 1962. *Death, Property, and the Ancestors*. London: Tavistock; Stanford, California: Stanford University Press.

HAYLEY, T. T. S. 1947. *The Anatomy of Lango Religion and Groups*. Cambridge: Cambridge University Press.

LIENHARDT, G. 1954. The Shilluk. In Daryll Forde (ed.) *African Worlds*. London: Oxford University Press for IAI.

MACKRELL, J. E. C. 1942. The Dinka Oath on Ashes. *Sudan Notes and Records* **25** (1): 131–4.

MYLES, MARGARET F. 1959. *A Text-book for Midwives.* Edinburgh: Livingstone.

OGOT, B. A. 1961. The Concept of Jok. *African Studies* **20**: 123–30.

OTTENBERG, S. 1968. *Double Descent in an African Society.* Seattle: University of Washington Press.

RICHARDS, A. 1956. *Chisungu: A girls' initiation ceremony among the Bemba of Northern Rhodesia.* London: Faber & Faber.

ROSCOE, J. 1911. *The Baganda.* London: Macmillan.

ROSCOE, J. 1923. *The Bakitara.* Cambridge: Cambridge University Press.

SCHAPERA, I. A. 1926. Customs Relating to Twins in South Africa, *Journal of the African Society* **26**: 117–37.

SELIGMAN, C. G. & B. Z. 1932. *Pagan Tribes of the Nilotic Sudan.* London: Routledge.

SOUTHALL, A. W. 1956. *Alur Society.* Cambridge: Heffer.

SOUTHALL, A. W. 1971. Cross-Cultural Meanings and Multi-lingualism. In W. H. Whiteley (ed.), *Language Use and Social Change.* London: Oxford University Press for I.A.I.

WAYLAND, E. J. 1931. Preliminary Studies of the Tribes of Karamoja, *JRAI* **61**: 187–230.

Belief and the problem of women

EDWIN ARDENER

The problem of women has not been solved by social anthropologists. Indeed the problem itself has been often examined only to be put aside again for want of a solution, for its intractability is genuine. The problem of women is not the problem of 'the position of women', although valuable attention has been paid to this subject by Professor Evans-Pritchard (1965). I refer to the problem that women present to social anthropologists. It falls into (1) a technical and (2) an analytical part. Here is a human group that forms about half of any population and is even in a majority at certain ages: particularly at those which for so many societies are the 'ruling' ages – the years after forty. Yet however apparently competently the female population has been studied in any particular society, the results in understanding are surprisingly slight, and even tedious. With rare exceptions, women anthropologists, of whom so much was hoped, have been among the first to retire from the problem. Dr Richards was one of the few to return to it at the height of her powers. In *Chisungu* (1956) she produced a study of a girls' rite that raised and anticipated many of the problems with which this paper will deal.[1] While I shall illustrate my central point by reference to a parallel set of rites among the Bakweri of Cameroon, through which women and girls join the world of the mermaid spirits, this paper is less about ethnography than about the interpretation of such rites through the symbolism of the relations between men and women.

The methods of social anthropology as generally illustrated in the classical monographs of the last forty years have purported to 'crack the code' of a vast range of societies, without any direct reference to the female group. At the level of 'observation' in fieldwork, the behaviour of women has, of course, like that of men, been exhaustively plotted: their marriages, their economic activity, their rites, and the rest. When we come to that second or 'meta' level of fieldwork, the vast body of debate, discussion, question and answer, that social anthropologists really depend upon to give conviction to their interpretations, there is a real imbalance. We are, for practical purposes, in a male world. The study of women is on a level little higher than the study of the ducks and fowls they commonly own – a mere bird-watching indeed. It is equally revealing and ironical that Lévi-Strauss (1963, p. 61) should write: 'For words do not speak, while women do.' For the truth is that women rarely speak in social anthropology in any but that male sense so well exemplified by Lévi-Strauss's own remark: in the sense of merely uttering or giving tongue. It is the very inarticulateness of women that is the technical part of the problem they present. In most societies the ethnographer shares this problem with its male members. The brave failure (with rare exceptions) of even women anthropologists to surmount it really convincingly (and their evident relief when they leave the subject of women) suggests an obvious conclusion. Those trained in ethnography evidently have a bias towards the kinds of model that men are ready to provide (or to concur in) rather than towards any that women might provide. If the men appear 'articulate' compared with the women, it is a case of like speaking to like. To pursue the logic where it leads us: if ethnographers (male and female) want only what the men can give, I suggest it is because the men consistently tend, when pressed, to give a bounded model of society such as ethnographers are attracted to. But the awareness that women appear as lay figures in the men's drama (or like the photographic cut-outs in filmed crowd-scenes) is always dimly present in the ethnographer's mind. Lévi-Strauss, with his perennial ability to experience ethnographic models, thus expressed no more than the truth of all those models when he saw women as items of exchange inexplicably and inappropriately giving tongue.

The technical treatment of the problem is as follows. It is commonly said, with truth, that ethnographers with linguistic difficulties of any kind will find that the men of a society are generally more experienced in bridging this kind of gap than are the women. Thus, as a matter of ordinary experience, interpreters, partial bilinguals, or speakers of a vehicular language, are more likely to be found among men than among women. For an explanation of this we are referred to statements about the political dominance of men, and their greater mobility. These statements, in their turn, are referred ultimately to the different biological roles of the two sexes. The cumulative effect of these explanations is then: to the degree that communication between ethnographer and people is imperfect, that imperfection drives the ethnographer in greater measure towards men.

This argument while stressing the technical aspect does not dispose of the problem even in its own terms, although we may agree that much ethnography (more than is generally admitted) is affected by factors of this type. It is, however, a common experience that women still 'do not speak' even when linguistic aspects are constant. Ethnographers report that women cannot be reached so easily as men: they giggle when young, snort when old, reject the question, laugh at the topic, and the like. The male members of a society frequently see the ethnographer's difficulties as simply a caricature of their own daily case. The technical argument about the incidence of interpreters and so on is therefore really only a confirmation of the importance of the analytical part of the problem. The 'articulateness' of men and of ethnographers are alike, it would appear, in more ways than one. In the same way we may regard as inadequate the more refined explanation that ethnographers 'feed' their own models to their male informants, who are more susceptible for the same technical reasons, and who then feed them back to the ethnographer. That something of this sort does happen is again not to be doubted, but once again the susceptibility of the men is precisely the point. Nor is it an answer to the problem to discuss what might happen if biological facts were different; arguments like 'women through concern with the realities of childbirth and child-rearing have less time for or less propensity towards the making of models of society, for each other, for men, or for ethnographers' (the 'Hot Stove' argument) are again only an expression of the situation they try to explain.

We have here, then, what looked like a technical problem: the difficulty of dealing ethnographically with women. We have, rather, an analytical problem of this sort: if the models of a society made by most ethnographers tend to be models derived from the male portion of that society, how does the symbolic weight of that other mass of persons – half or more of a normal human population, as we have accepted – express itself? Some will maintain that the problem as it is stated here is exaggerated, although only an extremist will deny its existence completely. It may be that individual ethnographers have received from women a picture of a society very similar to the picture given by men. This possibility is conceded, but the female evidence provides in such cases confirmation of a male model which requires no confirmation of this type. The fact is that no one could come back from an ethnographic study of 'the X', having talked only *to* women and *about* men, without professional comment and some self-doubt. The reverse can and does happen constantly. It is not enough to see this merely as another example of 'injustice to women'. I prefer to suggest that the models of society that women can provide are not of the kind acceptable at first sight to men or to ethnographers, and specifically that, unlike either of these sets of professionals, they do not so readily see society bounded from nature. They lack the metalanguage for its discussion. To put it more simply: they will not necessarily provide a model for society as a unit that will contain both men and themselves. They may indeed provide a model in which women and nature are outside men and society.

I have now deliberately exaggerated, in order to close the gap in a different way. The dominance of men's models of a society in traditional ethnography I take to be accepted. However, men and women do communicate with each other, and are at least aware of each other's models. It has been furthermore the study by ethnographers of myth and belief, collected no doubt, as formerly, largely from men, that has provided the kinds of insights that now make it possible to reopen the problem of women. Much of this material still discusses women from a male viewpoint. Women are classed as inauspicious, dangerous, and the like. But models of society as a symbolic system made from this kind of data are (it is no surprise to note) of a rather different type from the ethnographic (male) models deriving from the older type of fieldwork (e.g. Needham 1958, 1960, 1967). So much so that many social anthropologists are unable to accept them as 'true' models, that is 'true to reality', where 'reality' is a term of art for what fieldwork reveals. I suggest, on the contrary, that a fieldwork problem of the first magnitude is illuminated. Indeed the astounding deficiency of a method, supposedly objective, is starkly revealed: the failure to include half the people in the total analysis.

II

At the risk of labouring the obvious, but to avoid being buried in a righteous avalanche of fieldnotes, I say this yet again with a diagram (*Figure 1*).

Because of an interesting failing in the functionalist observational model, statements *about* observation were always added to the ethnographer's own observations. To take a simple case:

140 *Edwin Ardener*

Figure 1

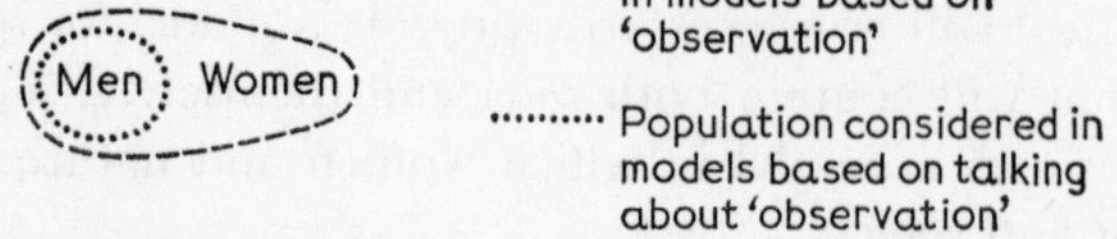

- - - - Population considered
in models based on
'observation'

·········· Population considered in
models based on talking
about 'observation'

typically an ethnographer 'observed' a number of marriages
and divorces, and heard a number of statements about the
frequency of divorce, and then cumulated these quasi-quanti-
tatively into a general statement about divorce frequency. So
he did in other less easily detectable ways, and in some of those
ways he may still do so today. This confusion had many serious
consequences; in particular the difficulty of dealing with
statements that were not about 'observation' at all (relegated
to 'belief' or the like). For our purposes here, it is enough to
note that statements made by the male segment were *about*
both males and females. The functionalist confusion of the
two levels at any time, obscured the inadequacy of the total
analysis as far as women were concerned. Since the analysis
was always thought to represent observation, or to be checked
by observation, it was hard for anyone with fieldnotes on
women to see that they were effectively missing in the total
analysis or, more precisely, they were there in the same way as
were the Nuer's cows, who were observed but also did not
speak.

The students of symbolism cannot be accused of any functionalist bias towards the primacy of observation. Functionalist
fieldwork was unhappy with myths precisely because they
made statements that conflicted with, could not be cumulated
to, objective measures of economic or political status. Not being
faced with this mistaken necessity, the symbolists, almost incidentally, rediscovered women, who loom rather large in their
material. In view of the absence of conscient women from the
older models, this gains further significance, and suggests a
further step, which is taken here. The study of symbolism un-
covers certain valuations of women – some of which make more

sense if women, not men, had made them (they conflict with the social models of men). Old women ('old wives' tales') or mothers (we may extend this analysis even to the lore and language of children) acquire in the world of symbolism something more like their demographic conspicuity. Furthermore, in a field situation poor communication with women in this area is not so often complained of. I here contend that much of this symbolism in fact enacts that female model of the world which has been lacking, and which is different from the models of men in a particular dimension: the placing of the boundary between society and nature.

I suppose in Lévi-Strauss's terms this would place women in an ideologically more primitive position than men. It is not a necessary conclusion. It means something like this: the notion of themselves in society is imposed by its members upon a relatively unbounded continuum in ways which involve the setting up of a multitude of bounded categories, the bounds being marked by taboo, ridicule, pollution, category inversion and the rest, so ably documented of late by social anthropologists (Douglas, 1966; Leach, 1961, 1964). The tension between 'culture' and 'nature' (the 'wild') is to be understood as an outcome of this struggle, from which no human beings are free. The appreciation of the symbolic stress on the division between society and nature derives from Lévi-Strauss (1949), and lies behind much of his later work, including the three volumes of *Mythologiques* (1964, 1966, 1968). Lévi-Strauss now prefers the terminology 'nature' and 'culture' (1967, p. 3; (trans.) 1969, p. 3). Of late he has also been concerned to state that the distinction lacks objective criteria (1967, p. 12). This concern seems surprising since it is easily resolved as Lévi-Strauss himself shows:

> [T]he contrast of nature and culture would be neither a primeval fact, nor a concrete aspect of universal order. Rather it should be seen as an artificial creation of culture, a protective rampart thrown up around it because it only felt able to assert its existence and uniqueness by destroying all the links that led back to its

original association with the other manifestations of life (1967, p. xvii; trans. 1969, p. xxix).

Within this wider task men have to bound themselves in relation both to women and to nature.

Since women are biologically not men, it would be surprising if they bounded themselves against nature in the same way as men do. Yet we have seen that the men's models are characteristically dominant in ethnography. If men are the ones who become aware of 'other cultures' more frequently than do women, it may well be that they are likely to develop meta-levels of categorization that enable them at least to consider the necessity to bound themselves-and-their-women from other-men-and-their-women. Thus all such ways of bounding society against society, including our own, may have an inherent maleness. The first level is still recognizable, however, in the tendency to slip back to it from the metalevel: that is, to class other men and their wives with nature; as the Germans say, as *Naturmensch* (cf. Lévi-Strauss, 1967, p. xvi). If men, because of their political dominance, may tend purely pragmatically to 'need' total bounding models of either type, women may tend to take over men's models when they share the same definitional problems as men. But the models set up by women bounding themselves are not encompassed in those men's models. They still subsist, and both sexes through their common humanity are aware of the contradictions. In the social anthropologist's data the process can be more clearly viewed.

III

According to a story of the Bakweri of Cameroon (in a male recension): 'Moto, Ewaki, Eto and Mojili were always quarrelling and agreed to decide by a test which of them was to remain in the town and which should go into the bush. All were to light fires in their houses in the morning and the person whose fire was still burning on their return from the farms in the evening was to be the favoured one. Moto being more cunning than the others built a fire with big sticks properly arranged, whereas they only built with small dry sticks, and so his was the only fire that was still alight on their return in the evening. Thus Moto remained in the town and became Man. Ewaki and Eto went into the bush and became the Ape and the Mouse. Mojili was driven into the water and became a water spirit.'[2] *Moto* (Common Bantu **muntu*) is the ordinary Bakweri word for 'human being of either sex', and thus includes 'woman'. Ewaki, Eto, and Mojili, who are opposed to Moto by reason of his special skill with fire, lack of which relegates them to the bush, are in Bakweri belief all associated with women and their children, whom they attract into their domain. Mojili is responsible for young girls becoming mermaids (*liengu*, plural *maengu*) who are dangerous to men, and whose husbands are *eto* (pl. *veto*), the rats; while the attraction of human children to the apes of the forest is so great that the word *ewaki* must not be mentioned in front of children under seven, in case they fall sick and die. Mojili's name has the same effect. Rites exist to control these manifestations (Ardener, 1956).[3]

The possible marginality of women when men are defining 'the wild' is evident. Thus the idea of the denizens of the wild, outside Moto's village, being a danger or attraction to women and their offspring is comprehensible in a male model of the universe, in which female reproductive powers do not fall under male control. This is, however, inadequate. Bakweri women themselves bound their world as including the wild that Moto excluded. They go through rites by which they become *liengu* mermaid spirits, or spirits of the forest, generally in adolescence, and retain this feature of womanhood throughout their lives. The story of Moto gives the clue, for the three excluded 'animal' brothers all have the human gift of fire. Although the men bound off 'mankind' from nature, the women persist in overlapping into nature again. For men among the Bakweri this overlapping symbolic area is clearly related to women's reproductive powers. Since these powers are for women far from being marginal, but are of their essence as women, it would seem that a woman's model of the world would also treat them as central. When we speak of Bakweri belief we must therefore recognize a man's sector and a woman's sector, which have to be reconciled. Thus the myth of Moto states the problem of woman for Bakweri men: she insists on living in what is for them the wild.

IV

The wild for the male Bakweri is particularly well differentiated, because of the many striking form sin which it expresses itself. This people occupies the southeastern face of the 13,000 foot Cameroon Mountain, on the West African coast of Cameroon – an environment of romantic contrasts. The mountain rises straight from a rocky sea coast through zones of forest, grass, and bare lava to the active volcanic craters of the peak. The Bakweri proper occupy the forest, and hunt in the grass zones. A deity or hero, Efasamote, occupies the peak. Congeners of the Bakweri (Mboko, Isubu, and Wovea Islanders) occupy the rocky strand and fish. The Bakweri proper are agriculturalists; the staple crop was traditionally the male-cultivated plantain banana, although since the introduction of the Xanthosoma cocoyam in the last century, this female crop has become the staple (Ardener, 1970). It should be added that the whole area is now greatly fragmented by plantations and a large migrant population now lives in the Bakweri area (Ardener, Ardener, and Warmington, 1960). The mountain is an extremely wet place, and visibility is often reduced to a few yards because of the clouds that cover it for much of the time.

The villages are traditionally fenced – people and livestock living inside the fence, the farms being outside the fence. This way of looking at it is not inaccurate. In the light of the subject of this paper it is, however, just as true to say: the men live inside the fence with their livestock (goats, cows, and pigs) and most of their plantains; the women go outside the fence for their two main activities – firewood-collecting and farming the Xanthosoma. The men and their livestock are so closely associated that the animals have characteristically lived in the houses themselves. I have myself visited in his hut an elderly man on his bed, so hemmed in by dwarf cows (still the size of ponies) that it was difficult to reach him. The women are all day in the forest outside the fence, returning at evening with their back-breaking loads of wood and cocoyams, streaming with rain, odds and ends tied up with bark strips and fronds, and screaming with fatigue at their husbands, with the constant reiteration in their complaints of the word *wanga* 'bush', 'the forest'. The Bakweri men wait in their leaking huts for the evening meal. It is no wonder that the women seem to be forest creatures, who might vanish one day for ever.

At the coast, the 'wild' *par excellence* is the sea, and its symbolism is expressed through the *liengu* water-spirits. The Cameroon coast provides a kaleidoscope of beliefs about *liengu*. They are found among the Kole, the Duala, the Wovea, the Oli, the Tanga, the Yasa, and many other peoples. Ittmann (1957) gathers together material from numbers of such sources.[4] The common theme is, however, used in the different belief systems of the various peoples in different ways. As I have tried to demonstrate elsewhere (1970), from a consideration of the Bakweri zombie belief, the *content* of a belief system can be analysed as a specific problem, by methods of the type used by Lévi-Strauss in *Mythologiques* (1964, 1966, 1968), as well as through those of more humdrum ethnographic aim. Among the latter, it is possible to discuss the geographical distribution of parts of the content of the belief, and consider, in the *liengu* case, questions such as whether the mermaids 'are' manatees or dugongs, which will not concern us here. The *realien* of the belief for each people are the elements plundered by the *bricoleur*: dugongs, mermaids are all to hand, but what dictates the particular disposition of elements in each system, the 'template' of the belief?

The Bakweri incorporate the *liengu* mermaids into a damp tree-ridden environment in which the sea is not visible, or is seen only far off on clear days, and in which the forest is the dominant external embodiment of the wild. The *liengu* beliefs and rites are in detail marked as a result by the inconsistency of a marine iconography with a non-marine environment. We have various different combinations producing a patchwork of several women's rites all of which are linked by the name *liengu,* some of which have content that links them with certain other West African rites. They are all enacted, however, as a response to a fit or seizure that comes mainly upon adolescent girls but also upon older women. For those men who participate in the rites, the stress is laid upon the 'curing' of the women. For, as we shall see, the men have their own view of the rites.

Liɛngu la ndiva (*ndiva*: 'deep water') appears to retain the closest connection with the water-spirits.[5] The sickness attacks a girl or woman, characteristically, by causing her to faint over the fireplace, so that she knocks out one of the three stones that are used to support the cooking pots. A woman versed in this form of *liengu* then comes and addresses her in the secret *liengu* language. If she shows any signs of comprehension, a *liengu* doctor (male or female) is called and given a black cock, on which he spits alligator pepper; he then kills it and sprinkles its blood in the hole made when the girl knocked out the hearth-stone, and replaces the stone. The patient then enters a period of seclusion. Drummers are called on a fixed evening, the girl herself staying in an inner room, dressed only in a skirt made of strips of bark of roots of the *iroko* tree, hung over a waist string. The doctor then makes her a medicine which she vomits, bringing up the black seeds of the wild banana; these are then threaded on a string and worn like a bandolier. The drummers stay all night and they and the doctor receive a fee. There are usually a number of visitors, especially *liengu* women, and these are given food.

During the period of seclusion which then follows, the girl has a woman sponsor who teaches her the secret *liengu* language, and gives her a *liengu* name. She is subject to a number of conventions and taboos during this period, which will be summarized later. After several months, the *liengu* doctor is called again, and, in the darkness before dawn, she is picked up and carried in turn, one by one, by men chosen for their strength until they reach the deep part of a stream, where the doctor pushes her in. Women who accompany them sing *liengu* songs, and the company try to catch a crab, representing the water-spirit. After this rite, the girl is regarded as being a familiar of the water-spirits and one of the *liengu* women. On the return of the party, the *liengu* drummers play and food is provided for the guests. After the visit to the stream the girl stays in her house for a further period. On the occasion when she finally comes out the doctor and drummers, and other women and visitors, come to the house, where she is dressed in new clothing. Traditionally she was rubbed with camwood. There is another feast, and she is regarded by the men as finally immune from any attack by the water-spirits.

Lisngu la mɔngbango differs from *ndiva* in several respects. For example, the first symptom is sometimes said to be the girl disappearing into the bush as if attracted by spirits. She is then sought by a group of female relatives singing to her in *liengu* language, and when she is found, taken to the seclusion room. There the doctor makes the vomiting medicine as in *lisngu la ndiva*. Details of the seclusion show little difference, but in this case it does not last the whole period of the rite. After a few months, a feast is made which is traditionally all eaten on the ground, after which the girl is allowed to go out, although still subject to taboos. After a further period of about nine months, a sheep is killed and a similar feast made, the girl and her *liengu* woman sponsor being secluded in an enclosure in the bush. She is now dressed in fern-fronds (*senge* or *njombi*) rubbed with camwood, and led through the village tied to the middle of a long rope held by her companions in front and behind. Outside her house, both sets of people pull the rope, as in a tug of war, until the rope comes apart, when the girl falls down, as if dead. She is revived by being called nine times in the *liengu* language, after which she gets up, and is dressed in new clothing.

A few weeks later, she is washed in a stream by the doctor to show that she is free from the taboos she observed during the rites. Both with *ndiva* and *mongbango* the rites extend over about a year.

A third version of the rite, *liengu la vefea*, reduces the procedure essentially to the killing of a goat and a young cock, and the drinking of the vomiting medicine followed by food taboos. The medicine is the same in all three rites. Among the upper Bakweri who live furthest from the sea, an even more generalized *liengu* rite seems to have existed in which the simple *rite de passage* aspect is very noticeable. It is said that formerly every daughter was put through *liengu* at about 8 to 10 years of age so that she would be fertile. She would wear fern-fronds and be secluded for a period, apparently shorter than in the above examples. Other variations in detail appear to have existed in different places and at different times.[6]

The reduced rites were at the time of my first acquaintance with the Bakweri (in 1953) the commonest. The people had, during the previous generation, been overwhelmed by their belief that they were 'dying out' – a belief not without some slight demographic justification. Their economy was stagnant. Public rites of all kinds had gone into decline. The people blamed the general condition of their country on witchcraft. The decline of the *liengu* rites was further blamed by many for the fertility problems of Bakweri women. Nevertheless, a celebration of the *mongbango* ceremony occurred in that same year. In 1958 a Bakweri *liengu* girl was even brought, with a *liengu* mother, to grace a Cameroon Trade Fair. Since then there has been a revival of all kinds of *liengu* rites (I was asked to contribute to the expenses of one in 1970). However, the great rites of *mongbango* and *ndiva*, because of their expense, were probably always relatively rare, compared with *vefea* and other reduced rites. The latter are also common now, because so many *liengu* celebrations are 'remedial', for women who did not pass through them in their adolescence – during the long period of decline. Nevertheless, even such women are told the ideology of the great rites: the immersion (of *ndiva*), the tug-of-war (of *mongbango*), the seclusion, and the secret language. Since we are concerned here with the dimension of belief, it may be added that the image of the *liengu* is a powerful one even for the many Christian, educated, and urban Bakweri women. Scraps of the secret language are common currency. It is as if the *liengu* rites are always 'there' as a possibility of fulfilment; and also as if the rites are themselves less important than the vision of woman's place in nature that appears in them: the template of the belief.

Despite the fact that *liengu* is a woman's rite, men are not immune to the precipitating sickness, especially if there are no women left in a man's extended family, and rare cases are cited in which men have gone through at least part of the rite. The fertility associations of the rite are uppermost in such cases, and the *liengu* mermaids have had to work through a male in the absence of viable females. *Liengu* doctors may be men or women. As we shall see, the participation of men does not obscure the symbolism of the rites for women. It does assist their symbolism for men. Thus the men who carry the *ndiva* girl have to be strong. Although men from her matrilineage (in practice, perhaps, her full brothers) would be favoured, a man from her patrilineage, or just a fellow-villager would be acceptable. Men see themselves as helping out with the treatment of morbidity (social and physical) in women. The domination of men as doctors in Bakweri medical rites means that the specialization as *liengu* doctors by men presents few problems. The major rites (*ndiva* and *mongbango*) have a public aspect, because of their relative expense, and a male doctor is likely to be involved. The female *liengu* doctors are associated with the less expensive, reduced rites. The 'medical' aspects of the rite have thus a somewhat 'male' aspect.

The female significance of the rites lies in the girl's acceptance by her fellow *liengu* women. In the fuller *ndiva* and *mongbango* forms, as already noted, it is customary for her to have a sponsor (*nyangb'a liengu*, '*liengu* mother') to teach her the mysteries. For the periods of seclusion, in both rites, the girl is not allowed to plait her hair but must let it grow uncontrolled, and rub it, as well as her whole body, with charcoal mixed with palm-kernel oil, so that she is completely black. This is supposed to make her resemble a spirit. She is forbidden to talk to visitors, but greets them with a rattle, of different types in *liɛngu la ndiva* (*njola*, made of wicker-work) and in *mongbango* (*lisonjo*, made of certain tree-seed shells). This is also used night and morning, when she has to recite certain formulae in the *liengu* language. While in the house, the *liengu*, as the girl herself is now called, treats rats (*veto*) with special respect as they are regarded as her husbands (compare the story of Moto above). If a rat is killed she must cry all day and wash it and bury it in a cloth; killing rats in her compound is forbidden. No man or boy can enter the *liengu* house wearing a hat or shoes, or carrying a book (all introduced by Europeans) or she will seize them, and return them only on the payment of a fine. If a person dies in the village the *liengu* must not eat all day. In *liɛngu la mongbango*, after her period of seclusion, and before the completion of the rite, the girl may go out only with her rattle, and should turn away if she sees any person not a Bakweri. If anyone wishes to stop her he has only to say the word *yowo* ('magical rite') and she must do whatever he says. However, the *liengu* has an effective retaliation if molested, as any male whom she knocks with her rattle is thought to become permanently impotent. The *liengu* may not go into any room but her own and dogs must not go near her. She should always be addressed by her special *liengu* name. Truncated forms of these requirements are also followed by women in the *vefea* rite. After all rites the participant is henceforth known by one of a standard series of *liengu* names.

v

It has been the intention here merely to indicate those aspects of the symbolism that are peculiar to the *liengu* corpus. This is not the place for an extended analysis, which I hope to attempt elsewhere. The male interpretation is that the *liengu* rites cure a spiritual illness. That is why male doctors take part. The women nod at this sort of interpretation in male Bakweri company but there is a heady excitement when the *liengu* subject is raised in the absence of Bakweri men. It is accepted that the *liengu* mermaid spirits do 'trouble' the women, and cause them physical symptoms. The trouble is solved when a woman becomes a *liengu*. The mermaid world is one of Alice through the looking-glass – no manmade objects, garments only of forest products; no imported goods, traded through men.[7] For the edible plantain banana, a male crop and consciously seen as clearly phallic, we find the inedible seed-filled, wild banana – a total symbolic reversal whose effect is a 'feminization' of the male symbol. The male doctor, who is perhaps only a half-aware participant in this, makes the medicine in an integument of (male) plantain leaves to hem in its harmful effects. The rites see the woman as attracted away into the wild. The domestic hearth-stone (*lio*) is the popular symbol of the household (a unit in the essentially patrilineal residence pattern). It is dislodged. In *mongbango* food is eaten on the earth, and not on the customary (male) plantain leaves. The mermaid's rattle destroys the potency of males. The men are reduced to the scale of little rats, her 'husbands'. She returns to the world through the symbolic tug-of-war at which she is in the middle. She falls senseless. The men assume the world has won. Yet she is revived by nine calls in the *liengu* language. There is surely little reassuring to men in her final incorporation in the wild outside the fence of the village.[8]

The interpretation of the Bakweri *liengu* rites as 'nubility rites', because they often (but not always) precede marriage, is not exactly an error, since it does not say anything. It merely draws attention to the question 'what after all *is* a nubility rite?' Passage through *liengu* rites shows that a girl is a woman; her fellow-women vouch for it. The men feel a danger has been averted; she has been rescued from the wild and is fitted for marriage with men. But she still continues to bear a spirit name, and converses with fellow-women in the mermaid language. The term 'nubility rite' implies for some that the rites have a social 'function'; the girl takes her place in the system of relations between corporate kin-groups. The rites no doubt can be shown to 'validate' this and that aspect of the structure in the normal 'functionalist' manner. Alternatively they prepare the girl for the role of exchangeable unit in a system of alliance. These are good partial statements, but we are left asking questions like 'why did she vomit the seeds of the wild banana?' The terms 'puberty rite' and 'fertility rite' would be just as useful and just as partial. 'Puberty' stresses the biological basis that 'nubility' obscures, but of course even when the rites are not delayed until after marriage, they may take place some years after the onset of puberty – the rigid association of puberty with the menarche is a result of our mania for precision. 'Fertility' at least takes account of the association of the rites with a whole period of the woman's life. They are also 'medical rites' because they 'cure' sickness, and share features in common with Bakweri medical rites for men and women. A set of overlapping analyses such as Richards makes for *Chisungu* (1956) would clearly be equally fruitful here.

The rites are open to analysis in the manner of Van Gennep as classical rites of passage. They fall like all such rites into stages of separation, transition, and incorporation, but the notion of passage is either self-evident (through the rite) or inadequately defined. An analysis in the manner of Turner (1967) could also be attempted, and it is evident that there is the material for such an analysis. The Turnerian method assumes that symbolism is generated by society as a whole. This is of course in a sense true: the very contradiction of symbolic systems, their 'multivalency', 'polysemy', 'condensation', and the like, derive from the totalitarian nature of symbolism. But as the Moto story shows, its surface structure may express the male view of the world, obscuring the existence at deeper levels of an autonomous female view. I feel also that Turner does not perceive the 'bounding' problem that male/female symbolism is about, and which introduces an element of ordering into the symbolic sets.

I have argued that Bakweri women define the boundary of their world in such a way that they live as women in the men's wild, as well as partly within the men's world inside the village fence. In modern times the world outside the fence has included the 'strangers', migrants who are allowed to settle there. Sometimes the stranger's quarter is larger than the Bakweri settlement. Bakweri women have long travelled from stranger-quarter to stranger-quarter, entering into casual liaisons, while the men have complained (Ardener *et al.*, 1960, pp. 294–308; Ardener, 1962). This fortuitous overlap of the old wild with the new urban jungle may well account for the peculiar sense of defeat the Bakweri showed for so many years, which made them come to believe that zombies were killing them off (Ardener, 1956 and 1970). For the women's part, it is possibly not sufficient to account for their notable conjugal freedom, as I have argued elsewhere (1962), merely on the grounds that there are nearly three males to every woman in the plantation area. The Bakweri system of double descent similarly expresses the basic dichotomy. The patrilineage controls residence (the village), the inheritance of land and cattle, succession to political office – the men's world. The matrilineage controls fertility, and its symbolic fertility bangle is found on a woman's farm outside the village fence (Ardener, 1956).

VI

The Bakweri illustration can only briefly document my theme. Men's models of society are expressed at a metalevel which purports to define women. Only at the level of the analysis of belief can the voiceless masses be restored to speech. Not only women, but (a task to be attempted later) inarticulate classes of men, young people, and children. We are all lay figures in someone else's play.

The objective basis of the symbolic distinction between nature and society, which Lévi-Strauss recently prematurely retreated from, is a result of the problem of accommodating the two logical sets which classify human beings by different bodily structures: 'male'/'female'; with the two other sets: 'human'/ 'non-human'. It is, I have suggested, men who usually come to face this problem, and, because their model for *mankind* is based on that for *man*, their opposites, *woman* and *non-mankind* (the wild), tend to be ambiguously placed. Hence, in Douglas's terms (1966), come their sacred and polluting aspects. Women accept the implied symbolic content, by equating *womankind* with the men's wild.

Figure 2

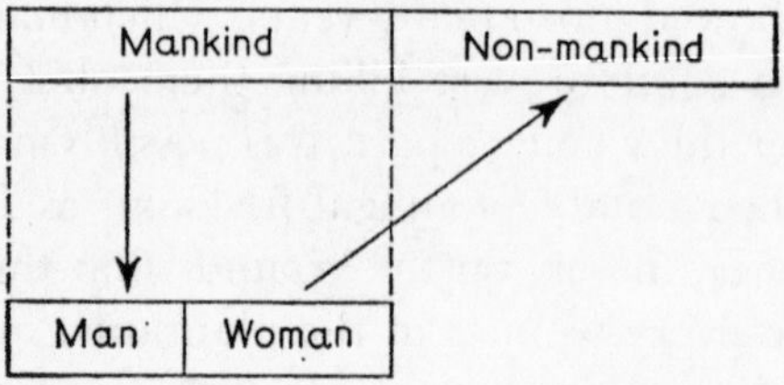

The topic of this paper is 'the problem of women'. Women, of course, have 'a problem of men', who may indeed live in a part of the wild that women bound off from themselves. With that world of hunting and war, both sexes are familiar. The men's wild is, of course, a threat to women. The *liengu* taboos of the Bakweri express some of this. The secluded mermaids hate European goods, which have increased male power. The tabooed 'male' animal, the dog (used in the chase), is an added danger because it can see the spirit world. Dogs walk purposefully on their own, although they have nowhere to go, and they frequently stare attentively into space. Bakweri men have their own symbolic zone of adventure and hunting beyond that of the women, on the mountain-top away from all villages and farms. This is ritually expressed in the men's elephant dance

(Ardener, 1959). Elephants sometimes emerge from the remote parts of the mountain and destroy the women's farms. Men and boys in many villages belong to an elephant society, a closed association that claims responsibility for the work of elephants, through the elephant-doubles (*naguals*) of its more powerful members. In their annual dance they enact their control over the elephant world. Women on such occasions form the audience, who clap out the rhythm for the men's virtuoso dancer. Some women rather half-heartedly claim the role of bush-pigs, but like Dames in an order of chivalry or girls at Roedean, they are performing a male scenario.[9]

It is a tragedy of the male life-position that, in the modern age, the men's wild is not now so easily accessible to them. For modern Bakweri as for American males the hunting fantasy at least is no longer entirely plausible. For if women still symbolically live in their wild, men have tried to ignore their own in the official symbolism of civilization. It will have emerged that the argument of this paper as it applies to women is a special but submerged case of the mode whereby self-identification is made. Obviously the different classes of men and of women, and individuals of all ages and both sexes contribute to that totality of symbolism – which merely appears a 'forest' when one fails to look at the trees.

To return then to the limited problem of my title, we need not doubt that the societies from which ethnographers come share the problem of all societies. If, as I suggest is the case, men's models of society accommodate women only by making certain assumptions that ignore or hold constant elements that would contradict these models, then the process may be traced further back into the ethnographer's own thinking and his own society. Our women ethnographers may then be expressing the 'maleness' of their subject when they approach the women of other societies.[10] It may well be, too, that their positive reluctance to deal with the problem of women is the greater because they sense that its consideration would split apart the very framework in which they conduct their studies.

NOTES

1. This paper was read at Dr Kaberry's seminar in University College, London in early 1969. I should like to take the opportunity, in presenting it for Dr Audrey Richards's festschrift, to acknowledge my debt to her for the main part of my early anthropological training. Her astringent humour and basic open-mindedness are qualities that I have respected ever since. I would also like to thank Dr Jean La Fontaine for her appreciative remarks on this paper, and for entering into the spirit of the analysis in her comments as editor.

2. This version was given in 1929 by Charles Steane, a Bakweri scholar, to B. G. Stone (ms 1929).

3. *Moto*, *eto*, and *ewaki* are the ordinary words for 'person', 'rat', and 'ape'. *Mojili* or *Mojele* is to the coastal Bakweri a spirit. For inland Bakweri his name is a euphemism for 'ape'. It is likely that the term belongs to the animal world, but is borrowed from the fishing peoples. Possibly it is the manatee.

4. When the term is used *in isolation* the spelling *liengu* will be used (not, that is, the 'Africa' alphabet spelling *liɛngu*, nor the occasional spelling with orthographic subscript *liẹngu*). The belief appears to be of coastal origin. There it is concerned with men, fishing, and the dangers of the deep. This paper is concerned with the *liengu* belief as utilized by the Bakweri. Elements of content are differently combined even between the coast and the mountain. Ittmann's rich material (1957) is to be used with caution because it combines several different systems. The pidgin English translation for water-spirit is 'mammy water'. The 'mammy water' myth has wide currency in West Africa in urban contexts. The ambiguity of the position of women in African towns makes this secondary elaboration of the belief very appropriate.

5. See also Ardener, 1956.

6. Various forms cited by myself (1956) and Ittmann (1957) are closer to 'fattening room' seclusion rites of the Cross River area in form and content. Their assimilation to the *liengu* belief is explicable because the latter belief most clearly organizes the women's world-view for the Bakweri.

7. Here is a subtle case of identical content yielding different meaning. The Duala mer-people hate European objects, but the *maengu* are often male. There they symbolize men's domination of the deep; they particularly detest paper (conceived of as the bible).

8. For the *liengu* language, see Ardener, 1956; and Ittmann, 1957. It is a code calqued upon Bakweri with vocabulary from various sources.

9. Dr La Fontaine commented on this paper that men plus wild = death, destruction; women plus wild = agriculture, fertility. She, a woman, thus expresses that faith in the female civilizing mission shared by so many reflective members of her sex!

10. For some unresolved puzzles of a new woman fieldworker see Bovin, 1966. For a resolution through literature see Bowen, 1954.

REFERENCES

ARDENER, E. W. 1956. *Coastal Bantu of the Cameroons*. London: Oxford University Press for International African Institute.

ARDENER, E. W. 1959. The Bakweri Elephant Dance. *Nigeria* No. 60: 31–8.

ARDENER, E. W. 1962. *Divorce and Fertility*. London: Oxford University Press.

ARDENER, E. W. 1970. Witchcraft, Economics, and the Continuity of Belief. In M. Douglas (ed.), *Witchcraft Confessions and Accusations*. ASA Monograph 9. London: Tavistock.

ARDENER, E. W., ARDENER, S. G., and WARMINGTON, W. A. 1960. *Plantation and Village in the Cameroons*. London: Oxford University Press.

BOVIN, M. 1966. The Significance of the Sex of the Field Worker for Insights into the Male and Female Worlds. *Ethnos* **31**: (supp.): 24–7. Stockholm.

BOWEN, E. S. 1954. *Return to Laughter*. London: Gollancz.

DOUGLAS, M. 1966. *Purity and Danger*. London: Routledge & Kegan Paul.

DOUGLAS, M. (ed.) 1970. *Witchcraft Confessions and Accusations*. ASA Monograph 9. London: Tavistock.

EVANS-PRITCHARD, E. E. 1965. The Position of Women in Primitive Societies and in Our Own. In *The Position of Women and Other Essays in Social Anthropology*. London: Faber & Faber.

ITTMANN, J. 1957. Der kultische Geheimbund djĕngú an der Kameruner Küste. *Anthropos* **52**: 135–76.

LEACH, E. R. 1961. Two Essays concerning the Symbolic Representation of Time. In *Rethinking Anthropology*. London: Athlone Press.

LEACH, E. R. 1964. Animal Categories and Verbal Abuse. In E. H. Lenneberg (ed.), *New Directions in Language*. Cambridge, Mass.: MIT Press.

LENNEBERG, E. H. (ed.), *New Directions in Language*. Cambridge, Mass.: MIT Press.

LÉVI-STRAUSS, C. 1949. *Les Structures élémentaires de la parenté*. Paris: Presses Universitaires de France (2nd. edn. 1967).

LÉVI-STRAUSS, C. 1963. *Structural Anthropology*. New York: Basic Books.

LÉVI-STRAUSS, C. 1964. *Mythologiques: Le Cru et le cuit*. Paris: Plon.

LÉVI-STRAUSS, C. 1966. *Mythologiques: Du Miel aux cendres*. Paris: Plon.

LÉVI-STRAUSS, C. 1967. *Les Structures élémentaires de la parenté*. Paris: Mouton.

LÉVI-STRAUSS, C. 1968. *Mythologiques: L'Origine des manières du table*. Paris: Plon.

LÉVI-STRAUSS, C. 1969. *The Elementary Structures of Kinship*. London: Eyre & Spottiswoode.

NEEDHAM, R. 1958. A Structural Analysis of Purum Society. *American Anthropologist* **60**: 75–101.

NEEDHAM, R. 1960. The Left Hand of the Mugwe. *Africa* **30**: 20–33.

NEEDHAM, R. 1967. Right and Left in Nyoro Symbolic Classification. *Africa* **37**: 425–52.

RICHARDS, A. I. 1956. *Chisungu: A girls' initiation ceremony among the Bemba of Northern Rhodesia*. London: Faber & Faber.

STONE, B. G. 1929. Assessment Report of Buea District. Ms. Victoria Divisional Office, Cameroon.

TURNER, V. W. 1967. *The Forest of Symbols*. Ithaca, NY: Cornell University Press.

Ritualization of women's life-crises in Bugisu[1]

J. S. LA FONTAINE

Audrey Richards's *Chisungu: A girls' initiation ceremony among the Bemba of Northern Rhodesia* is a major landmark in the analysis not only of *rites de passage* but of ritual in general. It is scrupulous in the presentation of ethnographic detail on the ceremony and its implications for Bemba society, yet far reaching in its general theoretical conclusions. While the Gisu, some of whose ritual I shall discuss here, are a patrilineal male-centred people, whose great ritual complex is based on the initiation of youths not girls, many of my insights into the meaning of that ritual derived from this classic analysis of the Bemba. It would not be feasible, within the confines of this paper, to attempt a full analysis of male initiation rites among the Gisu, and anything less would be a poor compliment. However, an interpretation of the *rites de passage* of women is both suitable as a tribute to the author of *Chisungu* and sheds light on some important elements of Gisu society and, indeed, on the initiation of men.

This paper, then, discusses the ritual accompanying first menstruation, marriage, and first childbirth, which can be seen as three stages in the progress from girlhood to full feminine maturity. The three rituals are characterized by different degrees of elaboration. The first and last are, today, ceremonials performed perfunctorily, and even in their traditional form were less elaborate than marriage. They could be called ceremonials in Gluckman's terms – 'any complex organisation

of human activity which is not specifically technical or recrea-
tional and which involves the use of modes of behaviour which
are expressive of social relationships' (Gluckman, 1962, p. 22)
were it not for the fact that traditionally they both involved
actions referring to 'mystical notions' (ibid.), in this case
ancestors. In the traditional form then they were rituals, although no Christian ritual has replaced the traditional offering
to the ancestors; in pagan as well as Christian homes they now
become merely ceremonies. The Christian ritual of baptism is
distinguished from the Gisu childbirth ceremonial and, in any
case, follows at some later date.

Marriage, by contrast, is clearly 'ritual' in Gluckman's
terms. It is symbolically more complex and has incorporated
into the traditional ceremony the religious elements of a
Christian wedding, though formerly offerings to the ancestors
involved on both sides were made to ensure the future prosperity of the new spouses. Yet the use of Christian ritual makes
the 'mystical notions' more obtrusive than they were in the
traditional ceremony, where they played a minor part in the total
complex. Thus traditionally the major difference in the three
rites de passage was that of elaboration, with marriage as a
public ritual and the other two rituals more domestic in
character, although they involved individuals outside the
domestic group. Yet today, marriage is still a ritual while the
other occasions are usually only ceremonial. Some distinction is
clearly involved. The problem to which this paper is addressed
is that of elucidating the nature of that distinction, and hence of
explaining the degree of symbolic elaboration in each case.

As an initial step I propose to take a rather different view of
ritual. Some distinction is usually made by anthropologists
between action that is regarded as technical and that which is
non-technical. Thus Goody (1961, p. 159) defines ritual as 'a
category of standardized behaviour (custom) in which the relationship between the means and the end is not "intrinsic", i.e.
is either irrational or non-rational'. Yet as Leach has pointed
out (1954, p. 12) technical acts are usually performed in a

manner peculiar to a particular culture and hence a technical act is, in some sense, symbolic, that is non-rational. Basketry, pottery, and other crafts show in their design not only the technical skills of their makers but the cultural tradition within which the craftsman works, which is also expressed in the art of that society. Experts can place artifacts as well as art objects in an artistic tradition and indeed it is often difficult to decide whether to call an object art or craft.[2] The artistic tradition is a means of cultural expression in certain symbolic forms. Ritual is also a form of symbolic action. Yet, if 'technical' acts include elements of the symbolic and expressive, how can the anthropologist differentiate 'technical' and 'ritual'? It is surely a question of proportion. A preponderance of symbolic over technical action (however technical the actors may consider the purpose of the rite) is what marks off ritual from the customary performance of technical acts. There is a continuum of action stretching from the purely technical to the purely symbolic. While the poles are clearly defined there are points between them that are difficult to place in either category. The term ceremonial seems to be useful here to indicate behaviour in which the symbolic element is clear and even emphasized, but there is less symbolic elaboration. However, it should be clear that the terms technical, ceremonial, and ritual are arbitrary distinctions among phenomena that are themselves not always easily classified.

The Gisu, whom I have described elsewhere (La Fontaine, 1959), are a Bantu-speaking people living on the southwestern slopes of Mount Elgon, an extinct volcano that straddles the Kenya–Uganda border some fifty miles north of Lake Victoria. Ultimately they see themselves as one great lineage descended in the male line from a single ancestor identified by name with the mountain, which they call Masaba. Lineages of lesser span are identified both with local areas and with variations in dialect and ritual practice within a single linguistic and cultural complex, whose major manifestation is the biennial cycle of circumcision ceremonies. Passage through these rituals makes full Gisu and lineage members of young men who without this ritual mark of manhood are deemed unfit[3] to perpetuate their lineage, or to participate in its affairs.

Traditionally, the ancestors of lineage segments were the most potent spiritual forces in the Gisu pantheon. While Gisu believed in a creator God and in refractions of this Great Spirit which manifested themselves in certain spots sacred to them, the ancestors were the main source of sufferings and blessings, both for lineage segments of varying span and for individuals. The ritual emphasized the predominance of men: precedence at ancestral rituals was accorded to those men whose first-begotten child was a son and the blessings these rites bestowed on the participants included, as the most important, the establishment of a flourishing male progeny. Women, although subject to the power of the ancestors, were to a large extent excluded from the rituals and participated only as spectators. It is important for the understanding of Gisu society to emphasize here that a woman is subject to the ancestors of her natal lineage all her life; she is not, unlike the married women of some other patrilineal societies,[4] transferred to the aegis of her husband's ancestors on marriage. Moreover, her children, while subject to the ritual jurisdiction of their father's ancestors, are influenced by the spiritual powers of the lineage that provided the source of their life, their mother. Thus, although emphasis on men and on descent through males is the overt theme of many Gisu rituals, fertility and procreative power is associated with and demonstrated by the women of the lineage. As sisters, women demonstrate through their fecundity the strength of their patrilineally given fertility and hence the power of their ancestors; as mothers they enable another lineage to perpetuate itself in their sons.

Thus it is intelligible that Gisu should manifest concern with the reproductive powers of women. The growing maturity and development of these powers is demonstrated by a series of biological events ending with the birth of children – to Gisu the fulfilment of women's social purpose and the mark of their maturity. The biological events can be invested with social significance by their ritualization, which can emphasize both the creative and destructive (dangerous) elements of the physical nature of women, and by the ritual seek to control it (Richards, 1956, p. 19; Douglas, 1966, p. 147). Biological changes that are thus marked by symbolic focus form *rites de passage* that dramatize not only physical changes but change in status. It has been well established that such *rites de passage* need not accompany any physical events in that either the events may go unmarked or the rites be held independently of physical changes (Richards, 1956, p. 52). Where the two aspects are associated, as they are in the *rites de passage* of women in Bugisu, it is clear that there is a meaningful relation between bodily changes and changes in social status, such that the two aspects of maturity are treated as indistinguishable. Since in Bugisu a woman's adult roles are those of wife and mother, and Gisu women represent the power of their lineages to perpetuate themselves, their social maturity is necessarily linked with their physical maturity. All changes from immature to mature result in a change in all the social relations in which the individual is concerned. Each individual is the focus of a unique set of these relations. For, although roles are socially defined and therefore similar, each individual can be distinguished by the particular roles he plays vis-à-vis particular persons and groups. The physical embodiment of this uniqueness is the body; hence bodily alterations whether natural or artificial seem appropriate to indicate major changes in the social status of an individual. For Gisu women a major element in all the roles they play refers to their child-bearing powers. Social recognition that a particular woman has partially or fully assumed these powers is important. Equally important is that these powers should be controlled by the men who are her guardians.

For Gisu women maturation is a transition marked by three *rites de passage*: at first menstruation; marriage; and when she bears her first child. The first and last are domestic events, although with wider extensions to the girl's kindred. They are more ceremonials than rituals, an elaboration of the formality of and emphasis on certain actions, some of which are performed at subsequent and all menstrual periods or childbirths. Marriage is the most elaborate event, although the social display at a wedding varies with the standing of the bride and groom. Unlike the other *rites de passage* it is unique in that it does not surround the first performance of a recurrent event but is performed once for each individual. (Second marriages, whether of widows or divorcees, are devoid of most or all of the symbolic actions of a first marriage.) The order of elaboration of symbolic acts is first menstruation, childbirth, marriage, but it is convenient to describe them in the order in which they occur in the life-cycle. After I have set out the ethnography I shall attempt to explain why elaboration should be greatest at marriage.

As in many societies blood has contradictory and powerful qualities for the Gisu (Richards, 1956, p. 19; Douglas, 1966, p. 121). It is associated with wounds and death, particularly in war, but also with life, for blood flows when an infant is born. Blood flowing from the female genitals is powerful in that it is associated with the natural power of women, their inherent physiological qualities which make them capable of childbearing. It is also dangerous, both to the woman herself and others. A menstruating woman must keep herself from contact with many activities lest she spoil them: she may not brew beer nor pass by the homestead of a potter lest his pots crack during firing; she may not cook for her husband nor sleep with him lest she endanger both his virility and his general health. A menstruating woman endangers the success of rituals by her presence. Menstrual blood is also highly vulnerable to sorcery worked upon it; a menstruating woman must take care lest drops of it come into the possession of persons ill-disposed towards her, for their sorcery could prevent her bearing children. Gisu recognize that a woman is capable of conceiving once she has menstruated and that cessation of menstruation is a sign of pregnancy. All these are natural events beyond human control, although mystical powers may interfere with them. Blood is then both beneficent and polluting.

A girl's first menstruation is the sign for Gisu that she has become a woman and is capable of child-bearing; henceforward she must observe the food taboos of women, although she might have assumed them before in order to show her maturity. These taboos prevent women eating chicken or eggs lest they become barren. A small girl of seven whom I knew well once refused an offer of a hard-boiled egg from me with the remark 'You should know that I am a woman and women do not eat eggs.' Her formality amused the women who heard her and they agreed that pre-pubertal girls could eat such things with impunity but that once menstruation had occurred it was dangerous not to observe the taboo lest one become barren. At first menstruation a girl becomes polluted with blood for the first time; it seems that the pollution is the greater by contrast with her former ritual purity.[5] She must be secluded at once from normal contacts, particularly from contact with men of the village, her agnates. During the time that she is menstruating she must not touch food with her hands; she eats with two sticks of the *lusoola* tree, identical with those used by initiates in the immediate post-circumcision period. Her mother must instruct her in the way she must comport herself during menstruation and stresses again, what the girl usually already knows, that she must take great care lest sorcery be used against her. As soon as the blood flow has ceased, the girl is washed with water in which herbs promoting fertility have been steeped, and dressed in new clothes. Traditionally she would have assumed for the first time the bunches of foliage covering genitals and buttocks, which were the garb of a mature but unmarried girl. Accompanied by her mother she must now pay formal visits to her kin; outside the village she visits her married sisters, father's sister, and, most important, she must visit her mother's brother, usually identified by Gisu as the brother whose wife was obtained with the bridewealth paid for the girl's own mother.[6]

The maternal uncle sacrifices to his ancestors and asks for their blessing on his sister's daughter. He must offer her the meal he would give an important guest, although he does not kill a chicken for her as he would for a male guest since she is now a woman and may not eat fowls. When she leaves to return home, she is presented with a gift, formerly a goat or a hen, nowadays money or cloth. When she returns to her natal village it is as a physically adult girl, marriageable and hence an asset to her father and brothers and, by extension, to the lineage of which she is a member. Her eventual separation from the community begins with her exclusion, at first menstruation, from the household of which she was a member, as far as sleeping arrangements are concerned. She must no longer sleep under the same roof as any man whom she calls father; traditionally the physically mature girls of a village slept in special huts, under the chaperonage of an elderly woman. A village might have several of these *isimba* in which girls might receive visits from suitors, although it was the chaperone's duty to see that her charges remained virgin until marriage.

First menstruation is thus clearly made a *rite de passage* for the Gisu girl; the physical event is accompanied by other events of a ceremonial and ritual nature which indicate the social significance of the transition. Formerly her appearance also proclaimed her change in status, for after first menstruation she assumed the distinctive garb of a mature unmarried girl. Her change in role vis-à-vis her agnates was and still is marked by her physical separation from them, both during menstruation and from then on in her permanent change of sleeping place. In particular we must note that while all non-agnatic kin ceremonially recognize a girl's maturity, the primary ritual figure, to the exclusion of her father or senior agnates, is her mother's brother. His blessing, and the blessing of his ancestors for whom he is an intermediary, is essential to the girl's future welfare and fertility. In a sense reaching maturity is a further manifestation of the procreative powers of her mother; hence her mother's agnates are those who must recognize and bless them if they are to develop well.

The ritual procedure, of seclusion, eating with sticks and cleansing are clearly a ceremonial underlining of the dangerous power of menstrual blood. The girl is in a polluted state, dangerous to the community and vulnerable herself, so that her isolation from normal life protects both her and the community. Clearly also the natural power inherent in woman's physical nature is made beneficent rather than dangerous by being subject to the social controls of the ceremonial. The ceremonial cleansing and the ancestral blessing both have the effect of bringing a natural event into the social order by controlling it. This is a theme that recurs in all the rituals.

The physical change marked by the ceremonies of marriage is that of the defloration of the bride. Traditionally, Gisu say, a girl would be a virgin at marriage, and even if she were to elope with a suitor of whom her father disapproved, he would leave her in the care of his kin, usually a maternal kinsman, so that her virginity was maintained intact. Whether this statement corresponds with what actually happened or not is immaterial, for the ceremonies are clearly based on the assumption that the bride is virgin. Defloration causes a flow of blood and is an essential prerequisite to conception, as Gisu recognize. It is thus an event of the same physical order as menstruation and childbirth; it is evidence of the dangerous and creative power of women. Yet it differs from other similar ritualized events in one very important particular. The defloration of a woman is not, in the same sense that menstruation and childbirth are natural events, a natural event. It involves a deliberate human act to induce it. It is thus the point at which control by the society of the physical power of women is greatest, for the timing and circumstances can be socially determined in a way that the other physical events in a woman's life cannot be. In a male-dominated society such as that of the Gisu this is vitally important and is, I suggest, the reason why defloration, rather than other events, is made the focus of the most important *rite de passage* for women.

I have written elsewhere (La Fontaine, 1962) of the significance of marriage choices in Gisu society and have emphasized the concern of two lineages in the alliance that marriage establishes. Here I am primarily concerned with marriage as a *rite de passage* for women and I shall not dwell on those elements of the ritual that symbolize its significance for men. This is not to say that the ritual is primarily that of a female *rite de passage*; on the contrary, it has many layers of meaning and those elements, whose reference to the nature of women I discuss, also have other symbolic meanings. However, in order to trace a single symbolic theme, it is clearer to set these aside.

After the conclusion of the bridewealth negotiations, when the agreement between the two groups of agnates concerned indicates that the marriage is to take place, some time elapses while preparations for the ceremonies are made by both sides. The foodstuffs must be assembled and beer brewed for the feasts that accompany the wedding. The bride-to-be is secluded for a period before the wedding. Although accounts differ as to the period the seclusion lasted, it is said to have been shorter formerly. While she is in seclusion she is fed particularly well with large amounts of food and her body is frequently greased with animal fat so that on her wedding day she shall be plump and beautiful, with the shining skin that Gisu admire. On the evening before, her father feasts his agnates and other kin, the men eating separately from the women. Among the women the most important is the girl's father's sister[7] who is the mistress of ceremonies, while the girl's mother plays a subordinate role. The father's sister is entitled to a substantial gift from among the items that have been paid as bridewealth for her brother's daughter; her due is usually described as a goat, although nowadays it is more likely to be money, chickens, or cloth for a dress. If she does not receive this or her help is not otherwise recognized and reciprocated, her ill-will may act to prevent the girl from conceiving or to kill her children. The father's sister thus controls, at least potentially, her agnate's child-bearing powers. As a member of the senior generation she may use this against her brother's child whose position is subordinate, in order to achieve recognition. It is significant that she does not threaten her brother directly but through his daughter's ability to fulfil her duties as a wife, that is by affecting the fertility of another lineage woman. No male agnate has these powers, although he may use sorcery against a sister or daughter. But a father's sister's power is direct since she has the same physical character as her brother's daughter, being both an agnate (of the same blood) and a woman.

The father's sister's duty at the wedding is primarily to deliver the ritual admonishment to the bride before she leaves her natal homestead, and conduct her to her bridegroom. On the morning of the wedding she 'dresses' the bride, that is she supervises her dressing and adornment and when the girl is ready she faces her and formally addresses her. All present must stop what they are doing and attend to what is being said; the speech is said to be harsh (*butafu*) and may make the girl cry. The father's sister speaks of their lineage, of its prestige and achievements; she then tells of the duties of a married woman and how the girl's behaviour in her conjugal home will reflect on her lineage. She is expected to make the future seem difficult and full of onerous responsibilities and ends with her blessing: may you bear many children, many sons. Nothing of what is said in the address is new to the listening bride, since she is already well aware of what a married woman's duties are and also of the representative position of a married woman in a village other than her own. As Audrey Richards has pointed out for similar 'instruction' of girls among the Bemba[8] these speeches do not impart new information, but they confirm the relevance of what is already known and make it legitimate. It thus takes on personal significance for the bride. The address emphasizes the authority and power of senior members of the lineage and in this respect, as in the emphasis it places on the fulfilment of adult roles, it exactly parallels the address given to the male initiand by a senior male agnate immediately before circumcision.

The bride then leaves her father's house accompanied by a group of agnates of her own generation under the leadership of her father's sister. They stop at all the households of the locality and will not move on until a present is given to speed the bride on her way. The bride's 'sisters' hold out baskets into which the gifts, sometimes the traditional gifts of millet, sometimes a few coins, are put. Thus the bride does not go empty-handed to her affines and the gift also signifies a blessing on her and her future. The grain is millet, the traditional staple cereal and the only one acceptable to the ancestors. It can be seen as symbolizing prosperity and abundance, as well as a recognition of the bride's departure.

At a point half-way between the homes of bride and groom the bridal party is met by a group from the groom's lineage, including the groom himself. The party rushes forward as though to attack and the bride's party surrounds the girl and pretends to defend her, refusing to let her go. Their reluctance ends when they are presented with gifts and the whole party then proceeds in procession either to church, if there is to be a Christian wedding or directly to the groom's homestead where there is feasting. The bride is expected to look downcast and sorrowful. She should not speak unless addressed and then should speak only in a low voice. When she is finally conducted into the bridal hut she is expected to show a similar reluctance as her 'sisters' prepare her for the night and see that no sorcery has been placed where it will endanger the sleeping mat or bed.

Traditionally, the bridegroom was expected to shout out his success when he consummated the marriage by deflowering the bride. The feasting guests would shout 'He has spoiled her' and the women would ululate. Some informants claimed that the bridal sleeping mat (a goat skin) would be inspected then for the blood stains that would proclaim the girl to have been a virgin; others said that it was always the custom to wait until the morning. The skin, with the evidence of virginity, was sent to the girl's parents with a trusted agnate of the groom's together with a gift in recognition of the fact that the girl's parents had guarded her well. The messenger was rewarded for his task with a substantial gift for should the bride not conceive then he might be suspected of allowing sorcery to be performed on the blood stains.

No ritual cleansing of the bride or groom on the morning after the wedding night seems to have been performed, although neither were allowed to resume normal life for a period. Although they were not secluded, their abnormal state was indicated by their abstaining from the normal activities of adult men and women, until a further ceremony was performed. They can thus be said to be in a marginal or abnormal state, but the theme of pollution by blood is not emphasized. As far as the bride is concerned, it is clear that in this intermediate stage, the *période de marge*, she is neither girl, nor yet married woman, for a married woman must have a kitchen in which to cook for herself and her husband and, ultimately, their children, yet she does no cooking and in many ways is treated, together with some of her sisters who have remained 'to keep her company' (and also to report on her treatment by her affines) as a guest.

A final ceremony completes the wedding as *rite de passage*. Accompanied by her new husband, her sisters, and some of her affines, the bride returns home to her parents, bearing gifts with her. There she is lavishly entertained as a guest and presented with gifts to take back to her affines. On her return with her husband she is presented by her mother-in-law with a hoe and shown where to hoe; she then ceremoniously hoes a few paces, and performs the other actions that typify the role of married woman – gathers firewood, light a fire, and cooks the first meal for her husband. These are practical actions but performed with an air of ceremony so that they symbolize her assumption of the full status of married woman. They confirm and legitimize a change of status which was achieved, both by her physical transfer and by her defloration – the change in her *physical* state which also causes blood to flow. The *rite de passage* uses the physical events as central features of what is the transfer to an individual of a new role. Thus the girl is divested of her role as unmarried daughter by being addressed by a female agnate, who has also married into another lineage, and then being removed from her parental home. Once the marriage is consummated there is no reversal of the process; an irreversible physical change has taken place. The value placed on virginity shows this clearly. If a girl proves not to be a virgin, she may be rejected and sent back to her parents; there is no marriage. If she is a virgin and for some reason, perhaps ill-treatment during the intermediate period, the marriage does not go well, then she may return to her parents' home and the return of the bridewealth may be negotiated. But this is then called a divorce.

The virginity of the bride is important because her loss of it is a further step in the development of her female power. It should thus, in Gisu eyes, be controlled by the men of those lineages concerned; that of her father and brothers who transfer this power to others with whom they create new ties, and that of her husband who will benefit from the legitimate children the woman will bear. An important aspect of marriage ceremonies then is the fact that this event occurs in the 'right' place and time. It thus testifies to the power of the girl's agnates to exercise control over their female members. In addition, the husband's right to deflower his bride is part of his right to control her powers of reproduction by initiating her reproductive life. A non-virgin bride has taken the control of her sexuality herself; she thus dishonours her lineage and is a potential danger to her husband.

It might be thought that defloration is a necessary physical act merely incidental to marriage, and we have sufficient evidence to indicate that in different societies the consummation of the marriage may either precede or follow what the members of the society recognize as the ceremonial of marriage itself.[9] It would seem that for the Gisu it represents male control of the female physical powers of creation, a dogma essential to the maintenance both of male dominance and patriliny, and hence it is the central ritual act of marriage.

When a woman changes her status at marriage from that of daughter subordinate to the men of one lineage to that of wife subordinate to the men of another lineage, she has still not achieved her full potential as a woman. Only after she has borne children is she entitled to the honorific '*umugyerema*', nowadays translated as 'Mrs' or 'Madam'. A childless married woman must defer to other women of the community, not only according to their age and generation relative to her own but according to whether they have borne children or not. As mother of her husband's child, particularly if it is a son, a woman has a secure status in his lineage and in the community of which it is the core. Similarly in her own lineage she has demonstrated the power of her lineage to bestow progeny on the men of other lineages. A true sister is one who gives to her brother sister's sons. In the only quarrel between brother and sister I witnessed, the man flung at his sister the charge that she was no true sister, shouting 'where are my sister's sons?' Thus childbirth is an event that (like menstruation) on its first occurrence is given cultural significance by making it the sign of a change in status.

Gisu men and women compare childbirth explicitly with circumcision; in the comparison both sexes emphasize the pain that must be endured and the fact that it makes full adults of the immature. Yet men claim, and most women tacitly agree (at least in public), that childbirth is the lesser agony. It is a natural event which a woman does not choose for herself and it gets progressively easier; circumcision on the other hand is a voluntary ordeal for which an effort of will is required, and the suffering, although endured only once, is prolonged through convalescence. (It is a characteristic feature of Gisu circumcision that no indication of suffering must be shown by an initiate during the operation of circumcision, but that in song and speech during the post-operative convalescent period the newly circumcised relate in detail and with emphasis the sufferings they have endured and are continuing to bear.) Childbirth then transforms girls into adult women through the medium of pain endured, but it does not thereby fit women to be the equals of men. Gisu claim that the circumcised women of the neighbouring Sebei are rude and disobedient to their husbands, and challenge their authority. Their wills are strengthened by the ordeal of the knife, so Gisu believe.[10]

In considering childbirth there are also ritual parallels with circumcision to be considered, for details of the ritual occur in both the ceremonial of childbirth, particularly first childbirth, and the ceremonial of circumcision.[11]

Childbirth should take place inside the hut, not in the fields or bush, and a woman who is near to delivering a child should take care lest she should come into labour at a distance from home. However, some homesteads are not appropriate; she should not give birth to her child in her father's homestead, it would be preferable to go into the fields. The newly born infant is in a ritually vulnerable condition and hence should not be exposed to the dangers of alien surroundings; it is most protected in its pater's homestead, under the aegis of his ancestors. The mother herself is both vulnerable and polluting, particularly to her senior agnates. It is a cardinal principle of Gisu social organization that the procreative life of successive generations must not come into contact, particularly if the kin concerned are also of opposite sexes. Yet a woman is thought of as a stranger among her affines; her co-wives, both her husband's spouses and the spouses of her husband's agnates, are the most likely to wish her harm so that they are not considered the most appropriate women to deliver her child without supervision. She should be accompanied by a 'sister', or father's sister, her own agnates, either real or classificatory. The husband of a woman who is tended only by her co-wives is severely criticized for risking the health of his new child and the future children of his wife by neglecting to arrange for her better care. A mother of several children may give birth to her children alone, either not wanting or feeling it unnecessary to summon her sisters, but for the first childbirth she is thought to need their presence.

During the first stage of labour a woman squats, or stands, holding on to the centre-pole of the hut. Her attendants (who usually include elderly affines, experienced in midwifery) show her the posture that is said to make the pain easier to bear, and exhort her to be brave and not to show fear. She is expected to endure her pains in silence as far as possible, but if these are unduly severe and she cries out or weeps she is accused of cowardice (she fears: *atyia*), and she may be beaten or insulted for this fault, for Gisu say that fear retards delivery. A prolonged period of labour may also give rise to suspicions either that the woman has committed adultery or that mystical influences are 'closing the way'. In the first case the woman is urged to confess so that appropriate antidotes may be given her; in the latter she is given protective medicines to drink. Both remedies are obtained from and administered by specialists, usually women. Abnormal presentations of the foetus are recognized as such by the Gisu but are not nowadays regarded as symptomatic of mystical influences. As far as I could discover no attempt is made to turn the child.

For delivery the mother squats, supported by her attendants. After delivery the cord is cut and the end bathed in water in which herbs have been steeped; more herbs are placed on the cut end of the cord in order to stop the flow of blood. The child is washed, the water it is washed in being taken charge of, together with the placenta and other vulnerable effluvia, by a senior female agnate of the mother. She must dispose of them safely, usually by burying them inside the hut or in a secret spot in the homestead's banana grove. For her services she is given a hen by the new father. He has been informed of the birth of his child but must not approach his wife or the baby for some time, since his strength may be affected by their polluted state. The woman must be washed and put on a new cloth before her husband may enter the house.

After childbirth a woman is secluded for several days, during which time she may be visited by women of the village but male affines, except her husband, may not go near her. Men say they are afraid of looking at a new-born child, it may diminish their strength. She may not cook for her husband, nor should he sleep in the hut, contact between him and mother and child being thought to endanger all three of them. During this time the mother must eat a special type of banana, whole not mashed, using sticks to eat with, not her hands. When the placental cord has dried and dropped off, the child is ceremonially brought out. Its head is shaved. The mother and father take it to the huts of neighbouring and nearby kin. The baby is formally greeted by members of the village, each household offering a small gift, usually a few small coins, which entitled them to 'see' the child. It is spoken of as a fee to 'see' the child, the payment of which averts evil from the child, by demonstrating the goodwill of the giver. We can see it also as the first act of hospitality to the child, symbolizing his social relation with the giver. The ceremony establishes the child as a separate social being and should take place not long before its formal naming, which alone gives it full status as a human being. The ceremony also lifts the restrictions on the mother and allows her to resume normal daily activities, although she may not sleep with her husband for a further period.

Since we are concerned with the mother, we need not describe the further stages that establish the child as bearer of legitimate kinship statuses. One can see in first childbirth the way in which a physical event, the birth of a child, is the focus of attitudes and actions that give it meaning in the social context. Labour is the ordeal that separates a woman from her former status as married but immature; after labour she is in a ritually impure and dangerous state since blood has flowed. Cleansing and the passage of time weakens this condition, and a final ceremonial ends the marginal period. Similarly, the newly circumcised are polluted by blood and may not be approached until they have been cleansed. When the blood ceases to flow then normal social contacts are possible, although initiates are secluded until completely healed, whereas a woman is considered to have healed when the bleeding ceases.

The ceremonial of childbirth consists of acts that protect the mother and her child, for they are still thought of as connected beings, from mystical attack, and emphasizes a transition in status. Yet the acts that can be called ceremonial are, for the Gisu, technicalities which ensure a proper outcome of an essentially natural act. They are also symbolic statements about underlying concepts similar to those at first menstruation and marriage: blood is evidence of life, its loss is dangerous but accompanies new life as well as death, hence blood pollutes. The appropriate steps are therefore taken to prevent harm ensuing. A clear parallel with the form of first menstruation ceremonies can be seen here. The same acts performed during circumcision are more clearly symbolic, for they are separated from the technical acts which they represent. I have already noted that the mother of an initiate takes up the posture of a woman in labour inside the hut outside which her son is being circumcised and hence 'reborn'. While her action symbolizes his birth as a mature man, it also identifies the socially imposed pains of circumcision with the natural creative pains of childbirth; it is seen as symbolic, as part of a sequence of rites laid down by the ancestors. Yet the posture of a woman who is actually giving birth is also culturally determined; the observer notes that the centre-pole of the hut is frequently identified as the seat of the ancestors of the homestead's owner.[12] Its phallic form could be said to represent the male share in procreation.

Menstruation is not associated with pain but its first occurrence is also marked by formal items of behaviour which give the natural events a ceremonial form and social significance. A girl's seclusion from adult men, and from the normal world, is seen by Gisu as a precaution taken to ensure that the creative rather than the dangerous quality of bleeding triumphs. Formal instruction is given to the woman going through the *rites de passage* of menstruation, marriage, and first childbirth so that responsibility for continuing the protective acts and proper behaviour in future situations is made clear and devolves on her. As I have already pointed out, Audrey Richards's *Chisungu* (p. 125–9) demonstrated that it is the legitimizing function of the instruction that is important not the educative.[13] In all three rituals there is an emphasis on the primary elements of kinship and the opposed though complementary nature of the sexes. At menstruation the emphasis falls on the division between male and female agnates, particularly of different generations; at first childbirth the distinction is made between affines, dangerous and endangered, and female kin, supportive and safe.

The ceremony of marriage differs from the other *rites de passage* we have been considering in scale and the elaboration of ritual procedures. I have already indicated why I think this is so: the physical change that denotes the change of a woman's status is the result of a deliberate act that is brought about by her new husband. While defloration is one step in the chain of physical events that result in the maturation of a child into a fertile woman, it is also the one step that can be controlled by the society. First menstruation and first childbirth can be ritualized into social significance, but no human act can determine when they will occur. Other factors in the physical maturation process can be taken as diacritical signs, which mark the passage to maturity. In our society chronological age is the marker: at 16 a girl may legitimately use her sexuality, at 18 she may marry without parental consent. Physical maturity in this society is distinguished from social maturity. In non-literate societies chronology is geared to events in the natural world, which are given significance by socially defined markers: the roles of men and women are distinguished by physical signs. Thus the events of change in the physical attributes of individuals can be invested with social significance and come to symbolize sex roles. In Gisu society, as in most such societies, a woman's role is to bear children, so that the development of her physiological power to do this is marked at various stages, to control and augment it.

The Gisu recognize in women a creative power that is *sui generis* natural. The sign of this power is a flow of blood from the genitals, which is a physiological process. The rituals we have been discussing control and harness the reproductive powers of women for the benefit of men, whose powers by contrast are social, not part of the natural order. We can say, in Lévi-Straussian idiom, that men's powers are part of culture, women's of nature. The natural powers cannot be exercised without men; Gisu are aware of the role played by the male in procreation. Moreover natural power, uncontrolled, is dangerous. Defloration is the point at which nature and culture meet. Ritual under the control of men brings about a necessary event in the process of physical maturation; it directs the natural flow of events. Hence in a society in which male control of power is a dominant cultural theme, a girl's loss of virginity is an event of major significance and defloration a central act in a major *rite de passage*.

We can thus arrange the rituals which mark a woman's passage to maturity in an ascending scale according to the degree to which the controllable or the uncontrollable element is strongest. First menstruation is preceded by other physical signs but its onset cannot be predicted or prevented. It is thus the most 'natural' of the events of female maturation. Childbirth can be predicted within rough limits. Gisu see it as the logical outcome of the preceding physical stages, but believe that conception can be prevented by mystical or other means; it is usually women who are believed to take action to prevent conception or procure abortions. Parturition is thus not fully within the control of men. Marriage, or rather defloration of the bride, is the demonstration of men's control over women and over the reproductive capabilities that give them value; hence, for Gisu, it becomes the central event in a ritual that demonstrates both men's power over women and the passage of a girl to maturity. While Gisu say that a girl is not fully a woman until she has borne children, the elaboration of marriage as a ritual belies this, although it would also be true to say that the birth of the first child is merely the demonstration or result of the success of the marriage ritual.

At various points I have noted the parallelism of ritual that occurs in the three *rites de passage* of women and the circumcision of youths.[14] In many ways the initiand is treated as a bride and this parallel is made unmistakeable when, after his foreskin has been severed the onlookers shout: he (the circumcisor) has spoiled you. They use the verb which when used of a girl means to deflower. The secluded initiate is polluted by the shedding of blood in the same way as a menstruating girl or a woman after childbirth; he eats with sticks until he is ritually cleansed. As I hope to show elsewhere,[15] from one point of view Gisu male circumcision rituals can be seen as a symbolic creation in men of the inherent physical power of women. The juxtaposition of the pain of childbirth and the pain of circumcision now takes on greater meaning: in women it is natural uncontrolled bleeding that denotes their (reproductive) power; in men it is social, controlled bleeding that both symbolizes and creates superior social power.

As far as women are concerned, the major *rite de passage* is that in which their physical development is most closely controlled by society; the scale and elaboration of the symbolism clearly indicates that it is a ritual rather than a ceremonial. The ordering of *rites de passage* for women in terms of scale and complexity thus parallels their ordering in terms of the most cultural, most natural continuum. It can be represented diagrammatically thus (*Figure 1*).

Parturition mediates between nature and culture as the product of the cultural control of nature (the husband's defloration of his wife). Yet conception is a natural event that Gisu cannot altogether control so that the birth of children comes more into the sphere of nature, which is that of women's inherent power.

This implicit indentification of women with nature, men with culture can be seen by juxtaposing the *rites de passage* of men and women. Men pass through a single rite, built up of a

Figure 1

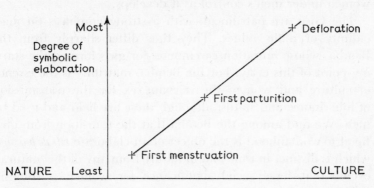

complex of symbolic elements referring to all three of the more simple *rites de passage* of women. These latter are ritualizations of natural events, of which the centre, both in sequential and symbolic terms, is the wedding, in which the natural power of a woman is controlled and directed by men for the ultimate purpose of the couple, the perpetuation of society by their children. Thus circumcision is to defloration as culture to nature; opposed yet inextricably linked by the cultural significance of natural events, and the control of nature's flow by cultural forces.

These oppositions are not permanent divisions or categories but principles of polarization. Thus defloration is part of culture when opposed to first menstruation but of the natural sphere when opposed to male circumcision. Symbolic elaboration appears greatest at the cultural pole. This would seem to be because symbols generate power and the greater the symbolic elaboration the greater the power. This power is directed to a specific purpose – it is intended to achieve a result (Richards, 1956, p. 113) – in this case a change in the state of the individual. For men this change is achieved by initiation, a single once-for-all complex ritual. For women culture marks out stages in their progress to maturity and surrounds the natural events with symbolism, which both defines their social significance and brings the natural power of women under men's control as it develops.

The Gisu are patrilineal, with a strong emphasis on masculinity or male values. They thus differ sharply from the Bemba, whose initiation ceremonies for girls formed the starting-point of this essay. For the Bemba, matriliny is the essence of culture and women the relevant sex for the transmission of inheritance and status, although these are held and used by men. We find among the Bemba that the transition from girlhood to womanhood is the object of an elaborate *rite de passage*, which is distinct in time and in nature from any of the 'natural' events that have social significance for women in Bugisu. *Chisungu* is celebrated before marriage; indeed, it is an essential prerequisite for marriage (Richards, 1956, p. 54). It follows first menstruation, but that physiological event is made the focus of a separate ceremonial. Nor does *chisungu* accompany defloration, for a girl may have been sleeping with her fiancé before her ceremony is performed, although it is true that she must not do so after her menstrual periods have begun (Richards, 1956, p. 19) lest she bear a child before her *chisungu*. It is quite clear that it is *chisungu* itself that makes girls into women (ibid., pp. 120–1); the ritual does not simply make the physiological changes significant.

One purpose of *chisungu*, as Bemba see it, is to protect a girl against the dangers of mature sexual intercourse. The first act of intercourse with the husband after *chisungu* is uniquely powerful and dangerous (Richards, 1956, p. 33) for it initiates the procreative life of the newly created woman. At many points in the ritual the dangers of intercourse and the strength of the link between husband and wife are referred to and symbolized (ibid., p. 140). One can say that in this matrilineal society husbands are aliens and therefore uncontrollable; they are also men and therefore powerful (ibid., p. 159). Husbands are necessary to the matrilineage in order that its women shall bear children, but they may also endanger and even kill those children. Bemba believe that adultery is mystically dangerous:

an adulterous husband may cause his wife's child to be born dead or his wife herself to die. The survival of children is a major preoccupation of the Bemba and Richards remarks (1956, p. 28) 'magic [of Bemba women] was very largely concerned with rites designed to save their babies' health'. It does not seem too much a distortion of the evidence to suggest that Bemba matrilineages protect their women, the source of their continuing existence, against the dangers inherent in the necessary, powerful contact with the uncontrollable (by the lineage, that is) powers of husbands.

Clearly the Bemba are not a mirror image of the Gisu; it would be distorting the evidence to suggest that the matrilineal society reverses the patrilineal opposition I have demonstrated, identifying men with nature and women with culture. Bemba women are also dangerous to their husbands and the fear of menstrual blood appears greater among the Bemba than among the Gisu. I am not suggesting that the mode of descent is the only structural principle determining the symbolic values associated with the two sexes. This would be contrary to the ethnographic evidence. To the east of the Gisu, in Kenya, live the Gusii, a patrilineal society who perform initiation rites for both boys and girls, of which rites for the latter are the more elaborate (see Mayer, 1953b, p. 26; Koloski, 1967, p. 7). Gusii society resembles that of the Gisu in many ways, but differs in that women are given ritual status in the lineage of their husbands and are more fully incorporated into them. Gusii are more concerned with the fertility of their wives than of their sisters, so that the nature of the opposition between the sexes is altered (Mayer, 1953a; Koloski, 1967, pp. 32–8).

It is clear then, that there is no simple correlation between patriliny and the pattern of elaboration in *rites de passage* for girls and for boys. There are patrilineal societies in which no initiation rites are performed for men; the examples of the various interlacustrine Bantu states would seem to indicate that in centralized societies achieved status or the ascription of rank may replace the simple categories of initiated and uninitiated with a more complex hierarchy. Yet I do not know of a cognatic society in which *rites de passage* reach the scale and elaboration of those I have discussed here. It would seem that in the selection of one sex to transmit, not only status, but incorporation into a group which is multifunctional in the society, a particular emphasis is given to a universal theme: the nature of men and women, their opposition and conjunction in procreation. For the Gisu this theme is linked with the distinction between nature and culture. The symbolic action of *rites de passage* is the means by which Gisu culture underlines the significance of related oppositions, which, when symbolically conjoined, ensure man's control over nature.

FOOTNOTES

1. This article was already in draft when I read a first draft of the article by Edwin Ardener in this volume, and I was struck by the parallelism in our views. However, I think it fair to record that his analysis has sharpened my own, and I would wish to record my debt to him. I have also profited from discussion with colleagues at the London School of Economics, and with Miss Anne Akeroyd to all of whom I offer my thanks and the assurance that I take full responsibility for the views expressed here.

2. This comparison was suggested to me by a lecture on the problem of distinguishing art from craft, given by Anthony Forge, in a course on Primitive Art.

3. Young men might father children before initiation but thereby incurred a state of ritual impurity that required a special cleansing ritual after circumcision, lest the wound fail to heal or render them sterile.

4. Cf. Hunter, 1936; Mayer, 1949; Koloski, 1967.

5. Pre-pubertal girls, being ritually pure, have special duties in certain rituals. They are the attendants of convalescent initiates in their post-operative stage, bringing them food. Pre-pubertal boys may also undertake these tasks, but it would be distorting Gisu ideas to say that such children are pure because they are considered to be asexual or neuter.

6. S. Heald, in an unpublished MS, notes that in central Bugisu a girl's mother took with her on this visit a few drops of her daughter's menstrual blood to show her brother. My informants in north

Bugisu did not refer to the need for such proof. The parallel with the demonstration of virginity at marriage is interesting (see p. 171).

7. Since Gisu kinship terminology emphasizes the lateral spread of kinship rather than lineal identification, some classificatory father's sisters are not of Ego's lineage; such a woman would not be allowed to undertake the role of sponsor at Ego's wedding. It is quite clear that she must be a senior agnate, if the 'real' father's sister is not available.

8. See Richards, 1956, pp. 125–9; and also Rosemary Firth, 1969.

9. See the essay in this volume by Monica Wilson (pp. 187–201) in which she states that the presence of the husband is not essential for the marriage to be celebrated.

10. It is interesting to note that the Sebei hold that clitoridectomy makes a girl humble and fit to be the subordinate spouse. They point to the (in their view) unruly promiscuous Gisu women as distasteful reminders of what uncircumcized women may become.

11. Turner (1969) has provided a summary account of this ceremony using material from my doctoral thesis as well as his own observations during the summer of 1966. Although the views that he attributes to me do not really represent my own arguments, I am in substantial agreement with his conclusions which, I feel, are nearly identical with those advanced in my thesis.

12. I disagree with Turner (1969, p. 240) that the centre-pole of the hut represents femininity and motherhood. As the seat of the patrilineal ancestors and the main support of the hut – which is identified with the nuclear family of which the man is the centre and authority, it is clearly a symbol of maleness and descent through males, cf. Rigby, 1966, p. 7.

13. In our own society, the phrase 'now you know' has overtones of a shift of responsibility from the speaker to the hearer.

14. In his book, *Symbolic Wounds*, Bettelheim explains male circumcision in Australia as an attempt to confer power on boys by inducing a male 'menstruation' in an operation that also excises that part of the male genitalia that could be said to resemble female organs. It should be clear that the parallel I am drawing is between all female *rites de passage* and the symbolism of the physiology of women in rituals of male initiation. Nor would I accept his reducing culture to the equivalent of the fantasies of mentally disordered children.

15. In an MS. (in preparation) on male initiation in Bugisu.

REFERENCES

BETTELHEIM, B. 1955. *Symbolic Wounds: Puberty rites and the envious male*. London: Thames & Hudson.

DOUGLAS, M. 1966. *Purity and Danger: An analysis of concepts of pollution and taboo*. London: Routledge & Kegan Paul.

DOUGLAS, M. 1970. *Natural symbols: Explorations in cosmology*. New York: Pantheon; London: Barrie & Rockcliff.

FIRTH, ROSEMARY 1969. Examinations and Ritual Initiation. *World Year Book of Education*.

GLUCKMAN, M. (ed.) 1962. *Essays on the Ritual of Social Relations*. Manchester: Manchester University Press.

GOODY, J. 1961. Religion and ritual: The definitional problem. *British Journal of Sociology* **12**: 143–64.

HUNTER, M. 1936. *Reaction to Conquest*. London: Oxford University Press for International African Institute.

KOLOSKI, E. 1967. Initiation Ritual in Selected African Societies: A study in social differentiation. MA thesis, University of London.

LA FONTAINE, J. S. 1959. *The Gisu of Uganda*. Ethnographic Survey of Africa: East Central Africa. London: International African Institute.

LA FONTAINE, J. S. 1962. Gisu Marriage and Affinal Relations. In M. Fortes (ed.), *Marriage in Tribal Societies*. Cambridge Papers in Anthropology. Cambridge: Cambridge University Press.

LEACH, E. R. 1954. *Political Systems of Highland Burma*. London: Bell.

MAYER, P. *The Lineage Principle in Gusii Society*. Memorandum 24. London: Oxford University Press for International African Institute.

MAYER, P. 1953a. Ekeigoriogoro: A Gusii rite of passage. *Man* **53**: 3–6.

MAYER, P. 1953b. Gusii Initiation Ceremonies. *Journal of the Royal Anthropological Institute* **89**: 9–36.

RICHARDS, A. I. 1956. *Chisungu: A girls' initiation ceremony among the Bemba of Northern Rhodesia*. London: Faber.

RIGBY, P. 1966. Dual Symbolic Classification among the Gogo of Central Tanzania. *Africa* **36** (1): 1–17.

TURNER, V. W. 1969. Symbolization and Patterning in the Circumcision Rites of Two Bantu-speaking Societies. In M. Douglas & P. M. Kaberry (eds.), *Man in Africa*. London: Tavistock.

The wedding cakes: a study of ritual change

MONICA WILSON

Audrey Richards is characterized by the quality of her field-work, and the range and variety of the material she has published. Her first field study on the Bemba is still unmatched in Africa for the detail provided on production and nutrition, and, in addition, the Bemba saga includes outstanding studies in depth of ritual and of political structure. Already in 1935, she was reflecting upon *how* to analyse changing societies, and in 1940 was writing on *Bemba Marriage and Modern Economic Conditions*, a pioneering study of change in kinship and ritual. The lines for future research in East Africa were already laid down, and were developed in comparative studies of: chieftain-ship; the shift from hereditary authority to appointed admin-istrators; village structure; patterns of migrant labour; and, changing patterns of farming.

A true scholar, Audrey Richards was eager to share her ideas and encourage the work of others. Innumerable students in Africa, in Britain, and in America benefited from her selfless and unstinting help. I was among the many she stimulated through discussion and careful criticism, and refreshed by her unquenchable gaiety. I gratefully acknowledge my debt, and offer in homage this fragment on change in marriage ritual.

In southern Africa a confrontation of religions and of cultural traditions has continued over a hundred and fifty years. Preliterate cattle-keepers and cultivators who had a lively belief in the power of ancestral shades, and slaughtered cattle in their honour encountered a literate people of Europe, explicitly Christian, with a culture shaped by Greece and Rome as well as Israel. The confrontation is reflected in ritual, in law, language, and music, in economy, and in political structure.

Ritual is commonly validated partly by its supposed antiquity, men say: 'it is the custom'; 'our fathers did this'; 'we follow the liturgy of the church'; 'it is part of the Catholic tradition'. The force of ritual comes partly from its antiquity, real or supposed, and the problem facing all who celebrate rituals in a fast-changing society is how to combine relevance to changing circumstances with the sanctity of tradition. Nowhere has the contradiction been clearer than in southern Africa, where the Nguni people identified piety with the observance of *amasiko*, i.e. traditional rituals and customs, and the Christian missionaries from nineteenth-century Europe whom they encountered were equally insistent on the celebration of rituals in the form customary in their church.

Here one ritual, universally important, is selected for analysis. It is the wedding. The change is described in the area of longest interaction: the frontier between Nguni and whites. There the wedding cake, borrowed from Europe, becomes two, one for the groom and one for the bride, whose health and fertility is felt somehow · to depend on the proper division and consumption of the cakes. The new rites take a set form and become obligatory, although the appearance of *two* ornately iced cakes suggestive of a French patisserie, seems wholly incongruous in a remote homestead, dominated by a cattle-byre. The anthropologist may well inquire why and how does this particular change occur? What is the symbolic content of the cake that becomes two? What other symbols are borrowed and why? What traditional rites are still celebrated and why are they felt to be important? Are any general principles of change in ritual discernible?

The people of the frontier were Xhosa, with Thembu, Mpondo, and others adjacent to them, and within thirty years of the first missionary work among the Xhosa, they were joined by refugees from Shaka's wars in Natal – Dlamini, Bhele, Zizi, and others, collectively known as Mfengu. The refugees were more receptive to mission teaching than the Xhosa who were fighting to retain their land and independence, so the new patterns were created by Mfengu rather than by Xhosa, and their Thembu and Mpondo neighbours (Wilson and Thompson, 1969, vol. 1, pp. 249, 252, 265). But the Nguni people as a whole, who stretched a thousand miles from the Ciskei to Swaziland, shared common patterns of ritual and language with relatively minor variations.

Variations occurred also in the forms of marriage introduced by missionaries who differed in denomination and in national origin, but again these were minor. In the common patterns that emerged, a strong German Moravian influence is discernible, for their customs percolated through their coloured converts who were the first interpreters and assistants to white missionaries of all denominations on the frontier (Wilson and Thompson, op. cit., pp. 246, 262). The Moravian women wore shawls and kerchiefs, black or white, the kerchiefs discreetly tied; still, in 1969, they wear them for communion services in the mother church in Cape Town; and a fringed alpaca shawl and kerchief – both black – came to play a part in the Christian marriage ritual of many Nguni. The aura of tradition characteristic of ritual quickly enveloped the new forms.

Marriage as celebrated by the pagan Nguni, and by the white missionaries and settlers who arrived on the frontier had many common elements. Both stressed agreement between the families concerned; betrothal; a public celebration of marriage; honouring virginity in the bride: and seeking from God, or gods, blessing and fertility. The ritual was accompanied by feasting, dancing, and admonition. Groom and bride each had an attendant or attendants – the groomsmen and bridesmaids (Maclean, 1866; Soga, nd; Hunter, 1936; Reader, 1954; Hammond-Tooke, 1962; Vilakazi, 1962; Krige, 1968).

But there were also diverse elements, Nguni marriage was

controlled by patrilineal clans, marriage within the clan of either parent and (among the strictest) of either grandmother, being prohibited. The legal bond, and control of children, depended upon the passage of cattle from the groom's group to that of the bride. This transfer of cattle in return for a girl concerned not only the groom and the bride and their parents, but members of both their lineages, living and dead: an individual was identified by his or her lineage and marriage was the affair of lineages. The marriage ritual, directed first to the shades of the bride and then to those of the groom, sought their blessing and celebrated the transfer of the bride from the care of her father's shades (the dead members of his lineage) to those of her husband. This was marked by the rite of *ukudlisa amasi*, giving her the milk of cattle of her husband's lineage, after which she ceased to drink milk from her father's cows. Sharing milk was the most intimate bond, and no one might drink the milk of an unrelated lineage except at their chief's homestead (Alberti, 1811, pp. 77, 130–1; Hunter, 1936, pp. 52–3, 200–1, 392). A bride was expected to bring with her a cow, 'the beast of the shades' (*inkomo yesinyanya*, or *inkomo youbulunga*) which represented her father's shades, and from which tail hairs were plucked for her to wear as a necklace. The wearing of such a necklace (*intambo yobulunga*) was a prayer to the shades (Hunter, 1936, pp. 234–40). If the bride were a virgin, one of the cattle handed over by the groom was recognized as a gift to her mother for guarding her virginity.[1]

The cleavage between the lineages was expressed in the celebration of *two* feasts, one at the home of the bride, and one at that of the groom; by competitive dancing between the bride's party and that of the groom on both occasions; and by the change in behaviour required of a girl when she moved from the homestead of her father to that of her husband. At her husband's homestead she showed respect (*ukuhlonipa*) by avoiding those parts of the homestead frequented by men – the courtyard, the cattle-byre, and the half of the hut on the right hand as one enters; by covering her head and breasts in the presence of her in-laws and looking down, rather than directly at them; by wearing the long skirt of a married woman in place of the short kilt of a girl; and by avoiding words resembling the name of her father-in-law and kinsmen identified with him. Modesty also required that a bride should weep at her wedding.

By traditional custom both groom and bride were individuals socially recognized as adult and fit to marry. This implied seclusion of the bride at puberty and the celebration of rites designed to bring the blessing of her shades, and ensure fertility, as well as making her plump and attractive with a good complexion. For men it had once implied circumcision among all the Nguni but by the mid-nineteenth century this survived only among those who lived farthest south – the Xhosa, Thembu, Mfengu refugees, and other smaller groups (Wilson and Thompson 1969, p. 125).

In the Christian ritual as introduced by the missionaries, there were six essential elements:[2] the public notification of intention to marry in calling banns; the public assent of the bride's father or guardian; the public assent of both bride and groom to a life-long union and sharing of wealth; placing a ring on the bride's left hand; seeking blessing on the union through prayer to God; and the legal bond established through registration by a marriage officer. Interwoven with these were conventions felt to be appropriate: an engagement ring; a white dress and veil for the bride if she were a virgin, and a change of clothes for her for travelling; a wedding cake and wine to toast bride and bridegroom; speeches complimenting both families; perhaps feasting and dancing; and the giving of gifts to bride and groom. Ancient conventions which no-one took very seriously also survived; these included reserving the right-hand side of the church as one enters for the friends of the groom, the left for those of the bride, sprinkling bride and groom with grain (or a symbol of grain), tying old shoes to their vehicle, and other horseplay. The marriage might be accompanied by transfer of property, a 'marriage settlement' of some sort, but this was not held necessary to the union.

From these two marriage rituals – that traditional among the Nguni, and that from Christian Europe – there emerged a new ritual characteristic of Christian Nguni, and felt by them to be obligatory and appropriate. This paper is concerned with what symbols were selected, why these symbols and not others were felt to be obligatory and appropriate, and how and why other symbols, traditional in one group or the other, were readily dropped.

Traditional Nguni marriage turned on the transfer of cattle from the groom's group to the bride's and the various return gifts made, the bride bringing with her presents for her in-laws, as well as her own household equipment which she received from kinsfolk and neighbours. In spite of opposition from many missionaries, most Christian Nguni continued to regard such a transfer of cattle as a condition of legal marriage. *Lobola* continued (Wilson *et al.*, 1952, p. 82) and where money replaced cattle it was still spoken of as if it were cattle, for cattle were symbolically associated with the lineage, and with the shades. The bride continued to bring with her both household equipment for her own use and gifts for her in-laws, but with rising standards of furnishing the provision of household equipment became more difficult, and many mothers joined clubs whose members pledged themselves to provide gifts for the daughter (or daughters) of each member when she married, on condition that she married with her parents' consent. Great prestige attached to the handing over of gifts to the bride at a party given by her parents shortly before her marriage, and a careful record was kept of what personal friends, relatives, and each member of the gift-club provided (Wilson *et al.*, 1952, pp. 165–9; Hammond-Tooke, 1962, p. 129; Hunter, 1936, pp. 215–16).

Clan exogamy continued to be observed (except among a handful of sophisticated people in town), and among the Xhosa, Thembu, and Mfengu, as opposed to the Zulu and Swazi, circumcision of the groom was a precondition of any marriage negotiations. Rituals specifically directed to the shades[3] and seeking their blessing were difficult to reconcile with Christian teaching, but traditional ritual killing was reinterpreted as secular feasting and the slaughter of an ox or goat commonly continued on traditional occasions, as for example when a family said farewell to a daughter about to be married; or 'to lay the mat' in her new home; and when she began to drink milk in her husband's homestead. The Christians argued that these were conventional feasts and not obligatory ritual, and that Christians did not fear lest the bride be sterile or fall ill if they were omitted, but still the feeling remained that it was somehow much more appropriate to 'slaughter at home' than to buy meat from a butcher on such occasions. The 'beast of the shades' was not brought by a Christian bride, that was altogether too closely associated with the shades for it to be appropriate at a Christian marriage, but it was whispered in Pondoland that *sometimes*, if a Christian bride were ailing, she would slip back to her father's homestead to beg the tail hairs of a cow, and wear them wrapped in a cloth so that none should see them.

Among Christians the long seclusion of a girl at puberty was replaced by a brief seclusion from the time the banns were called until the marriage was celebrated, and the explicit intention was that she should become plump, and care for her complexion with modern cosmetics (such as cold cream) during that time. The rite of *ukudlisa amasi*, making the bride drink milk, became the *idinala yomtshakazi*, the 'bride's dinner' (Hunter, 1936, pp. 214, 220), just as the pagan rites of Europe were baptized or secularized when Christianity spread among pagans there.

Old rites thus faded and became of less account though they did not vanish altogether, and new rites, felt somehow to be more potent, were added. In borrowing new rites three processes are apparent. First, the religious rites laid down by each denomination, and legal procedures for registering a marriage, were taken over complete, almost without modification.

Second, some of the conventions of western marriage were taken over piecemeal, and details copied, notably the dress for the bride and groom (down to orange blossom, bouquet, buttonhole, and white gloves for both partners), and their formal parade, the bride taking the groom's arm or holding his hand (Hunter, 1936, plate XXVIIIb). Third, other conventions, such as that of the wedding cake, were borrowed and transformed.

The dichotomy between the groom's lineage and the bride's, which was so clear in the pagan ritual, reappeared in the Christian ritual. Again there were two feasts, one at the home of the bride and one at the home of the groom. Bride's party and groom's party again danced in competition, but the form of dancing changed, for pagan dances were bitterly opposed by the early missionaries. One of the ironies of culture contact is that each group often regards the art, and particularly the dancing, of the other as *immoral*, as well as distasteful. The girls' initiation dance (*intonjane*) and the boys' circumcision dance (*ukutshila*) of the Xhosa were actually prohibited by law in the Ciskei, as being 'contrary to good morals', and quivering of the muscles which played a major part in the ordinary dances of young people was forbidden to Christians at least in some communions (Hunter, 1936, p. 375). For their part, many Nguni regarded western ballroom dancing in which partners held one another as highly indecent, and indeed one independent African state in which people of Nguni origin wield power, Malawi, has prohibited it. The Christian wedding dances and songs were therefore new-made, and the wedding cake, so conspicuous at the weddings of white missionaries and settlers, was seized upon as the focus of the dance. One was provided by the bride's family and one by the groom's, each had three tiers, but the bride's cake was iced in white, the groom's in blue. The two families vied with each other to provide a magnificent cake and, first at the homestead of the bride and then at that of the groom, bride's friends and groom's friends danced separately, each grouped round their cake, which was carried by one of the women dancers (Hunter, 1936, pp. 216–217; Hammond-Tooke, 1962, pp. 131–2). They danced with the cakes, displaying them, before either was cut. Then, at the conclusion of the feast at the groom's home, the bride cut into the middle of each cake, and this was distributed to the guests to eat. The bottom layers of the cakes were divided in two: the groom's mother took half of each and having cut them up sent a piece of each to kinsfolk unable to attend; the bride's mother was likewise given half of the bottom layer of each cake to distribute among her kin. This distribution of cake by the mothers was held to be important, and it was essential that they act with goodwill. One case was reported in which an educated Christian and his wife had no child, and according to gossip among their friends this was because the groom's mother had not favoured the marriage and had not given cake to her kin. When no child was born the groom himself, a devout Christian, was reported to be anxious about his mother's failure to distribute the cake. The 'head' of each cake was kept for the christening of the first child, and bride and groom ate of the cakes together. Here the pattern differed from that in parts of Europe in that two cakes were kept and bride and groom were required to eat of them together. The wedding cake was therefore transformed. It became two, and for some people at least it became a sacramental food. Eating together sacred food was familiar both in the traditional feast for the shades and the Christian communion. Traditional ideas about the dichotomy between lineages and the control of senior relatives over fertility (Hunter, 1936, pp. 174, 194, 245) were thus expressed in new symbols.

But Christians were also part of the new world in which black and white were constantly interacting, and African Christians sought status in the new world. Whites exercised authority as administrators, employers, and teachers; they had prestige. The *display* at a Chrisian wedding – the clothes worn and the parade of bride and groom – was a copy so far as resources permitted of white patterns of display. Advice and help in securing appropriate clothes, flowers, and cakes were commonly sought from a local white trader or, on farms, from a white employer. On no other occasion did a Xhosa woman take her husband's arm or hand in public. As in Zambia (Wilson, 1941; and Mitchell, 1956) clothes were used partly as an assertion of status in the new civilized world; the white gown was understood as a symbol of virginity. But the bride who did something so strange as to take her husband's arm was still bound in some measure by traditional conventions: she *must* look modestly down; she *should* look sad; and often she wept. And after the wedding was over and she lived as a bride in the homestead of her husband's father, she showed respect (*ukuhlonipa*) on formal occasions, such as going to church on Sunday, by wearing a long skirt, a fringed black alpaca shawl, and a kerchief suitably tied to indicate her status. The style taken over by the *first* converts tended to become the norm, and the black fringed shawl and kerchief survived a century longer among Nguni women then they did among the whites with whom they originated. In speech the bride might still avoid the name of her husband's father and 'words very like it', but the stringency of this taboo diminished. Instead she was required to be circumspect in her language, and use less earthy terms than a pagan might do without offence[4] (Hunter, 1936, pp. 460, 534).

Public admonition to groom and bride on the behaviour expected of them as married people was part of the traditional Nguni marriage, and the wedding speeches customary in Europe were readily assimilated to the admonitions, which were made at both ceremonies – that at the home of the bride, and that at the home of the groom. The Nguni expectation that the bride should live, at least for a period, at her husband's father's homestead, and that she should work under the supervision of her mother-in-law did not change. No idea that the groom and bride should seek privacy on a holiday, or set up an independent homestead at once was entertained. The period during which a married man lived in his father's homestead tended to get shorter and shorter, but the formal taking of his bride 'home' was still required (Wilson *et al.*, 1952, pp. 50–1).

Traditionally the Nguni recognized no divisions of the month other than phases of the moon, but a seven-day week was something quickly accepted, and the wedding was geared to the week. The church ritual was *expected* to take place on the Tuesday, following the third calling of banns, and the conventional time was 11.00 am. This expectation epitomizes the fact that within a short space of time *new* forms are accepted as 'traditional' in ritual. Some of the details of the contemporary marriage ritual described derive from traditional Nguni patterns, others from Europe, and others (such as *two* cakes) are brand new, but they are spoken of as *customary* among Christians, with an implication of antiquity.

The process of change in ritual is highly selective and we still know little about the principles governing selection (cf. Bartlett, 1946). For example, sprinkling the bride and groom with grain (or a paper symbol of it) might have been expected to 'catch on' since fertility was so important in the traditional Nguni rites, but it did not. Perhaps the symbolism was never grasped, though grain is thrown into a basket carried by the bride's mother in traditional marriage rites further north in Africa (Wilson, 1957, pp. 95, 109). When people of different languages and cultures interact failures of communication are legion, and are perhaps most numerous when they involve symbols of which the users are only half-conscious. Furthermore, strangers sometimes suppose a symbolic content that does not exist. Thirty years ago, in Pondoland, many pagans believed that when white traders or administrators or missionaries went to holiday at the coast they were honouring their shades 'who had come from the sea' (the first whites in Nguni country were survivors from shipwrecks). As one Mpondo commented 'They [the whites] *always* take their children to the sea when they have been ill.'

One of the marks of increased scale is increased diversity in a society and this is obvious in regard to marriage in South Africa.

Not only are pagan and Christian marriage rituals celebrated, but some couples choose to marry by civil rites, before a magistrate, to avoid family opposition, long negotiations, or the expense of the elaborate marriage gifts and feasts. Sometimes bride and groom simply elope and seek the services of a magistrate to marry them. More often a drama of 'marriage by capture' is enacted, the groom and his friends carrying off the bride, because it is still felt that it is hardly becoming for a bride to run off with a man *willingly* (Wilson *et al.*, 1952, pp. 84–7).

What a Xhosa witness who was giving evidence before the 1883 Commission on Native Laws and Customs referred to as 'this thing called love' has relatively more weight in the new forms of marriage than in the old. One of the moral requirements enforced by missions and embodied in colonial law was that a woman should not be forced into marriage against her will, and in Natal Sir Theophilus Shepstone devised a legal form whereby a bride was required to express her consent before a state witness. The legal change expressed a difference in the traditional Nguni view of marriage and that of nineteenth-century Europe. In the Nguni view it was primarily a contract between lineages, the dead members of two lineages – the shades – being involved as well as the living (Vilakazi, 1962, pp. 69–70); in the European view it was primarily the concern of individuals. In traditional custom the marriage ritual could be celebrated even in the absence of the groom, so long as members of his lineage played their part (Hunter, 1936, p. 199); but at a Christian marriage the groom himself was expected to be present for the negotiations as well as the marriage ritual itself (Vilakazi, 1962, p. 69). Marriage became more the affair of individuals and less the business of lineages, though the lineages' concern did not disappear altogether.

The anthropologist studying society selects facts relevant to a hypothesis. He can make no study without a hypothesis, explicit or implicit; he can never observe or record *all* facts. And likewise, men everywhere, reflecting on their world and dramatizing events, select social facts, ignoring some and elaborating others. To analyse change in ritual it is necessary to understand how men in a given community ordered social relationships, how they viewed their world, and how all this changed. Traditionally, Nguni thought in terms of kinship, of patrilineages that included living and dead, in which men identified themselves with cattle, and cattle sacrifices were offered as feasts in which living and dead joined. Lineages were bound together by the exchange of wives and of cattle, and senior members of a lineage living and dead, exercised just authority over junior members. In particular, senior members of a lineage controlled fertility. Because these were basic categories of thought *lobola* continued, and one of the symbols prominent in the new type of marriage demonstrated to Christian Nguni in the marriage of whites was seized upon and reinterpreted in terms of lineages, and of the power of senior members over fertility. At the same time Nguni society was being transformed by interaction with whites, and Christians sought recognition as civilized men, distinguished from illiterate pagans. They asserted their status through the clothes they wore, and, since Christians were forbidden to dance the traditional pagan dances, they created new styles for themselves that were foreign to pagans. It sometimes happened that both sorts of dancing took place at one wedding. Christians and pagans dancing in opposition just as groom's and bride's lineages danced in opposition, but the pagan-Christian cleavage was not static – it had all but disappeared from some districts of the Ciskei by 1950 – and this division was only explicit at certain periods and in certain places.

Men living in small societies classify their world, as do men in large societies, but the categories they use differ (Lévi-Strauss, 1962a, 1962b). The opposition of pairs of lineages is plain enough in Nguni ritual and is reasserted at Christian marriages, and in addition a further dichotomy in the new community, that between pagan and Christian, is reflected in marriages when Christians differentiate between what they do and what pagans do, and dance separately.

What particular symbols are retained, or borrowed, or transformed depends upon what catches the imagination. A poet's associations always lie within the frame of his experience as a member of a particular society within a given culture, but inside that frame his imagination roves; the symbols used in rituals are poetic or dramatic forms accepted by a community, through time.

NOTES

1. Local variations – here called dialect variations – existed in regard to this custom (see Hunter, 1936, p. 192).

2. This account is based on fieldwork in Pondoland and the Ciskei in 1930–3 (Hunter, 1936, pp. 10–14, 213–22) and occasional attendance at weddings in the Ciskei during the past thirty-five years (cf. Hammond-Tooke, 1962, pp. 124–37: Wilson *et al.*, 1952, pp. 76–93).

3. There can be no doubt that the traditional Nguni rituals at birth, puberty, and marriage, as well as in sickness and at death, were specifically directed towards the shades. The demonstration of this lies outside the scope of this paper.

4. Direct observation in the Ciskei.

REFERENCES

ALBERTI, L. 1811. *Des Cafres*. Amsterdam: E. Maaskamp.

BARTLETT, SIR F. C. 1923. *Psychology and Primitive Culture*.

BARTLETT, SIR F. C. 1946. Psychological Methods for the Study of Hard and Soft Features of Culture. *Africa* **16**: 145–55.

HAMMOND-TOOKE, W. D. 1962. *Bhaca Society*. Cape Town: Oxford University Press.

HUNTER, MONICA. 1936. *Reaction to Conquest*. London: Oxford University Press for International African Institute.

LÉVI-STRAUSS, C. 1962 a. *Le Totémisme aujourd'hui*. Paris: Presses Universitaires de France. (Trans. R. Needham) *Totemism* 1964. London: Merlin Press.

LÉVI-STRAUSS, C. 1962 b. *La Pensée sauvage*. Paris: Plon. (Trans. 1966) London: Weidenfeld and Nicholson.

KRIGE, E. J. 1968. Girls' Puberty Songs and their Relation to Fertility, Health, Morality and Religion among the Zulu. *Africa* **38**: 173–85.

MACLEAN, COLONEL. 1866. *Compendium of Kaffir Laws and Customs.* Cape Town: Saul Solomon.

MITCHELL, J. C. 1956. *The Kalela Dance.* Manchester: Manchester University Press for Rhodes-Livingstone Institute.

RICHARDS, A. I. 1940. *Bemba Marriage and Modern Economic Conditions.* Livingstone: Rhodes-Livingstone Paper 4.

READER, D. H. 1954. *Makhanya Kinship Rights and Obligations.* Cape Town: School of African Studies.

READER, D. H. 1966. *Zulu Tribe in Transition.* Manchester: Manchester University Press.

SOGA, J. H. (nd) 1931? *The Ama-xosa: Life and Customs.* Lovedale: Lovedale Press.

VILAKAZI, A. 1962. *Zulu Transformations.* Pietermaritzburg: University of Natal Press.

WILSON, G. 1941–42. *An Essay on the Economics of Detribalization in Northern Rhodesia.* Livingstone: Rhodes-Livingstone Papers 5 and 6.

WILSON, M. 1957. *Rituals of Kinship among the Nyakyusa.* London: Oxford University Press for International African Institute.

WILSON, M., KAPLAN, S., MAKI, T., & WALTON, E. M. 1952. *Social Structure.* Keiskammahoek Rural Survey, Vol. III. Pietermaritzburg: Shuter and Shooter.

WILSON, M. & THOMPSON, L. 1969. *The Oxford History of South Africa*, Vol. I. Oxford: Clarendon Press.

The significance of kava
in Tongan myth and ritual

ELIZABETH BOTT AND

EDMUND LEACH

Psychoanalysis and ceremony[1]

ELIZABETH BOTT

I am convinced that a knowledge of unconscious mental processes gained from the practice of psychoanalysis can deepen
and enrich understanding of social behaviour. But I have not
written this paper to prove or even to illustrate this conviction.
I have written it in an attempt to understand a particular
event, the kava ceremony of the Kingdom of Tonga in the
South Pacific. This ceremony is a social event and as such involves groups, roles, and social differentiation as well as
conscious and unconscious feelings. In order to understand it
to my satisfaction I found I had to use ideas derived both from
social anthropology and from psychoanalysis.

What I am saying, in effect, is that the problem in question
should take priority over one's loyalty to a particular pro-
fession or professions, whether that problem is concerned with
the understanding of a patient, of a ceremony, of social stratification, of political behaviour, or whatever it may be. Of course
professional training shapes one's interests and limits one's
selection of topics for study. In view of my double training as
an anthropologist and a psychoanalyst it is not surprising that
I have selected a problem that concerns both professions. The
analysis of ceremonies falls within the traditional domain of
anthropology, but it has also stirred many psychoanalysts to
speculative efforts in applied psychoanalysis.[2]

In the course of trying to understand and interpret the kava
ceremony it has repeatedly occurred to me that a ceremony has
much in common with a dream. A dream is a condensed and

disguised representation of unconscious thoughts and wishes. A ceremony is a condensed and partially disguised representation of certain aspects of social life. A dream and a ceremony both serve a double and contradictory function: they release and communicate dangerous thoughts and emotions; but at the same time they disguise and transform them so that the element of danger is contained and to some extent dealt with. An effective ceremony protects society from destructive forms of conflict; an effective dream protects the sleeper from anxiety.

Of course there are important differences between a dream and a ceremony. A dream is the product of an individual; a ceremony is the product of a group. Dreams reflect unconscious thoughts. Some of the ideas and emotions expressed in ceremonies are unconscious, but many others are not so much unconscious as unformulated. Just as one can speak a language correctly without being able to formulate its grammatical rules, so one can play one's part in social life and in a ceremony without understanding how all the parts and principles fit together. Further, many of the symbolic statements made in a ceremony concern social norms and values of which the participants are consciously aware.

The basic events of the kava ceremony are very simple. A group of people pound up the root of a kava plant, mix it with water, and drink it. But all this is done according to a fixed ceremonial procedure that has hardly varied for at least 160 years. We have a good description of the ceremony dating from 1806 (Mariner, 1818, vol. 2, pp. 172–96) and the verbal orders and the actions performed have hardly changed at all, with one important exception. The kava root used to be chewed and then mixed with water, whereas nowadays it is pounded with stones.

The botanical name of the kava plant is *Piper methysticum*. It contains several chemical constituents and there is considerable controversy about their physiological effects. The general conclusions are that it has a slight tranquillizing and anaesthetic action, though the effects are very mild. Tongans, however, treat kava as if it were strong stuff. And so it is, but the strength comes from society, not from the vegetable kingdom.[3]

Before I describe the ceremony, here are a few background facts about the Kingdom. Tonga is a Polynesian society consisting of about 150 small islands with a population of about 70,000 people. It has a Treaty of Friendship with Great Britain, but has always been independent, never a colony, a fact of which Tongans are very proud. The people have been Christian for 130 years and virtually everyone can read and write. Tongans practise subsistence farming on small holdings, with coconuts and bananas as the main cash crops. There are no extremes of wealth or poverty. For the past 100 years government has assumed the form of a constitutional monarchy. Anyone who saw Queen Sālote of Tonga at the coronation of Queen Elizabeth in 1953 will not be likely to forget her. She is as memorable in Tonga as she is in Britain. She died in December 1965 and was succeeded by her eldest son, the present King Taufaʻahau Tupou IV.

DESCRIPTION OF THE CEREMONY

The basic form of the kava ceremony is always the same, though it may vary from a small informal gathering of four or five people to a huge assemblage of several hundred people. It can be dressed up or down as the occasion requires. It takes place on many different sorts of occasion: when men visit each other just to talk; when welcoming home relatives who have been away; in courtship; at weddings; at certain points in a funeral; at the appointment of a king and later on at his coronation; and similarly at the appointment of a chief and on the occasion when he first presents himself and his villagers to his King.

Figures 1 and *2* show the seating at an informal and at a formal ceremony. The participants sit cross-legged, with the chief whose title is genealogically the most senior at the head of the circle. He has an official called a matāpule on either side of

IR—P

Figure 1   Schematic diagram of seating at small informal kava ceremony

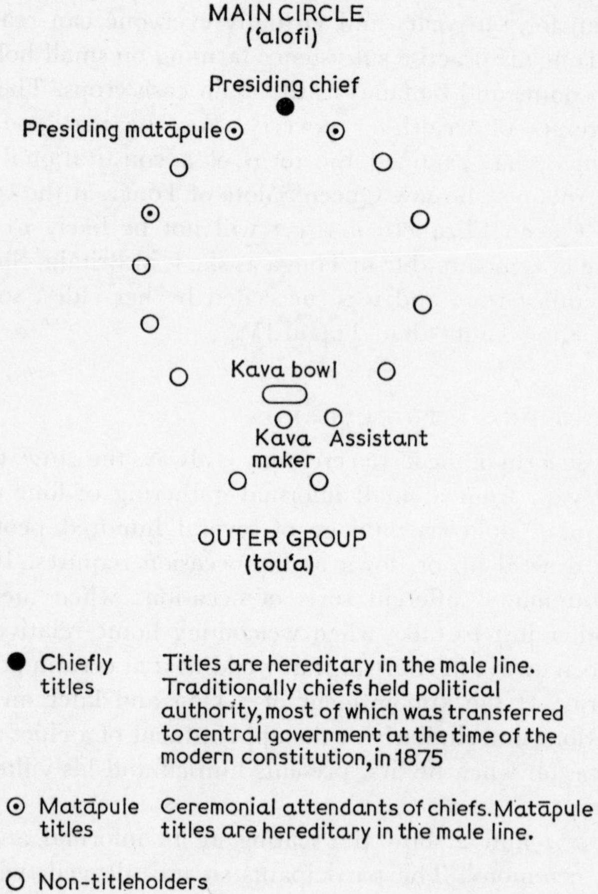

MAIN CIRCLE
('alofi)

Presiding chief
●

Presiding matāpule ⊙   ⊙

       ○   ○

   ⊙   ○

  ○   ○

  ○   ○

    ○   Kava bowl   ○
              ⬭
           ○   ○
        Kava Assistant
        maker

      ○   ○

OUTER GROUP
(tou'a)

● Chiefly   Titles are hereditary in the male line.
  titles   Traditionally chiefs held political
                 authority, most of which was transferred
                 to central government at the time of the
                 modern constitution, in 1875

⊙ Matāpule   Ceremonial attendants of chiefs. Matāpule
  titles   titles are hereditary in the male line.

○ Non-titleholders

Figure 2 Schematic diagram of seating at formal royal kava ceremony

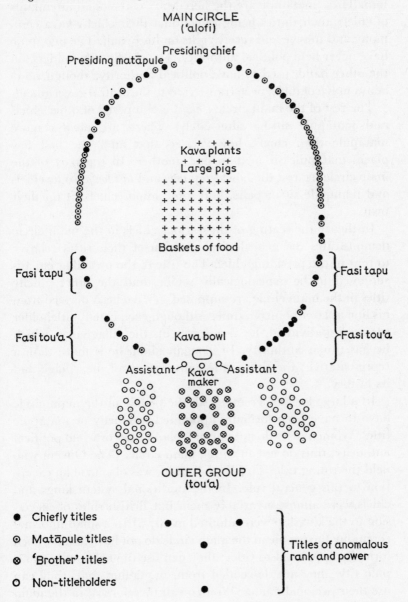

MAIN CIRCLE
('alofi)

Presiding chief

Presiding matāpule

Kava plants

Large pigs

+ + + + + + +
+ + + + + + +
+ + + + + + +
+ + + + + + +
+ + + + + + +
+ + + + + + +
+ + + + + + +

Baskets of food

Fasi tapu

Fasi tapu

Fasi tou'a

Kava bowl

Fasi tou'a

Assistant

Kava maker

Assistant

OUTER GROUP
(tou'a)

● Chiefly titles
⊙ Matāpule titles
⊗ 'Brother' titles
○ Non-titleholders

Titles of anomalous
rank and power

him. These matāpule are the hereditary ceremonial attendants of chiefs, their duties being to conduct their chief's kava ceremony and to give and receive gifts on his behalf. The matāpule have never held political authority. The chiefly title holders, on the other hand, used to have political authority, though nowadays much of it has been transferred to the central government.

The rest of the main circle (*'alofi*) is composed of other chiefs and matāpule sitting alternately. There are always more matāpule than chiefs, however, so that after the first few places matāpule sit next to one another. In the part of the main circle nearest the bowl (*fasi tapu* and *fasi tou'a*) some chiefs and matāpule sit in pairs, and some minor chiefs sit on their own.

In theory the seating of the various chiefs in the main circle demonstrates the genealogical position of their titles relative to that of the presiding chief. The title of the presiding chief is supposed to be genealogically senior, and the other chiefly titles in the main circle are supposed to have been derived from his line at later points in time. Although each chiefly titleholder sits as an individual, he also represents the village over which he has titular authority. In Tongan idiom he is more than a representative; the title is the embodiment of the village and its history.

In a large formal ceremony all the people in the main circle have to have been formally appointed to chiefly or matāpule titles. Women, who do not normally hold titles or wield political authority, thus do not sit in the main circle. (The Queen, who held the ruling title, Tu'i Kanokupolu, was of course an exception to this general rule. In the traditional system kings and chiefs were almost invariably men, but British rules of succession to the kingship were adopted in 1875.) In a small informal ceremony the people in the main circle do not have to have been formally appointed to titles; they can use the name of a matāpule title they are descended from, or, failing that, they can use their personal names. Women can therefore sit in the main circle on such informal occasions if they want to.

The kava bowl is opposite the presiding chief. The bowl is three or four yards away from the chief in a small ceremony, some two hundred yards away in a large royal ceremony. The kava maker sits behind the bowl with an assistant on either side of him. There is a group of people behind the bowl who help to make and serve the kava (the 'outer group' – *tou'a*). In a small informal ceremony the outer group is often very small. It is sometimes reduced to the bare minimum necessary to carry out the ceremony – the kava maker, one assistant, and someone to serve the kava. In a large formal ceremony the outer group is larger and more elaborately structured.

In a very large royal kava ceremony, such as that represented in *Figure 2*, the outer group is divided into three parts. In the centre group sit men who are the holders of minor titles that stand in the relation of 'younger brother' (*tehina*) to certain of the titles in the main circle. It is the titles that are brothers, not the men. In the beginning, when the titles are supposed to have originated, the first titleholders are said to have been actual brothers, and this relation has continued to exist between the titles even though the men who hold the titles may no longer be linked by kinship. 'Our titles are brothers but we are not related', as Tongans put it.[4]

The right-hand portion of the outer group (that is, the portion to the right of the presiding chief) is composed of people without titles. In theory anyone can sit in the outer group at a kava ceremony, but at a formal ceremony most of those who attend are the 'children' (*fānau*) of the titles in the main circle, meaning that they are descendants of former holders of the titles. Some of the people who sit in this part of the outer group serve the kava during the ceremony. Others are called 'grandchildren of high rank' (*makapuna 'eiki*). This means that they had a grandfather who held one of the titles in the main circle, and their kinship relation to the present titleholder is such that they have higher personal rank than the current titleholder. They play an important part in the cere- monial distribution of food during the ceremony. Many of the

'children' and 'grandchildren' in this part of the outer group
are women.

The left-hand portion of the outer group is also composed of
'children' of the titles. Most of the people in this group are
men, and they do the heavy work of the ceremony – carrying
the kava, pigs, and other food in and out, dividing the food
for distribution, and so forth. The path between this group
and the central group is called the 'path of work' (*hala ngāue*),
whereas the path between the right-hand group and the centre
group is called the 'sacred path' (*hala tapu*).

Finally, at a formal royal ceremony, there are certain very
important chiefly titles that are seated right at the back, behind
the outer group (see *Figure 2*).

To summarize the salient facts about the seating: the chief
whose title is genealogically senior sits at the head of the main
circle; the rest of the main circle is made up of formally appointed titleholders, chiefs and matāpule, sitting alternately.
The titles of the chiefs in the main circle are supposed to be
genealogically junior to the title of the presiding chief. The
outer group is composed, first, of men who hold minor chiefly
titles that stand in the relation of 'younger brother' to the titles
in the main circle and, second, of men and women without
titles who are the 'children' and in a few cases also the 'grandchildren' of the titles in the main circle.

The first thing that happens in the ceremony is that people
come in and seat themselves. Kava plants and sometimes food
are presented to the presiding chief and placed in the centre
of the circle (see *Figure 2*). The traditional food to go with the
kava is sugar cane, but vast quantities of pigs and other cooked
food are presented along with it. Nowadays the sugar cane is
often omitted. In a formal ceremony the food is meticulously
counted and thanks for it are chanted by the matāpule. Then
the presiding matāpule tells someone on the outer group to take a
kava plant from in front of the presiding chief down to the
bowl end, where it is split up, cleaned, and then pounded by
the kava maker. (Traditionally small bits of the kava root were

handed to people in the outer group who chewed it, spat it out neatly on to a leaf, and then handed it back to the kava maker who put it in the bowl.) The kava maker puts the pounded kava root in the bowl and begins to knead it with his hands, and water is poured in by the kava maker's assistants – all of these actions being carried out according to fixed ceremonial orders chanted by the presiding matāpule. The pouring in of the water is one of the most sacred moments of the ceremony and all conversation stops. Then the matāpule calls out to mix the kava and to strain it. While the kava maker is straining the kava conversation is resumed, speeches may be made, and if there is food some of it is ceremonially divided and distributed to each titleholder in the main circle. The titleholders do not eat their food, however. They call for their respective 'grand-children of high rank' to come from the outer group and take the portions of food away. Then all the remaining food is ceremonially given to the matāpule on the left of the presiding chief, who orders men from the outer group to take it away. After the ceremony is over this food is divided among the participants.

Eventually, after the flurry of activity in distributing and removing the food, the kava maker's assistant calls out that the kava is clear and the matāpule gives the order for servers to come from the outer group with cups. A cup of kava is taken to each person in the main circle and to several in the outer group. Generally when the serving is completed the ceremony is ended. It may be continued, but in this case the second serving is directed by the matāpule on the chief's left. An informal kava ceremony may go on all night, alternating from right to left.

To recapitulate the sequence of ceremonial operations: the participants seat themselves; kava and food are presented and counted; a kava root is pounded and placed in the bowl; the kava is kneaded and water is poured in; the kava is strained, to the accompaniment of conversation or speeches and the distribution and clearing away of food; finally, cups of kava are served.

The first kava ceremony I saw was a small informal one, so informal that I did not realize it was a ceremony. I noticed an old man mumbling away from time to time – in fact he was giving ceremonial orders – and I saw that there were occasional lulls in the conversation, but I thought they were natural pauses not especially sacred moments in a ceremony. The first royal ceremony I saw was an entirely different affair. From the first moment when the food and kava were brought in with cries of 'Tue, tue, tue, tue, tue – e – e', and the matāpule chanted their thanks, the atmosphere was electric – charged with an intense feeling of being together in a group. The kava, the ceremony, and the group were sacred – *tapu*. I have never felt anything like it in our own society except at the coronation of Queen Elizabeth, where it seemed to me that our mutual indifference to anything outside our own little circle was lost for a moment in a common feeling of being one nation.

How does one set about understanding such a ceremony? It is not much use asking people point-blank what it means any more than it would be useful to ask an individual what his dream means. To such questions Tongans reply politely, 'It is our custom,' and that is the end of the matter. What one should not do, either with a dream or a ceremony, is plunge headlong into arbitrary interpretations of symbolism. While this may be a useful intellectual exercise for the anthropologist or the psychoanalyst, it does not bring him much closer to the new and unique bit of reality he is trying to understand. It would be like trying to interpret a dream without knowing anything about the dreamer – no associations, no transference, no background knowledge of the dreamer's current life and childhood.

To understand a ceremony one needs to know something about the social context. One can also learn a lot by listening to what people say spontaneously and following up their leads. One can ask certain direct questions, such as why people sit where they sit, why the kava is used instead of another plant, or what the properties of kava are, without running into the blank wall of 'It is our custom.' One can ask people to explain the differences between one type of kava ceremony and another. I think this process of exploration is analogous to the use of patients' associations to dreams.

In the course of talking around the ceremony several informants told me the myth of the origin of kava, which proved to be a useful lead. I recorded two versions of the myth and there are others in the literature (Gifford, 1924, pp. 71–5). Their points of similarity and difference helped to clarify the central theme of the myth but I only have time for one version, which is the one recorded by the late Queen Sālote.

THE MYTH OF THE ORIGIN OF KAVA

One day the King of Tonga went fishing with a friend. They did not catch anything, and as they were tired and hungry they called in at the little island of 'Eueiki to get something to eat. At that time there was only one couple living on the island and they had one child, a daughter, whose name was Kava'onau. (In some versions the name is abbreviated to 'Kava'.) She had leprosy. It was a time of famine and the only food the couple had left was a large kape plant (Alocasia macrorrhiza) which stood near the beach. When the King landed he sat down to rest against this plant. When the couple realized who their guest was they set about making an earth oven, but when they came to get their sole remaining food plant they could not use it because the King was leaning on it. The King's friend saw the couple hit something in their house and bring it out to be baked in the earth oven. He saw that they had killed their daughter because they had nothing else to give their King. The King's friend told the King what the couple had done. The King was deeply moved by their sacrifice. He rose up immediately and returned to the main island, telling the couple to bury their child properly.

Two plants grew from the grave, one from the head and one from the foot. One day the couple saw a mouse bite the first plant, stagger a bit, and then bite the second plant, after which he recovered his balance.

One day Lo'au came to the island and the couple told him all that had happened. (Lo'au is a figure who turns up in Tongan legend and mythology at times when social institutions are being established or changed. He tells the people how to organize their social life and then fades from view. He is thought of as human, not a god, and he is called the 'carpenter of the land', which, freely translated, means the establisher of social customs.)

When Lo'au heard the couple's story he sat in silence for a time, deeply moved, and then he spoke in poetry telling them what they should do. They must take the two plants to the King and give him Lo'au's instructions about how the plants should be used. The one from the head was to be used to make a drink, and that was the kava, and the other was to be eaten with the drink, and that was the sugar cane. The couple did as Lo'au had told them. At first the King thought their plant might be poisonous. He had one of his matāpule taste it first. But on finding it was all right he directed the people to carry out Lo'au's instructions.

And so kava was made for the first time and the rules and procedures for making it were established.

Tongans say that the origin of the kava from the leprous girl explains some of its properties. The shoots of the kava plant grow, split, and become limey and grey like the skin of a leper, and the skin of those who drink too much kava becomes grey and scaly like the skin of a leper. There are other linguistic links with the idea of kava as a poison. *Kavafisi* and *kavahaha* are creepers used as fish poisons. The word *'kavahia'* means to be nauseated. Some informants told me that they felt nauseated when they drank strong green kava, and nausea is said to have been the Tongan reaction to attempts to copy the Fijian custom of *actually* eating human flesh.[5] At the same time, in other contexts Tongans said that kava loosened the tongue and made one feel pleasantly relaxed. Thus there is a series of associations between kava, tranquillity, leprosy, poison, nausea, and cannibalism. It may seem odd that tranquillity should appear alongside ideas of poison, nausea, and cannibalism, but I hope the reasons for this strange juxtaposition will become clearer as the exposition proceeds.

INTERPRETATION

The first point is that *the kava ceremony is one of a series of ceremonies that clarify social principles and social roles.* In the kava ceremony the principle of stratification by titles is marked off as clearly as possible from all other forms of social differentiation. This aspect of the ceremony is conscious and explicit. Many Tongans told me, 'Everything in the kava ceremony goes by titles.'

In the traditional political system, chiefly titles carried formal political authority. A chiefly titleholder had the right and obligation to rule and to represent all the inhabitants of a given territory. The kava ceremony displayed the political relationships of titles to one another.

This emphasis on titles only makes sense when one knows that in the traditional system, and to a considerable extent today as well, there were two other systems of social differentiation that were very important in everyday life though they played a very minor role in the kava ceremony; these two other systems of social differentiation were political power and personal rank.[6]

Any man who could gather about him a large and industrious group of relatives and friends could become a political leader in the traditional system. This dimension of political power cut across the system of titles. Some powerful leaders did not hold titles. Some chiefly titleholders were strong leaders of large and powerful local groups; others were politically unimportant.

The third system, that of personal rank, is the same today as it was in the traditional system. The rewards of high rank are gifts of food and elaborate gestures of deference from people of lower rank. By and large, high rank is more highly esteemed than political power or political authority. Power and authority mean work and responsibility; high rank means pure privilege.

Personal rank depends not on whether one holds a title, but on sex, seniority, and descent. Sisters have higher rank than their brothers; elder siblings have higher rank than younger siblings; and the descendants of sisters have higher rank than the descendants of their brothers. Unlike a system of social class such as we are familiar with in our society, the Tongan system of rank is such that no two individuals can have the same rank. The society is not divided into ranked groups or categories; rather the conception is one of a line from the person of highest rank at the top to the person of lowest rank at the bottom. Moreover, personal rank is relative to the relationships involved. A man may be an 'aristocrat' (*'eiki*) at one funeral and a lowly kitchen worker at another, depending on how he is related to the deceased.

Unlike titles, which are normally inherited in the male line, personal rank is inherited from both parents. To be a great aristocrat means that one is descended, preferably through a line of eldest sisters, from the eldest sister of the former sacred King, the Tu'i Tonga, a title that is now defunct. Even the principles of rank in themselves may sometimes conflict. If a man marries a woman who is a great aristocrat and his sister marries a lowly commoner, the children of the respective marriages will be in a contradictory situation. According to one principle the children of the sister will have higher rank than the children of her brother, but according to the other principle (that descent from the Tu'i Tonga's sister confers high rank) the children of the brother will have higher rank. The resolution of such contradictions depends on the situation and the people involved, and gives rise to much gossip, ill-feeling, and amusement.

Like the dimension of political power, personal rank cuts across the other dimensions of stratification. This tendency was very marked in the traditional system. Many men of high rank did not hold titles or political power. Some titleholders were of high rank, some of low rank. Some powerful leaders were of high rank, others of low rank.

The discrepancy between rank and political power was incorporated into the traditional political hierarchy. The sacred king, the Tu'i Tonga, held the most senior title and was of very high personal rank; only his sisters and their children were of higher personal rank. But his political power was very limited. Secular authority was wielded by a second king, the Tu'i Kanokupolu, which is the title of the present ruling line. The Tu'i Kanokupolu title was genealogically junior to that of the Tu'i Tonga, and the individual incumbents of the Tu'i Kanokupolu title were of much lower personal rank than the sacred king, but their political power was much greater. They were supposed to rule the kingdom on behalf of the Tu'i Tonga. The recurrent practice of a particular type of marriage between the two royal houses ensured that the sacred king continued to be of higher personal rank than the secular king; personal kinship ties thus reinforced the relationship between the titles.

In the traditional system the object of the social and political game was to use one's standing in one system to increase one's standing in the others, marriage being one of the main devices for doing so. The process took several generations. Increasing the rank of one's descendants was the ultimate goal, but it was unwise in the long run to concentrate on rank alone. The disappearance of the former sacred kingship is a case in point. The kava ceremony provided a snapshot of the process; it showed where the manœuvring for position had got to at any particular moment, at least as far as the system of formal titles was concerned.

In the modern social and political system the principle of independent but overlapping dimensions of stratification has been retained, though the content has changed. The system of personal rank continues unaltered. Education, however, has supplanted the old system of power and unofficial political leadership. Education is the new pathway to political authority and to higher rank for one's descendants.

The system of chiefly titles and political authority has also changed. In 1875 at the time of the Constitution most of the authority of the chiefly titleholders was transferred to the central government. In compensation for their loss, about forty of the more important and powerful chiefs were given the new European title of 'noble' (*nopele* in Tongan) and were given a special position in the central government. They could elect seven of their peers to the legislative assembly. At the present time being a noble gives one a considerable initial advantage in acquiring political authority, though one must also be educated.

The system of noble titles thus provides a link between the old and the new systems of formal government. The kava ceremony has changed accordingly. It used to be a ceremonial statement of political authority; now it is a statement of continuity between the new political system and the old. As before, principles of personal rank and political power are almost entirely excluded from the ceremony. People are seated and served according to their titles, not according to their personal rank, education, or position in government.

In the beginning I found the constant contradictions of rank, titles, and government authority difficult to grasp. Tongans assured me it was perfectly simple if one had grown up with it. But one thing that helps to keep it simple is ceremonies. Ceremonies mark off one social principle from the others and keep each principle clear in everyone's mind. At government feasts people are seated primarily according to their position in government; a commoner of low rank who is a Cabinet minister will be seated at the Queen's table. At funerals, duties depend mainly on the principles of kinship and personal rank. In the kava ceremony titles are what matter, and power and personal rank play a very minor role. Thus, if the same set of people were involved in the three types of ceremony, they would assume different positions and would have very different relationships with one another in each ceremony. Hence the kava ceremony cannot be understood on its own; it is part of a complex of ceremonies.[7]

I have repeatedly said that power and personal rank are 'virtually' excluded from the kava ceremony. The qualifying objective needs explanation. Although titles are dominant in the ceremony and are supposed to be seated and served according to their genealogical seniority, there are certain features of the seating and the ceremonial procedure that link the system of titles to the principles of political power and personal rank.

Certain important titles are in an anomalous relation to the present kingship. Two of these titles were originally senior to the title of the present king. A third title had a good claim to the throne at one period. A fourth title, although always junior to the present ruling line, had a remarkably able and ambitious series of incumbents in the eighteenth and early nineteenth centuries. One of them broke away from the secular king (the Tu'i Kanokupolu) and became a virtually independent ruler of the northern islands. The power of this particular titleholder, in other words, far outstripped the official political authority of his title. By a series of marriages to aristocratic women, the line increased the personal rank of its incumbents until, in the late nineteenth century, the personal rank of the current incumbent was considerably higher than that of the King himself. In the royal ceremony at the present time, all four of these titles are seated far away at the back, twenty yards or so behind the outer group (see *Figure 2*). Both their distinctiveness and their anomalous position are thus emphasized. They do not fit in.

There is one event in the ceremonial procedure itself that draws attention to the principle of personal rank. This is the moment when the 'grandchildren of high rank' are called from the outer group to collect the portions of food allocated to the titleholders in the main circle. It is a reminder to all concerned that although the chiefs and nobles hold the titles, they have relatives who are of higher personal rank.

The kava ceremony thus displays the system of titles, with passing references to the two other principles of social differentiation, personal rank and political power. It demonstrates the separateness of the three principles and at the same time shows how they co-exist.

We have no historical information on how this particular form of differentiated social principles developed. It was in full flower at the time of Captain Cook's visits. He confessed himself bewildered by the system, though he gives a clear description of behaviour from which the operation of the three principles of authority, power, and rank can be inferred.

Although the historical development of the system remains obscure, some of its effects can be observed in operation. It preserves social continuity while at the same time providing opportunities for flexibility and individual initiative. For individuals it provides a ready-made defence and a mode of adaptation to a general problem that Freud outlined long ago in *Totem and Taboo*: how are subordinates to reconcile themselves to the fact that they hate and envy the authority ('father') whom they also need and love. In the Tongan system 'authority' is split up and dispersed so that no one, not even the King, can be on top all the time. However great a man may be in one dimension, someone else will be greater in some other dimension or some other context. What you lose on the swings you gain on the roundabouts. Further, the system is such that it is difficult, even today, to mobilize consistently opposed groups of 'haves' and 'have-nots'. But it would be a mistake to regard the splitting of authority, rank, and power as a 'solution' to the problem of ambivalent feelings towards authority, for it seems very likely that each of the three systems generates its own complex of envy and rivalry. The system may generate more hatred than it disperses.

There are many indications in everyday life that Tongans are very sensitive about problems of authority and conflict. People avoid open expression of disagreement, while at the same time seeing to it that the authorities concerned find out indirectly about the issues involved. For example, people will agree to fulfil what they consider to be unreasonable demands by a person in authority or a person of high rank, but they will then fail to carry out the desired activity. If confronted by their lack of conformity, they disappear, or find a reasonable excuse or say they did not understand what was required of them. 'They have been leading us around for generations' as one eminent noble put it.

Possibly one factor in this general sensitivity to conflict and avoidance of open expression of it is that Tonga is an island, or rather a group of islands in close communication with one another. In a comparatively isolated group of islands more of an effort has to be made to contain and resolve internal conflicts than on a large land mass where dissidents and persecuted groups can move away without actually leaving the society. And if the controls break down and violence actually breaks out on an island, as it did in Tonga in the early nineteenth century, the island is in for a blood bath that few can escape.

The second major point about the kava ceremony is that *it is a conserving and conservative institution*. This aspect of the ceremony is less explicit than the emphasis on titles. It is unformulated though certainly not unconscious.

The seating and serving order of the kava ceremony are a partial substitute for a written history, for the seating of each title, especially in the royal kava ceremony, is supposed to be explainable in terms of actual historical events. I was so intrigued by this aspect of the ceremony that I spent many months asking titleholders why they sat where they did in the royal kava ceremony. My husband and I were frustrated and puzzled to find that many titleholders did not know why they sat where they did. Eventually it dawned on us that this in itself was the significant point. Forgetting is selective. The seating of titles that are still politically important is known and understood. The reasons for the seating are forgotten if the titles are politically unimportant today.

Personal rank and political power can change very quickly in Tonga; it takes a long time for the titles and the kava ceremony to catch up. Two or three generations of 'bad' marriages can drastically reduce the personal rank of the man who holds a title, but the title itself and its position in the kava ceremony are hardly affected. Once a drop in personal rank is combined with a drop in the political power and influence of the title-holder, however, the rank of the title and its position in the kava ceremony gradually begin to decline as well. People start to forget the reasons for the seating of the title. Its position in the circle may be changed to accommodate a more important title. Eventually unimportant titles cease to be appointed and even their ceremonial place is forgotten.

Occasionally there is a massive reshuffle of seating arrangements to take account of changes in political power. This happened after the death of the last sacred king in 1865. While the sacred kingship was still in existence, the kava circle of the secular king, the Tuʻi Kanokupolu, included only those titles that were derived from the Tuʻi Kanokupolu line and were genealogically junior to the Tuʻi Kanokupolu title. But when the sacred kingship lapsed in 1865 and the Tuʻi Kanokupolu became the sole king, the titles derived from the Tuʻi Tonga line had to be fitted into the Tuʻi Kanokupolu's kava circle, even though many of these titles were genealogically senior to the title of the Tuʻi Kanokupolu. This conflict between actual political power and the genealogical seniority of titles was surmounted by a sort of legal fiction. Before he died the last Tuʻi Tonga transferred his sacred prerogatives to the Tuʻi Kanokupolu. There is some doubt, however, about how he disposed of his kava prerogatives. Some say that he handed these over to the 'King of the Second House', a very ancient title that stands in the relation of 'brother' to the Tuʻi Tonga title. The difficulty was solved by a marriage between the Tuʻi Kanokupolu line and the 'King of the Second House' line, the end result being that the 'King of the Second House' title is now held by the Royal Family, and the present incumbent is the King's younger brother.

Thus the kava ceremony changes to take account of changes in the power of titles, but it changes more slowly than the rank and power of individuals, and the changes are phrased as much as possible in the idiom of titles and their genealogical seniority.

The third major point about the ceremony is that *it expresses a fundamental contradiction.* We were first alerted to this aspect of the ceremony by comparing the many different social contexts in which it takes place. One thing all these social situations have in common is a confrontation of people of different status. In everyday life these people can be expected to harbour feelings of jealousy and resentment about their differential privileges. At the same time, in spite of the antagonisms, during the ceremony there is a strong feeling of being at harmony to-gether in a group. As Tongans put it, 'You do not drink kava with an enemy.'

In brief, the ceremony says, 'We are all united,' but it also says, 'We are all different.' And the element of difference contains another contradiction, for it makes two contrary communications. It says, 'We are differentiated and inter-dependent,' but it also says, 'We are unequal. Our titles differ in seniority. And some of us do not have titles at all.' In other words the kava ceremony expresses ambivalence – the simul-taneous presence of contradictory feelings. I do not mean that each participant in the ceremony becomes consciously aware of the sort of emotional ambivalence that I have described. Most people seemed to be more aware of feelings of unity and harmony than of feelings of antagonism and rivalry – or at any rate more willing to talk about feelings of unity and harmony. The feelings of antagonism showed themselves more in what people did than in what they said. At formal ceremonies we observed many minor breaches of *tapu.* One's hands should be clasped in one's lap throughout the ceremony, for example, but our photographs show that people often moved their hands about. Similarly people are not supposed to talk in a very formal ceremony, but people were whispering away al-most all the time – usually uncomplimentary remarks about the way the ceremony was being conducted.

Within the prescribed events of the ceremony there is only a little scope for the formal expression of conflict, envy, and jealousy. For example, there is one titleholder whose duty it is to see that the kava is well prepared and that everyone behaves properly. In 1959 the incumbent of this title was a man of comparatively low personal rank; he aimed his sharpest reprimands at two titleholders of very high personal rank, men whom he would never have dared to challenge in any other social context. But he was not alone; all the men of low rank relished his performance. Even in this case, the titleholder concerned was not ceremonially obliged to abuse the men of high rank. What he did was left to his own initiative.

In other words, the formal, prescribed events of the ceremony emphasize unity and harmony. Rivalry, jealousy, and envy are widely and consciously felt, to varying degrees, but their expression is either unofficial or is left to individual initiative.[8]

The myth of the origin of the kava helps to elucidate the contradictory attitudes implied in the ceremony. When the late Queen was reflecting on this myth she said it expressed the mutual sacrifice and understanding between ruler and subjects that was essential to keep Tonga united and strong. It was this mutual sacrifice and understanding the kava ceremony was commemorating. I agreed with this interpretation, but said I thought the myth also expressed suspiciousness and hostility between ruler and subjects. The couple sacrificed their most precious possession, their daughter, but she did have leprosy; eating her might have harmed the King. The King's refusal to eat her was partly an act of generosity, but he was also protecting himself. And when the couple brought in the plant, he thought at first that it might be poisonous. If I had thought of it at the time, I might have added that the couple's sacrifice was an insult to the King, for to call someone a 'man eater' is a common insult in Tonga. And, in addition to everything else, spitefulness is implied in the couple's heroic act. It is as if they were saying to their King, 'Look at the dreadful thing you have made us do.'

After some discussion the Queen said that such suspiciousness between ruler and subjects was probably inevitable and natural. Perhaps what the myth and the ceremony meant was that mutual understanding and sacrifice were possible in spite of doubt and suspicion.

This was as far as I got with the myth while we were still in Tonga. After we left I wished I had asked many other questions about it, for it now seems to me that there are many other levels of meaning and feeling in it. If I were doing the study again I would ask why the little island of 'Eueiki? Why the famine, the cannibalism, and, above all, the leprosy, all of which are known in Tonga but have always been rare. Why the particular food plant, the kape, and what of the many different triangular situations mentioned in the various versions of the myth? There is one issue that I think worth including even though I did not explore it fully at the time. The myth seems to deal with the progression of psychic experience from a very primitive level in which good and bad are confused and contaminated to one in which good and bad are better differentiated, so that it becomes possible to distinguish the symbol from the object. The burial, in other words, transforms the contaminated, sacrificed girl into the two plants, the kava, which is still potentially poisonous, and its antidote, the sugar cane.[9]

The kava myth helps to understand what the plant symbolizes and why Tongans regard it as strong stuff, but it does not throw much light on the actual events of the ceremony – the pounding, pouring in of water, serving, etc. For this we must turn, very briefly, to another myth that almost paraphrases some of the events of the kava ceremony. The explicit claim of this myth to relevance in connection with the kava ceremony is that it is concerned with the origin of the system of titles that the kava ceremony ceremonially displays. None of my informants pointed out the close parallel between the events of the kava ceremony and the events of the myth, though I was told the myth in the context of discussing the ceremony so that there was obviously an associative link. I myself was only half aware of the connections between the myth and the ceremony while I was still in Tonga, I think this half-awareness is similar to Tongans' feeling about the myth. A connection is dimly felt without being explicitly thought out.

The story of the myth is simple and melodramatic. A god from the sky has intercourse with a woman of the earth and a son is born, called 'Aho'eitu. When he grows up he wants to see his father and, following instructions from his mother, he climbs up to the sky by a giant ironwood tree. 'Aho'eitu is enthusiastically welcomed by his father, who thinks at first that 'Aho'eitu is a god of even higher rank than himself. The father then sends his new-found son, without introduction, to see his other sons in the sky, presumably the sons of sky mothers. When 'Aho'eitu's half-brothers see everyone admiring 'Aho'eitu because of his beauty, and when they hear rumours that he is their father's son, they tear 'Aho'eitu to pieces and eat him up. The father suspects what they have done. He calls for a wooden bowl and makes his sons vomit into it. This is very reminiscent of the former custom of chewing the kava, of the statements that kava sometimes makes people feel like vomiting, and of the linguistic association with nausea. The sons vomit up 'Aho'eitu's flesh and blood, they confess, and the father sends people to collect the bones and the head, which are also put in the bowl. Water is poured into the bowl, as in the kava ceremony. The pouring in of the water, as I have noted above, is one of the most sacred moments of the ceremony. After some time 'Aho'eitu begins to take shape and finally sits up in the bowl. Then the father calls all his sons together and tells them that 'Aho'eitu will go back to the earth to become the first king of Tonga, the first Tu'i Tonga. At this point, the myth says, affection awakens in the hearts of the brothers, and they plead with their father to be allowed to go with 'Aho'eitu. The father agrees. Four of the brothers go down to earth to serve 'Aho'eitu as his matāpule. The fifth and eldest brother cannot be king, the father says, because he is guilty of murder, but he will be the King of the Second House (Tu'i Fale Ua). If 'Aho-'eitu's line should die out then the King of the Second House will become King. (This is the rationale for the belief, mentioned above, that the last Tu'i Tonga bequeathed his kava prerogatives to the King of the Second House.) There are several other myths and legends that purport to show that all through Tongan history the descendants of the King of the Second House tried to murder 'Aho'eitu's descendants in order to wipe out his line.

Using the leads provided by this myth, I think that the chewing or, nowadays, the pounding of the kava is a symbolic repetition of psychic cannibalism, representing a desire both to get possession of the qualities of the beautiful envied brother and son and to destroy him. This mixture of admiration, greed, and destructive envy is a familiar theme from the analysis of the cannibalistic fantasies of patients. But of course in the ceremony it is kava that is pounded or chewed, not a person; this symbolic transformation is taken up in the kava myth.

The idea that the pounding of the kava may represent cannibalistic destruction of an envied object, a brother or son, is consistent with the fact that the people in the outer group, who used to chew and now help to pound the kava, stand in the relation of 'child' or 'younger brother' to the titleholders of the main circle.[10] In other words, the kava plant is presented to the presiding chief as 'Aho'eitu was presented to his father. The father then sends the kava/son to be destroyed. The destruction is carried out by 'children', though perhaps also by 'younger brothers' (of the 'father') – an indication that people in the 'father' category are involved in the destruction. The father's envy and destructiveness are hinted at in the myth, for the father at first thinks his son is of higher rank, and then sends him to his other sons without introduction. He immediately suspects his other sons of murder and cannibalism, as if the thought were not far from his own mind. So far as I could discover none of this is conscious. That is, participants in the ceremony are aware to some extent of their envy and jealousy of one another, and most of them know the two myths, but they do not consciously link the two sets of knowledge.

In the 'Aho'eitu myth incorporation and destruction are followed by healing water and the awakening of good feeling. Once this has taken place the kava is served, that is, the experience can be re-incorporated in a form that is soothing and tranquillizing. But the transformation is not always successful, for strong green kava sometimes makes people want to vomit. In other words, the method of preparing the kava can be seen as an effort to convert envy and jealousy into remorse and affection, to change poisonous feelings into feelings of tranquillity and harmony. But other myths and legends make it clear that envy and jealousy can never be overcome entirely and permanently, just as they can never be eradicated from everyday life. The feelings appropriate to cannibalism are here to stay. Envy, greed, and jealousy are always with us, but so are admiration and remorse. Conflict is inevitable. The kava ceremony states the particular Tongan variant of this general human dilemma and tries to communicate the idea that the forces of love can be made stronger than the forces of hate, at least temporarily. Once again, people do not think all this out consciously. They feel there is something good about the ceremony, something healing, but no one phrases it in terms of reparation to a damaged object and the re-incorporation of the whole experience.

As with the kava myth, there are many other possible interpretations of the 'Aho'eitu myth. One version of the myth, for example, goes into considerable detail about the way the brothers threw 'Aho'eitu's head into a bush, which caused the bush to become poisonous. Perhaps this is a way of talking about castration, with the customary theme of power residing in the cut-off head/phallus. There is a great deal of ambiguity in the myth about who is killing whom. Obviously the half-brothers kill 'Aho'eitu, but he is the father's favourite so they are attacking the father as well. The father himself sends 'Aho'eitu to his death, as I have indicated above. And what of the mother far away in Tonga? 'Aho'eitu is her only son, so she is being attacked and perhaps destroyed. But it is she who tells 'Aho'eitu how to get to heaven in the first place. And what of the link with the kava myth itself in which a daughter is destroyed? Is it a daughter only or also a mother in disguise?

I do not think one can select any particular interpretation as the 'right' one. None of them can be 'proved' or 'disproved', at least not by the methods appropriate to the consulting-room, nor by any other method that I could think of at the time. In the consulting room, where the two partners to the relationship are supposed to be discovering psychic truth, however painful and improbable, one can make interpretations about unconscious cannibalism or unconscious desires to castrate a brother, and judge from the patient's reactions whether the interpretations are close to home or wide of the mark. One always has the transference situation, of which one has direct experience, as a yardstick against which the manifest content of the patient's material can be compared. In Tonga I was often aware of transference, especially of the more obvious aspects of it: the attitude that I was a foreigner with whom a cultural 'front' had to be kept up; attempts to 'use' me in one way or another to gain some social end; the feeling that I was a sympathetic outsider with whom emotional burdens could be shared. But I never felt it appropriate to interpret the transference. I found I was prepared to raise such issues as the likelihood of hostility between rulers and subject, particularly with a very secure and much-loved monarch, but I was not prepared to try out interpretations of cannibalism or castration with anyone, so unprepared, in fact, that I could hardly think of such interpretations intellectually until I had left the field. The social situation I was in did not sanction such endeavours.

From among the many possible interpretations, I have emphasized the theme of cannibalism and reparation, of the destruction and restoration of a brother/son, because it seemed to me the most obvious, the most consistent with the events and the status differentials of the ceremony, and the most in accord with constellations of envy and rivalry in other aspects of Tongan social life. It helped to order the facts in a new and comparatively simple pattern that I had not seen before. But it seems very likely that at various times and to various Tongans any or all of the variants described above might be unconsciously meaningful. The ambiguity of myths and ceremonies is part of their point. It gives individuals some leeway to play with experience, to make culture their own possession.

The particular beauty of the kava ceremony, at least for me, is that it deals with problems on so many different levels at the same time. It clarifies social principles and roles. It puts a temporary brake on certain types of rapid change. It states and partly resolves problems of dependence and envy, and of interdependence and rivalry, some aspects of which are generated by the peculiarly Tongan system of social stratification, and some by the universal human attributes of having a capacity for thinking and feeling and being brought up in a society.

Small-scale societies tend to have multidimensional ceremonies of this type more frequently than we do. This suggests that time and continuity of shared experience are needed to build a ceremony that can transmit messages on many different levels at the same time. A long history of interpersonal contact and conflict makes possible the development of a symbolic statement in which universal human experiences are meaningfully linked with unique social circumstances.

In conclusion, I hope that I may have been able to interest you in taking a fresh look at ceremonies in our own society – at the coronation, for example, or at the elaborate ceremonial installation of the Lord Mayor of London as compared to the absence of ceremony in the installation of the head of the Greater London Council, at the Communion Service, at weddings, funerals, New Year's Eve parties, and so forth. Are roles dramatized and clarified? Is there a sense of continuity with the past? Is a symbolic form of expression provided for unspoken, or unformulated, or unconscious thoughts? Does the ceremony show other aspects that the kava ceremony does not display?

Even in the lecture situation in which we find ourselves, it seems to me there is a ceremonial component. There is some dramatization of roles, though it is not nearly so complex as in the kava ceremony. There is not much sense of continuity with the unique past history of British society, but there *does* seem to be symbolic expression of unspoken thoughts. I would gather from your presence and your attentiveness that you are here because of sympathetic interest in the subject, but it would be surprising if interest and curiosity were not accompanied by criticism, doubt, and at least some measure of hostility both towards the subject and towards the speakers. Similarly, the speakers experience a complex mixture of feelings. The conventional arrangements of lectures like these – the raised platform, the physical distance between speaker and audience, the loudspeakers, the chairman, the introductions, the applause, the questions – are partly necessary for purely practical reasons, but they also provide a setting that both expresses contradictory feelings and keeps them under control.

NOTES

1. The paper was originally given in 1967 as one of the Winter Lectures on Psychoanalysis to members of the general public interested in psychoanalysis. It was first published in 1968 (Sutherland, 1968). The Foundations Fund for Research in Psychiatry generously provided me with a fellowship to analyse and write up the material. I am deeply indebted to the many Tongans who helped me to record and understand the ceremony and to the several colleagues with whom I have discussed the interpretations of it, especially Miss Pearl King, Miss Isabel Menzies, Mrs T. T. S. Hayley, and my husband, James Spillius.

If I had been writing for an anthropological audience or specifically to contribute to a festschrift in honour of Dr Audrey Richards, I would doubtless have written the paper somewhat differently. However, since Dr Leach's critique and his own analysis of the myths and the ceremony were initially based on this version of my paper, it seems best to publish it in its original form.

2. Many anthropologists, especially in Britain, do not share Audrey Richards's and my view that understanding of unconscious mental processes is relevant to the analysis of social events. They are particularly apprehensive that psychoanalysts will attempt to explain social events in terms of individual needs. Their attitude is paralleled by the psychoanalyst's conviction that the complex events of the consulting room cannot be reduced to the level of neuro-anatomy. See especially Leach (1958); Lévi-Strauss (1964), especially Chapter 3; Gluckman (1964); Turner (1964); and Fox (1967).

3. For discussion of the chemical constituents and physiological action of kava see especially Keller and Klohs, 1963. Dr C. R. B. Joyce, Reader in Psycho-Pharmacology at the University of London has very kindly reviewed the literature for me and reports the following conclusions: 'All in all, my impression remains firm that this substance is not remarkable for its pharmacological activity; that such active properties as it contains have not been isolated so far (there is more activity on animals in the watery or chloroform extract, for example, than in any so far identified substance); and that the whole situation is a remarkable example of the placebo phenomenon in a wide and important social setting.' Personal communication, May 1967.

4. A similar institution is found among certain Bantu tribes. A. I. Richards (1950) calls it 'positional succession'; I. Cunnison (1956) calls it 'perpetual kinship'.

5. Tongans say that cannibalism was not indigenous to Tonga, but that early in the nineteenth century groups of young Tongan warriors visited Fiji, adopted the practice of eating slain enemies, and continued to practise this custom when they returned home to Tonga. The new custom was not adopted with enthusiasm and was soon abandoned.

6. The analysis of these three principles of social differentiation, political authority (titles), political power, and personal rank was first worked out by my husband, James Spillius, and was presented to the Tenth Pacific Science Congress at Honolulu in 1961 in a paper entitled 'Rank and Political Structure in Tonga'.

7. This complex of ceremonies is a striking example of what Max Gluckman has called the 'ritualization' of social relations in small-scale ('tribal') societies. He attributes this 'ritualization' to '. . . the fact that each social relation in a subsistence economy tends to serve manifold purposes . . . it is from this situation that I see emerging the relatively great development of special customs and

stylised etiquette to mark the different roles that a man or woman is playing at any one moment' (Gluckman, 1962, pp. 26–7).

8. In recent years anthropologists have devoted much attention to conflict and ambivalence and their expression in religion and ritual as well as in everyday affairs. See especially Fortes (1959); Gluckman (1955), (1963) especially the Introduction and Chapter 3 entitled 'Rituals of Rebellion in South-East Africa' and (1965), especially Chapter 6 entitled 'Mystical Disturbance and Ritual Adjustment'; Leach (1965); Turner (1957) and (1964).

One problem of particular relevance is that some rituals incorporate conflict directly into the prescribed events of the ritual whereas others, like the kava ceremony, imply conflict but do not prescribe its enactment. But a comparative discussion of this topic would lead me too far from the immediate problem of the kava ceremony.

9. On the differentiation of 'good' and 'bad' as part of normal psychic development, see especially W. R. Bion (1957), (1958), and (1962). See also Hanna Segal (1964). On the differentiation of symbol from object see Hanna Segal (1957).

10. The early accounts of kava ceremonies in which the kava was chewed instead of pounded do not specify whether the chewing was done only by the 'children' in the outer group or also by the 'younger brothers'. All we know is that the people who did the chewing were in the outer group and that a considerable number of them took part in the chewing. Nowadays only the kava maker does the actual pounding.

REFERENCES

BION, W. R. 1957. Differentiation of the Psychotic from the Non-Psychotic Part of the Personality. *International Journal of Psycho-analysis.* **38**.

BION, W. R. 1958. On Hallucination. *IJP.* **39**.

BION, W. R. 1962. The Psycho-Analytic Study of Thinking. *IJP* **43**.

CUNNISON, I. 1956. Perpetual Kinship. A Political Institution of the Luapulu Peoples. *Rhodes–Livingstone Journal* No. 20.

FORTES, M. 1959. *Oedipus and Job in West African Religion.* Cambridge: Cambridge University Press.

FOX, R. 1967. *Totem and Taboo* Reconsidered. In E. R. Leach (ed.), *The Structural Study of Myth and Totemism.* ASA Monograph 5. London: Tavistock.

FREUD, S. 1913. *Totem and Taboo*. In *The Standard Edition of The Complete Psychological Works of Sigmund Freud* Vol. 13. London: Hogarth.

GIFFORD, E. W. 1924. *Tongan Myths and Tales*. Bernice P. Bishop Museum Bulletin 8, Honolulu.

GLUCKMAN, M. 1955. *Custom and Conflict in Africa*. Oxford: Blackwell.

GLUCKMAN, M. 1962. Les Rites de Passage. In M. Gluckman (ed.), *Essays on the Ritual of Social Relations*. Manchester: Manchester University Press.

GLUCKMAN, M. 1963. *Order and Rebellion in Tribal Africa*. London: Cohen & West.

GLUCKMAN, M. (ed.) 1964. *Closed Systems and Open Minds*. Edinburgh and London: Oliver & Boyd.

GLUCKMAN, M. 1965. *Politics, Law and Ritual in Tribal Society*. Oxford: Blackwell.

KELLER, F. & KLOHS, M. W. 1963. A Review of the Chemistry and Pharmacology of the Constituents of Piper methysticum. *Lloydia* **26** (1).

LEACH, E. R. 1958. Magical Hair. *J. Roy. Anthrop. Inst.* **88** part 2.

LEACH, E. R. 1965. The Nature of War. *Disarmament and Arms Control* **3** (2).

LÉVI-STRAUSS, C. 1964. *Totemism*. (Trans. R. Needham). London: Merlin Press.

MARINER, W. 1818. *An Account of the Natives of the Tonga Islands*. (2nd edn.) 2 vols. (ed. John Martin.) London: John Murray.

RICHARDS, A. I. 1950. Some Types of Family Structure amongst The Central Bantu. In A. R. Radcliffe-Brown and D. Forde (eds.), *African Systems of Kinship and Marriage*. London: Oxford University Press.

RICHARDS, A. I. 1956. *Chisungu: A girls' initiation ceremony among the Bemba of Northern Rhodesia*. London: Faber & Faber.

SEAGAL, H. 1957. Notes on Symbol Formation. *IJP* **38**.

SEGAL, H. 1964. *Introduction to the Work of Melanie Klein*. London: Heinemann.

SPILLIUS, J. 1961. Unpublished paper, Rank and Political Structure in Tonga presented to the Tenth Pacific Science Congress, Honolulu.

SUTHERLAND, J. D. (ed.) 1968. *The Psychoanalytic Approach*. London: Baillière, Tindall, & Cassell.

TURNER, V. W. 1957. *Schism and Continuity in an African Society.* Manchester: Manchester University Press.

TURNER, V. W. 1964. Symbols in Ndembu Ritual. In M. Gluckman (ed.), *Closed Systems and Open Minds.* Edinburgh and London: Oliver and Boyd.

The structure of symbolism

EDMUND LEACH

Although I am exclusively responsible for what is said in this paper I wish to express from the start my great indebtedness to Dr Elizabeth Bott who has had the generosity to make many careful and extremely helpful comments on an earlier draft. A number of Dr Bott's observations have been incorporated into this final version without specific acknowledgement. I would also express my thanks to Dr La Fontaine and Dr Tambiah for their helpful critical comments on earlier drafts.

A principal theme in Audrey Richards's *Chisungu* (1956) is that in the study of ritual symbolism the various interpretative procedures adopted by different brands of anthropologist and psychologist should be regarded as complementary rather than mutually inconsistent. Elizabeth Bott has recently argued in similar vein. In a paper devoted to the analysis of Tongan kava ceremonial (see pp. 205–37 above) she supplements interpretations of a fairly straightforward functionalist kind (pp. 217–27) with the intuitions of a psychoanalyst, e.g.: 'I think that the chewing or, nowadays, the pounding of the kava is a symbolic repetition of psychic cannibalism, representing a desire both to get possession of the qualities of the beautiful envied brother and son and to destroy him' (p. 229).

Now I concede that the intuitions of functionalist anthropologists are no more likely to be right (or wrong) than the intuitions of psychoanalysts so that if we accept either style of analysis we should accept the other, but if anthropologists wish to be taken seriously as scientists they need to develop methods of analysis that are less dependent upon private hunch, and it is primarily on this account that I feel they should pay close attention to the work of Lévi-Strauss. If structuralism has any advantage over the alternative techniques considered by Richards and Bott it is precisely because it can claim to be, relatively speaking, 'intuition free'.

The basic issue is one of methodology. Are there operations by which we can analyse sequences of myth and ritual and say quite positively that 'the evidence shows that this and this is the case', or must we always fall back on some equivocating personal formula – 'it seems to me that' or 'it is surely obvious that'?

From this point of view the distinctive characteristic of structuralist procedure is that the analyst tries to avoid making symbolic substitutions which are not already quite overtly specified in the evidence. It is this aspect of structuralist analysis that I shall seek to demonstrate in this essay. Unlike some practitioners of the technique I share with Bott the functionalist assumption that myth is a charter for ritual performance and that we can only understand what is being symbolized in the ritual if we take note of what is being 'said' in the mythology. However, unlike Bott, I assume that it is the structural patterns embedded in the mythology rather than the superficial content that conveys the significant message.

Here is a preliminary example of what I mean. In one of the myths cited below (Bott II, p. 253), we are told how older brothers of a common father from a foreign land kill and eat their younger Tongan half-brother. In another myth (Gifford V, p. 251), which is in all structural respects the converse of the first, an elder half-brother of a common mother runs away to live in a foreign land from which he returns at the time of his younger Tongan half-brother's death.[1] One way of describing this antithesis is to say that the two stories present a contrast between 'the overemphasis of kinship bonds' (death associated with mutual identification) and 'the underemphasis of kinship bonds' (death associated with mutual separation). This contrast is presented to us by the evidence itself; it does not require 'interpretation' by the analyst (cf. Lévi-Strauss, 1963, p. 215). In the course of the essay that follows I shall constantly revert to this contrast, which is expressed in the actual ritual by a marked ambivalence in the relationship between the presiding chief and the presiding matāpule (cf. Bott, pp. 225–6 above).

The distinctiveness of this procedure may be seen if we compare it with that employed by Bott who interprets the mythology by resort to intuition. Thus she claims that the myth (Bott II)' mentioned above, represents a symbolic displacement of parental envy or castration symbolism (Bott, p. 230 above). Plainly she is here introducing an element of Freudian dogma which is quite external to the evidence as such.

All the same, we should not too hastily assume that Bott's conclusions must be false. The skeletal structural analysis that I have proposed above is precisely analogous to one which Lévi-Strauss applied in 1953 to a series of incidents in the classical Theban saga (cf. Lévi-Strauss, 1963, p. 215). In that case the 'overemphasis of kinship bonds' was exemplified by the love of Oedipus for Jocasta and of Antigone for Polynices whereas the 'underemphasis of kinship bonds' was exemplified by the hostility between Oedipus and Laios and between Eteocles and Polynices. Since the Theban saga contains within itself all the basic complexes of the Freudian dogma it is hardly surprising that Bott should have got a whiff of ancient Thebes when contemplating the Tongan drama of 'Aho'eitu! But this, of course, raises the more general question of what is the relation between structuralist 'objective' analysis and psychoanalytic 'intuitive' analysis? The following material is designed to pursue this problem rather further.

I must first draw attention to a difficulty that Bott herself ignores. Her paper is, in the main, an analysis of 'royal' kava ceremonials as performed during the reign of the late Queen Salote. Bott observed such ceremonials and discussed them with the Queen in person. One of the myths that she describes is in a version that comes direct from the Queen. In one sense, therefore, we are discussing ethnographic facts as they existed around 1960. But Queen Salote was a highly educated woman, very well versed in the English language accounts of her own society. This makes me sceptical. Bott says of the kava ceremonial:

> But all this is done according to a fixed ceremonial procedure that has hardly varied for at least 160 years. We have a good description of the ceremony dating from 1806 (Mariner, 1818, Vol. 2, pp. 172–96) and the verbal orders and the actions performed have hardly changed at all. . . . (p. 206).

But this continuity is surely hypothetical? The various ethnographic sources, notably Gifford (1929, pp. 156–68) and Williamson (1939, pp. 70–87), provide a step-by-step instruction book on how to run a 'traditional' kava ceremonial, and it is at least possible that the whole business in its present form is quite recent and self-consciously archaic. Moreover, we need to remember that whereas the genuine 'traditional' kava ceremonial was part of an elaborate 'traditional' religious complex, the population of Tonga has been thoroughly Christian for nearly 150 years. Even if the form of the present-day kava ceremonial resembles that described by Mariner, it is hardly possible that it can, in any but a rather superficial sense, possess the same 'meaning'. In such circumstances, is *any* interpretation of the symbolism justifiable?

So also in the case of the mythology. Bott's informants had presumably read Gifford (1924) just as she had done herself; does this affect the legitimacy of such materials for the purposes of ethnographic analysis? I don't know. So far as the main body of this paper is concerned I will accept Bott's unstated presupposition that *all* the evidence (whether it comes from Mariner, or Gifford, or Bott, or any other source) belongs to a single 'ethnographic present', but this assumption is suspect. I shall return to this issue at the end.

However I must, even at this point, intrude a special note of ethnographic caution which stems from known facts about the details of Tongan institutions. Bott's principal informant was the ruling monarch of Tonga, Queen Salote, son's daughter's son's daughter of King George I who assumed the powers of a constitutional monarch of the British type in 1845. In pre-European times there was no such unified office, though the dignitary known as the Tu'i Tonga might reasonably have been described as the 'ritual king'. In the early part of the nineteenth century the most powerful chiefs, in a political sense, were those who held the title of Tu'i Kanokupolu, and King George I was one of these. At this period, before 1845, the titles of Tu'i Tonga and Tu'i Haa Takalaua were both notionally 'superior' to that of the Tu'i Kanokupolu, but King George I obliterated these titles and since his day they have not been employed. However, in 1865, on the death of the last properly entitled Tu'i Tonga, King George I went through a ritual whereby he himself formally assumed the office and prerogatives of the Tu'i Tonga, so that he would seem to have *absorbed* the office of Tu'i Tonga rather than to have *abolished* it (see Gifford, 1929, pp. 60, 86, 93, 98). Now, since Queen Salote's 'proper' title was that of Tu'i Kanokupolu, it might appear that the 'royal kava' that Bott observed and which is discussed in the following pages was the 'kava of the Tu'i Kanokupolu'. On the other hand the mythology that justifies this ceremony and forms the main subject matter of this paper is plainly appropriate to the 'kava of the Tu'i Tonga' rather than to that of the Tu'i Kanokupolu. It may be relevant therefore that Queen Salote could, by a fiction, have claimed the prerogatives of either title. It also seems relevant that, for several generations prior to 1845, the Tu'i Tonga had regularly been married off to the daughter of the Tu'i Kanokupolu and a son of this marriage had regularly succeeded as the next Tu'i Tonga. Thus, at this period, the holder of the Tu'i Tonga title was not only the son of a previous Tu'i Tonga, he was also the daughter's son of a previous Tu'i Kanokupolu (see *Figure 1*, p. 244)

Figure 1 Perpetual succession and affinity of Tongan titles (numerals indicate rank order of titles)

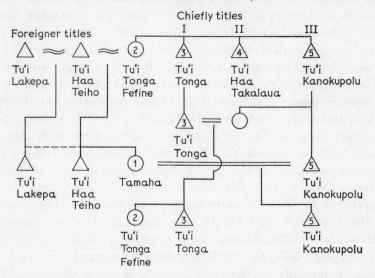

The essential features of a Tongan kava ceremonial appear to be the following:

The participants seat themselves in a circle in the manner shown by Bott in *Figure 1*, p. 208. The order of seating is precisely determined by the rank of the title held by the individual concerned. (Tongan titles are transmitted patrilineally in accordance with a system of positional succession. For example, certain titles are in younger brother relation to other titles 'but it is the titles that are brothers, not the men' (Bott, p. 211). Kava plants and food (traditionally sugar cane) are presented to the presiding chief and placed in the centre of the circle. The presiding matāpule[2] then gives orders that a kava plant be taken from in front of the presiding chief down to the kava bowl end of the circle where it is

> split up, cleaned, and then pounded by the kava maker. (Traditionally small bits of the kava root were handed to people in the outer group who chewed it, spat it out neatly on to a leaf, and then handed it back to the kava maker who put it in the bowl.)

The kava maker puts the pounded kava root in the bowl and begins to knead it with his hands, and water is poured in by the kava maker's assistants – all of these actions being carried out according to fixed ceremonial orders chanted by the presiding matāpule. The pouring in of the water is one of the most sacred moments of the ceremony and all conversation stops. Then the matāpule calls out to mix the kava and to strain it. While the kava maker is straining the kava conversation is resumed, speeches may be made, and if there is food, some of it is ceremonially divided and distributed to each title holder in the main circle. In a large scale ceremonial the title holders do not eat their food, however. They call for their respective 'grandchildren of high rank' to come from the outer group and take the portions of food away. Then all the remaining food is ceremonially given to the matāpule on the left of the presiding chief, who orders men from the outer group to take it away. After the ceremony is over this food is divided among the participants.

Eventually, after the flurry of activity in distributing and removing the food, the kava maker's assistant calls out that the kava is clear and the matāpule gives the order for servers to come from the outer group with cups. A cup of kava is taken to each person in the main circle and to several in the outer group. When the serving is completed the ceremony is ended. Or it may be continued, but in this case the second serving is directed by the matāpule on the chief's left. An informal kava ceremony may go on all night, alternating from right to left (Bott, pp. 212–13).

Bott's problem (and mine) is to determine what this ritual sequence is all about.

Certain facts of Tongan ethnography are clearly relevant. All accounts of Tongan society lay stress on the Tongans' almost obsessive interest in the twin, though distinguishable, concepts of 'rank' and 'title'. *Rank* in Tongan terms is a personal attribute that depends upon the individual's ancestry through both male and female lines; *titles* are offices that an individual may inherit by patrilineal succession (or usurpation). Titles are themselves ranked in a hierarchy that is, in theory, unalterable and depends upon the circumstances in which the title first came into being in mythological times. It is very relevant for

what follows that Bott was told by her Tongan informants
(p. 217) that 'Everything in the kava ceremony goes by titles.' As
has been indicated above, the three highest ranking titles in
the pre-European society were the Tu'i Tonga, the Tu'i Haa
Takalaua and the Tu'i Kanokupolu in that order. This ranking
of titles was expressed by saying that the first Tu'i Haa Takalaua was a younger brother of the Tu'i Tonga and that the
first Tu'i Kanokupolu was a younger brother of the Tu'i Haa
Takalaua (Gifford, 1929, p. 82), and today the relative status
of titles is expressed by saying that the one is the elder or the
younger brother of the other. But the relationship is between
the titles, not between the holders of the titles.

In matter of *personal* rank, a sister always ranked above her
brother; hence, at any particular time, the male Tu'i Tonga
was outranked, as an individual, by his sister, the female Tu'i
Tonga (Tu'i Tonga Fefine).[3] In personal terms certain children
of the Tu'i Tonga Fefine might rank even higher.

In pre-Christian Tonga no clear distinction was made between regular marriage and temporary liaison. The offspring
resulting from a casual sexual encounter between an important
man and a woman of low status might be classed as 'children
in the bush', which implied that they were of low rank but
they were not, in any meaningful sense, illegitimate. By the
same token the offspring of a high ranking woman by a lower
ranking man might have very high personal status.

In particular, the Tu'i Tonga Fefine was entitled to sleep
with anyone she chose. When she cohabited in this way with
the holder of one or other of the 'Fijian' titles, Tu'i Lakepa and
Tu'i Haa Teiho, a resultant son would inherit one of these titles
and a daughter would become the Tamaha, who was the
highest ranking individual in the whole system.

The Tamaha was often married to the Tu'i Kanokupolu, who
ranked third in the chiefly hierarchy of titles but was the most
powerful chief in a political sense. It will be noted that the
adult Tu'i Lakepa or Tu'i Haa Teiho would then be the Tu'i
Tonga Fefine's cross-cousin – Father's sister's son (see Gifford,

1929, pp. 80–1: also Bott, personal communication). Notionally it should have been possible to generate an individual of even more exalted personal status than the Tamaha by having this lady cohabit with the Tu'i Tonga. Tongan myth actually provides for such a possibility (Gifford, 1929, p. 81) but significantly no such alliance seems to have occurred in history (see *Figure 1*).

It will be seen that although the political leader, the Tu'i Kanokupolu, held a lower ranking title than the ritual leader, the Tu'i Tonga, the pattern of marriage was such that the personal rank status of the Tu'i Kanokupolu, derived through maternal links, might be as high or higher than that of the reigning Tu'i Tonga.

The net result of these complex games of status is thus summarized by Bott (p. 218):

> Unlike titles, which are normally inherited in the male line, personal rank is inherited from both parents. To be a great aristocrat means that one is descended, preferably through a line of eldest sisters, from the eldest sister of the former sacred King, the Tu'i Tonga, a title that is now defunct. Even the principles of rank in themselves may sometimes conflict. If a man marries a woman who is a great aristocrat and his sister marries a lowly commoner, the children of the respective marriages will be in a contradictory situation. According to one principle the children of the sister will rank higher than the children of the brother, but according to the other principle (that descent from the Tu'i Tonga's sister confers higher rank) the children of the brother will have higher rank.

This statement suffices to provide us with an initial hypothesis. The kava ceremonial contains only two classes of operations. First, the participants must seat themselves in the right order. Second, the kava and food must be ritually prepared and handed round. The position in the circle of present-day title-holders is determined by patrilineal succession in accordance with the relative ranking position of the hereditary titles, but the personal rank of the holders of these titles may be widely discrepant from the relative ranking of the titles themselves, because the personal rank contains the added element of matrilineal succession from a Tu'i Tonga Fefine.

My hypothesis is that the kava ceremonial provides a charter for this discrepancy. I postulate that although the seating arrangements are strictly by title the actual presentation of the kava represents the legendary maternal ancestry of the individual recipients.

With this possibility in mind let us turn to consider the mythology.

Bott tells us that she recorded two versions of 'The Myth of the Origin of Kava' and draws the reader's attention to four other versions printed by Gifford (1924, pp. 71–5). The version that Bott herself provides is as follows:

Bott I

One day the King of Tonga went fishing with a friend. They did not catch anything, and as they were tired and hungry they called in at the little island of 'Eueiki to get something to eat. At that time there was only one couple living on the island and they had one child, a daughter, whose name was Kava'onau. (In some versions the name is abbreviated to 'Kava'.) She had leprosy. It was a time of famine and the only food the couple had left was a large kape plant (*Alocasia macrorrhiza*) which stood near the beach. When the King landed he sat down to rest against this plant. When the couple realized who their guest was they set about making an earth oven but when they came to get their sole remaining food plant, they could not use it because the King was leaning on it. The King's friend saw the couple hit something in their house and bring it out to be baked in the earth oven. He saw that they had killed their daughter because they had nothing else to give their King. The King's friend told the King what the couple had done. The King was deeply moved by their sacrifice. He rose up immediately and returned to the main island, telling the couple to bury their child properly.

Two plants grew from the grave, one from the head and one from the foot. One day the couple saw a mouse bite the first plant, stagger a bit, and then bite the second plant, after which he recovered his balance.

One day Lo'au came to the island and the couple told him all that had happened . . . When Lo'au heard the couple's story he sat in silence for a time, deeply moved, and then he spoke in poetry telling them what they should do. They must take the two plants to the King and give him Lo'au's instructions about how the plants should be used. The one from the head was to be used to make a drink, and that was the kava, and the other was to be eaten with the drink, and that was the sugar cane. The couple did as Lo'au had told them. At first the King thought their plant might be poisonous. He had one of his matāpule taste it first. But on finding it was all right he directed the people to carry out Lo'au's instructions.

And so kava was made for the first time and the rules and procedures for making it were established.

Bott glosses this with the comment:

Lo'au is a figure who turns up in Tongan legend and mythology at times when social institutions are being established or changed. He tells the people how to organise their social life and then fades from view. He is thought of as human, not a god, and he is called the 'carpenter of the land' which, freely translated, means the establisher of social customs (p. 216).

In Gifford's variants the following are the principal points of difference:

Gifford I

The 'King of Tonga' is referred to as the Tu'i Tonga, but this Tu'i Tonga is then merged with Lo'au. The couple living on 'Eueiki are named Fevanga and Fefafa, and Fevanga is a friend and attendant (*takanga*) of the Tu'i Tonga. The Tu'i Tonga visits 'Eueiki at Fevanga's invitation, and it is a return visit since Fevanga has previously visited the Tu'i Tonga at Mua. Fevanga and Fefafa manage to get the Tu'i Tonga away from the *kape* plant so they are able to dig it up and they bake the *kape* along with their murdered daughter. When the food is placed before 'the chief Lo'au' he immediately identifies it: 'Why have you destroyed your child? Did you not know it was a kava plant?' After the body has been buried the kava plant grows from the head, the sugar plant from the intestines (not the foot). The detail about the King thinking the kava was poisonous and testing it on a *mātāpule* is omitted.

Gifford II

'The King' is referred to throughout as 'a chief called Lo'au' who lives at Ha'amea (i.e. he is Tu'i Ha'amea). The story follows

Gifford I rather than Bott I. The buried corpse is cut into two parts, the head being buried in one place and the rest somewhere else; *both* the magic plants grow from the head.

Gifford III

'The King' is specifically described as 'The Tu'i Tonga named Lo'au'. The story follows Bott I rather than Gifford I in that it implies that Lo'au and Fevanga are mutual strangers. There is no reference to the sugar plant. When the kava plant which has grown from the buried body has been dug up and taken to Lo'au he identifies it as 'Kava, child of Fevanga and Fefafa, the leper from Faimata ['Eueiki]'.

Gifford IV

The events take place at Eua[4] not at 'Eueiki. No reference to Lo'au. 'The King' is described as Tu'i Tonga throughout. No reference to the *kape* plant. No reference to the sugar. This last is a fairly early version but derived second-hand from a missionary.

TU'ITĀTUI, MOMO, AND NUA

Elsewhere Gifford (1929, p. 71) identifies the Tu'i Tonga or Gifford I as Momo, the tenth Tu'i Tonga. According to tradition this Tu'i Tonga married Nua, the daughter of Lo'au, the Tu'i Ha'amea, by whom he had a son Tu'itātui who was the eleventh Tu'i Tonga (Gifford, 1929, p. 60). Tu'itātui is a prominent figure in Tongan myth/legend (see Gifford, 1929, pp. 52–3). Among other things he committed incest with his elder sister Latūtama, the Tu'i Tonga Fefine (Gifford, 1924, p. 46). Heketa, the reputed locale of this adventure, is a real place on the island of Tongatabu (Gifford, 1929, p. 52) but, after the death of Tu'itātui, his sons are said to have moved to a new home because Heketa 'is bad, for it is rocky and rough' (Gifford, 1924, p. 46; cf. note 4, below).

It seems relevant that Gifford (1924, p. 47) cites a story that attributes to Tu'itātui the origin of the present arrangement of seating at a kava ceremonial.

The island of 'Eueiki, which figures in Bott I and in Gifford I–III, turns up again in another story about Tu'itātui

(Gifford, 1924, pp. 47–9). This time he seduces not his sister but a lady with the same name as his mother.

Tu'itātui is passing the island of 'Eueiki and sees a beautiful girl. At first he is not sure whether she is human or spirit. As in Bott I, there is again a suggestion (Gifford, 1924, p. 48) that there is no food on 'Eueiki. In the end Tu'itātui abducts the girl and they have children. The girl's name is Nua.

Gifford (1924, pp. 43–6) also gives two very similar versions of a myth relating to the marriage of Momo and Nua (the mother of Tu'itātui). The second of these runs as follows:

Gifford V
There was a Tu'i Tonga named Momo, who sent his attendant Leha'uli to the chief of Ha'amea (in Tongatabu) who was named Lo'au, telling him that he wanted 'new yams and old yams' to complete the planting of his little yam patch. Leha'uli did not understand the meaning of the message he bore. He really thought that the Tu'i Tonga wanted yams. Before he spoke to Lo'au, however, Lo'au guessed what he had come for. So Leha'uli delivered his message.

Lo'au told him to tell the Tu'i Tonga that he had 'no new yams but he had an old yam and bush yams', meaning one married daughter and 'daughters in the bush', i.e. illegitimate daughters.[5] The attendant took this message to the Tu'i Tonga, who again sent him to Lo'au to tell him that he wanted Nua, Lo'au's married daughter. She was married to Ngongokilitoto of Malapo, Tongatabu, who was chief of Ha'angongo (probably a clan or other group of people).

So Lo'au came to Malapo and spoke to Ngongokilitoto, telling him that the Tu'i Tonga wanted Nua. Ngongokilitoto told Lo'au to go and wait on the road until he had talked with Nua, for their marriage was a marriage for love.

Ngongokilitoto told Nua that he released her from marriage in order that she might go to the Tu'i Tonga, but he would visit her regularly. He told her that if she heard water dripping on a *kape* (*Arum costatum*) leaf as on a rainy night that it was a sign that he was outside.

Lo'au then took his daughter to the Tu'i Tonga. For some time Ngongokilitoto visited her. Whenever she heard the dripping on the *kape* leaf she went out to meet her husband. Nua had already born Ngongokilitoto a son called Fasiapule. She was anxious to bear a child to the Tu'i Tonga, so she told Ngongokilitoto that he had better cease his visits. She wanted to have a child that was without doubt the Tu'i Tonga's. After Ngongokilitoto ceased his visits to Nua she became pregnant to the Tu'i Tonga. She bore a son who was named Tu'itātui.

The story then continues at length about the relations between Tu'itātui and his half-brother Fasiapule. The beginning of this part of the story runs as follows:

When the Tu'i Tonga died, Tu'itātui became king. Tu'itātui did not know that he had a brother. One morning they had a ceremony in which the Ha'angongo people presented yams and other products to the Tu'i Tonga. Fasiapule came with the people. He brought a basket in which he carried a piece of charcoal, one ripe *mamae* (a sort of banana), one *toto* (a fruit), and the pithy inside of a banana tree through which a fibre ran.

During the kava drinking Fasiapule came inside the kava ring with his basket. Then he made a speech. First he picked up the banana pith and broke it in half, but it was still united by the fibre within. He told Tu'itātui that it was like themselves, that they could not break away from each other because they were born of the same woman. Then he picked up the *mamae* to show that the two half brothers will pity each other. If Fasiapule were to commit a wrong, Tu'itātui would have pity for him in his mind.

Then Fasiapule picked up the *toto* and told the Tu'i Tonga that they too were of one blood and united like the *toto*. Then he picked up the charcoal and told the Tu'i Tonga that his mind was dark like the charcoal, for he did not know until now that he had a brother in Fasiapule.

In the latter part of this story Fasiapule runs away to Fiji and returns just as Tu'itātui is about to be buried on the island of Eua. Fasiapule kills his Fijian companion and substitutes his corpse for that of Tu'itātui. He then takes Tu'itātui's corpse away to the island called Moungatapu (Sacred Mountain) and thence to a place unknown, by some identified as Heketa, the locale of his seduction of his sister Latūtama (*supra*, p. 250).

Three unobtrusive details in this story deserve the reader's attention. First, certain foods presented at a kava ceremonial are said to symbolize the solidarity that exists between an aristocrat and his chief by virtue of links of common maternal ancestry. Second, there is the charcoal symbolism of latent hostility between chiefs and aristocrats. Third, there is the marginality of Eua and Heketa.

In Gifford IV (p. 250) Eua is a substitution for 'Eueiki hence there is a recurrent association between 'Eukeiki and Heketa. Both are unpleasant 'sacred' places associated with sin and death. Both have real existence in modern geography but mythologically both seem to stand for 'the other world' of spirits rather than this world of living men.

In her paper Bott records a myth that is much more explicitly concerned with the polarization of this world and the other world (see p. 228). Bott considers that this myth relates to the origins of certain details of the kava ceremony itself. Her text is as follows:

Bott II

The story of the myth is simple and melodramatic. A god from the sky has intercourse with a woman of the earth and a son is born, called 'Aho'eitu. When he grows up he wants to see his father and, following instructions from his mother, he climbs up to the sky by a giant iron-wood tree. 'Aho'eitu is enthusiastically welcomed by his father, who thinks at first that 'Aho'eitu is a god of even higher rank than himself. The father then sends his new-found son, without introduction, to see his other sons in the sky, presumably the sons of sky mothers. When 'Aho'eitu's half-brothers see everyone admiring 'Aho'eitu because of his beauty, and when they hear rumours that he is their father's son, they tear 'Aho'eitu to pieces and eat him up. The father suspects what they have done. He calls for a wooden bowl and makes his sons vomit into it. This is very reminiscent of the former custom of chewing the kava, of the statements that kava sometimes makes people feel like vomiting, and of the linguistic association with nausea.[6] The sons vomit up 'Aho'eitu's flesh and blood, they confess, and the father sends people to collect the bones and the head which are also put in the bowl. Water is poured into the bowl, as in the kava ceremony. The pouring in of the water, as I have noted above, is one of the most sacred moments of the ceremony. After some time 'Aho'eitu begins to take shape and finally sits up in the bowl. Then the father calls all his sons together and tells them that 'Aho'eitu will go back to the earth to become the first king of Tonga, the first Tu'i Tonga. At this point, the myth says, affection awakens in the hearts of the brothers, and they plead with their father to be allowed to go with 'Aho'eitu. The father agrees. Four of the brothers go down to earth to serve 'Aho'eitu as his matāpule. The fifth and eldest brother cannot be king, the father says, because he is guilty of murder, but he will be the King of the Second House (Tu'i Fale Ua). If 'Aho'eitu's line should die out then the King of the Second House will become King. (This is the rationale for the belief, mentioned above, that the last Tu'i Tonga bequeathed his kava prerogatives to the King of the Second House.) There are several other myths and legends that purport to show that all through Tongan history the descendants of the King of the Second House tried to murder 'Aho'eitu's descendants in order to wipe out his line.'

According to Bott (personal communication) this version of the story is compounded from the accounts of several distinguished informants including the Queen Salote herself. Gifford (1924, pp. 26–9, 38–43) gives us two alternative versions. Both are considerably longer than Bott II but contain much the same elements. Bott (p. 230) mentions that in one version of this myth 'the brothers threw 'Aho'eitu's head into a bush, which caused the bush to become poisonous', and she sees this as 'perhaps a way of talking about castration'. Both of Gifford's versions contain this detail and in one of them the point is made that – 'they threw the head among the plants called *hoi*. This caused one kind of *hoi* to become bitter. There is another kind that is sweet. The bitter kind became so because 'Aho'eitu's head was thrown into it. That kind of *hoi* is not eaten because it is poisonous.'

I have already commented (p. 240) on certain similarities and contrasts between elements in Bott II and 'corresponding' elements in Gifford V (p. 251). In Bott II the relationship between the Tu'i Tonga ('Aho'eitu) and his murderers is that of half-brother through a common father; in Gifford V, the relationship between the Tu'i Tonga (Tu'itātui) and Fasiapule is that of half-brother through a common mother. In the 'Aho-'eitu case it is the heavenly half-brothers who might reasonably be considered of high status, it is the Tu'i Tonga who is of low status – 'the son in the bush' (hence perhaps the story about the *hoi* bush?).[7] In Bott II, the half-brothers kill 'Aho-'eitu in the other world and assimilate themselves to him by eating his body; the end of the story has both 'Aho'eitu and his half-brothers in this world with 'Aho'eitu as Tu'i Tonga and the half-brothers permanently linked to him as his subordinate matāpule. In Gifford V this sequence is precisely reversed. The story starts with Tu'itātui and Fasiapule in the relationship of Tu'i Tonga and subordinate in this world, emphasis being given to the permanence of this link; it continues with the death of Tu'itātui and the substitution of his body by Fasiapule and ends with Fasiapule assimilating himself to the dead Tu'itātui and removing himself and the dead half-brother to 'the other world' (cf. *supra*, p. 253).

These similarities and inversions establish in an objective (non-intuitional) sense that the Gifford V and Bott II stories are closely associated. But Gifford V also ties in with the 'Origin of Kava' stories (Bott I, Gifford I–IV), which involve links between the Tu'i Tonga (Momo), the Culture Hero semi-deity Lo'au, and the wife-mother-daughter Nua. The stories I have mentioned are thus *demonstrably* all members of a single set. This is an important point. Several other stories in Gifford (1924) have elements of similarity with those that I have given here, but none of them are tied into a single complex in the same way through multiple cross-references.

Certain additional observations on the half-brother theme in the Bott II and Gifford V stories deserve attention. In the Bott II version the half-brothers, who are related through a common *father*, only begin to act as kinsmen after the murder and the complete physical assimilation; in Gifford V, where the link is through a common *mother*, it is emphasized from the start that the bond of kinship is indissoluble despite differences of titular status and physical separation. Furthermore, in Bott

II it is the divine father who allocates to the half-brothers their respective titles while in Gifford V the half-brothers are of different titular status *because* they have different fathers.

Bott II and Gifford V both lay stress on the same feature of real life social organization, namely that while (a) titles are passed from father to son and not from mother to son and no two individuals can simultaneously hold the same title, nevertheless (b) a quality of personal rank (as distinct from title) is passed from mother to son, so that two sons of the same mother will always share an element of this personal rank even if they are of different titular status (*supra*, pp. 246, 247).

When Bott wrote her paper she was evidently unable to see any very direct connection between her myth about 'Aho'eitu (Bott II) and the story about the murdered leprous girl (Bott I) but she recognized that somehow there ought to be such a connection. Her comment on the 'Aho'eitu story (Bott II) is as follows:

> There is a great deal of ambiguity in the myth about who is killing whom. Obviously the half-brothers kill 'Aho'eitu, but he is the father's favourite, so they are attacking the father as well. The father himself sends 'Aho'eitu to his death . . . And what of the mother far away in Tonga? 'Aho'eitu is her only son, so she is being attacked and perhaps destroyed. But it is she who tells 'Aho'eitu how to get to heaven in the first place. And what of the link with the kava myth itself in which a daughter is destroyed? Is it a daughter only or also a mother in disguise? (pp. 230–1).

As we have already seen, there is quite independent evidence of a structural kind that 'the daughter is also a mother in disguise'.

There is no need to guess about a possible relationship between the two myths. The relationship palpably exists, and an analysis item by item will enable us to see what it is. In both stories 'this world' of ordinary human activity is contrasted with an 'other world' of mythical happenings. In Bott I and the 'other world' is 'Eueiki (*supra*, p. 253); in Bott II it is a Land in the

Sky. Now it is the characteristic of 'other worlds' that the events that happen there are altogether strange. So when Bott asks herself (p. 227) – 'Why the famine, the cannibalism, and above all the leprosy, all of which are known in Tonga but have always been rare?' she has provided her own answer. In part, these details simply serve to demonstrate that 'Eueiki is 'other' – 'In the Land of the Dead, Man stands on his Head', life goes back to front and upside down. But certainly there is more to it than that.

Let us suppose that both stories are not merely interrelated but that, at a certain level, they are, more or less, identical, and see where we get to. In the following tabulation I assume that each story consists of a series of 'bits' (binary digits) of information that might be coded onto a suitably designed computer programme as $+/-$ alternatives. These 'structural elements', which are common to both stories, are listed in the left-hand column; the nature of the contrast or similarity between the treatment of these structural elements in the two stories is indicated in the two right-hand columns.

Structural element:	BOTT I *myth detail:*	BOTT II *myth detail:*
1. The other world is	the island 'Eueiki	a land in the sky
2. It is reached by	a boat made of wood that floats	a tree made of wood that sinks (iron wood)
3. The visitor to the other world is	the Tu'i Tonga (Momo) or Lo'au	'Aho'eitu, the future Tu'i Tonga
4. The victim is	a leper girl who belongs to the other world	a beautiful boy ('Aho'eitu) who belongs to this world
5. The host is	*either* a stranger *or* the visitor's matāpule	the visitor's father
6. The murderer is	the victim's parent	the victim's half-brothers
7. Attitude of host to visitor is	deferential	deferential
8. Visitor and Victim are	different	identical

(*cont'd*)

Structural element:	BOTT I myth detail:	BOTT II myth detail:
9. Host and Murderer are	identical	different
10. The Victim is killed	by beating (pounding)	by rending and chewing
11. The Victim is	cooked by baking	is not cooked
12. The Victim's body is	not eaten	etaen
13. It is then	buried	vomited up and ritually mixed with water
14. Then	two plants grow from the body	the Victim is reconstituted from the vomit
15. and	while the plant from the head becomes kava, the other growing from the intestines (or the feet, or the head) becomes sugar cane	the Victim becomes the first Tu'i Tonga
16. The murderers are	persons in the other world who had the status of matāpule in this world (see below p. 268)	persons in the other world who later acquire the status of matāpule in this world
17. they	gather kava from the residuum of the victim and offer it to the Tu'i Tonga, but he gives it to his matāpule to prepare and distribute ritually	become the first matāpule in relation to their reconstituted victim, the Tu'i Tonga. As matāpule one of their principal duties is the preparation of the kava. However, the eldest of the murderer brothers, the Tu'i Fale Ua does not become a matāpule but rather a kind of Deputy Tu'i Tonga

Further correspondences associate both these myths with Tu'itātui stories (*supra*, pp. 250–3).

In Bott I, Lo'au is a distinct person from the Tu'i Tonga and is associated with the parents of the murdered girl. It is

Lo'au who sends the kava plant from 'Eueiki to the Tu'i Tonga.

In contrast, in Gifford I–III, Lo'au is merged with the Tu'i Tonga (Momo). But Momo married Nua the daughter of Lo'au. So Lo'au married his own daughter! This is all of a pattern with the fact that Tu'itātui, the Tu'i Tonga who was the son of Momo and Nua, not only commits incest with his full sister the Tu'i Tonga Fefine (*supra*, p. 250), but also 'marries' Nua, a spirit girl from 'Eueiki (p. 251).

Thus the murdered leper girl of 'Eueiki who becomes kava (Bott I) is associated in multiplex fashion with a complex theme of compounded incest. The leper girl is taboo because of her physical condition; Nua is taboo both because of her association with incest and because she is a 'spirit'. Both girls come from 'Eueiki, and both are given by Lo'au to the Tu'i Tonga, who is Lo'au himself.

This overall confusion between the giver and the receiver of the kava plant, which appears in all the variants of Bott I, is matched at the end of Bott II by the statement that the eldest of 'Aho'eitu's two murderers becomes, as Tu'i Fale Ua, the deputy for his former victim.

To summarize in one or other of the stories I have mentioned the following explicit identifications are made:

$$Nua = Lo'au's\ daughter$$
$$Nua = Tu'i\ Tonga's\ mother$$
$$Nua = Tu'i\ Tonga's\ wife$$
$$Tu'i\ Tonga's\ wife = Tu'i\ Tonga's$$
$$sister\ (Tu'i\ Tonga\ Fefine)$$
$$Lo'au = Tu'i\ Tonga$$
$$Nua = a\ beautiful\ (spirit)\ girl\ from\ 'Eueiki$$
$$Kava = an\ ugly\ (leper)\ girl\ from\ 'Eueiki$$

The myth does not explicitly state that Nua, the spirit girl from 'Eueiki, who becomes the ancestress of the Tu'i Tonga, is 'the same as' the leper girl from 'Eueiki who is later consumed sacramentally as kava, nor does the myth anywhere explicitly assert that Nua is the Tu'i Tonga Fefine, but it comes as close as possible to making both these identifications. In any case both myths seem to imply equations between the murdered victim and human title holders through the medium of the kava, as in *Figure 2*.

Figure 2 Mythical transformations in Bott I and Bott II

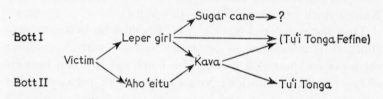

Further 'equivalences' seem to be implied by the various references to the *kape* plant and to yams. The *kape* root could be used as a food of last resort and the implication of the reference to *kape* in Bott I is that the victim is substituted for the *kape* as an offering of food to 'the King'.

We meet with *kape* again in Gifford V where the girl Nua, who has previously been described as 'an old yam' and has been offered as sexual consort to the Tu'i Tonga, is told by her lover that 'the dripping of water on the *kape* leaf' is to be treated as a sexual invitation.

In the pre-Christian Tongan society 'by far the most important ceremony at which the Tu'i Tonga functioned was the great annual *inasi* or offering of first fruits to the gods' (Gifford, 1929, p. 76). The central feature of this ritual was the offering of yams to the Tu'i Tonga. Finally, perhaps we should notice Bott's observation (*supra*, p. 213) that 'the pouring in of the water (onto the masticated kava root) is one of the most sacred moments of the ceremony'.

We need to notice two particular features of this concatenation of symbolic associations. First, there is a quite definite, though somewhat obscure, association between incestuous sex relations with a tabooed woman and the drinking of kava as a sacrament. Second, this whole complex of myth fits in admirably with a well-known generalization by Lévi-Strauss who has argued (Lévi-Strauss, 1963, p. 216) that there is always a logical contradiction in any story of first ancestors, particularly in patrilineal systems. For how can 'a first man' beget children except by cohabiting either with his mother or his sister? But if he had a mother, how could he be the first man? The logical contradictions of the coalescence and distinction between Lo'au (Tu'i Ha'amea) and Lo'au (Tu'i Tonga) seem to betray precisely such a problem. A somewhat similar ambiguity is implicit in the circumstance that although both the main myths make a close identification between the murdered victim and the Tu'i Tonga, Bott I makes the victim female and Bott II male; in the female case the associations of the chewing and preparation of the kava are sexual, in the male case the context is straight aggression.

Taken together a set of equivalences and symbolic associations of the following sort seems to be implied (*Figure 3*).

Figure 3 Kava/sugar polarity and symbolic equivalents

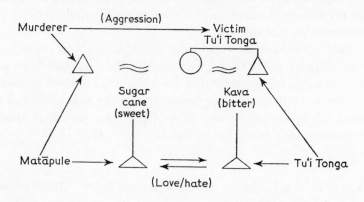

Let us return to my hypothesis (p. 248) that in the actual ceremonial the offering of kava is an expression of ancestral ties with high-ranking women.

In real life, Tongan titles can be distinguished as falling into one or other of two categories: (i) chiefly titles, which are all in the last analysis 'younger brothers' of the Tuʻi Tonga title (*supra*, p. 246) and (ii) matāpule titles, which are all considered to have been derived from 'foreigners' (Fijians, Samoans, etc.) who married with Tongan women. In the mythology the relationship between titles of class (i) and titles of class (ii) is treated as a relationship between half-brothers marked by ambivalent attitudes of love and hate.

Explicit examples of this ambivalence are provided in Gifford V (*supra*, pp. 251–2) especially in the story of Fasiapule, the *toto*-fruit, and the charcoal. Another story about Tuʻitātui has just the same implication. Gifford (1929, p. 53) records a tradition about this Tuʻi Tonga to the effect that he used a long stick to hit the knees of his matāpule when they came too close. 'His reason for this practice is said to have been fear of assassination because several Tuʻi Tonga had been killed at kava ceremonies by their matāpule.'

It is thus rather striking that whereas the formal appearance of the real life kava ceremonial exhibits extremely cordial relationships between the holders of chiefly and matāpule titles, the mythological counterpart is a set of stories about incestuous relationships and murder.

Taking the mythology and the ritual in combination we encounter two types of transformation. On the one hand there are permutations that occur within the body of the mythology itself; on the other there are representations in the real life ritual of incidents occurring in the mythology. The principal transformations may be set out as follows:

A. *Main transformation and identifications in the ʻAhoʻeitu Story* (Bott II)

I. Transformations occurring within the text of the myth itself

   (i) ʻAhoʻeitu (who has a divine father and a human mother)

is converted into a kava offering *in the other world* but becomes Tuʻi Tonga *in this world*.

(ii) 'Ahoʻeitu's divine (paternal) half-brothers are kava makers *in the other world* but becomes matāpule *in this world*, except for the Tuʻi Fale Ua, a chiefly title, ranking as Deputy for the Tuʻa Tonga.

II. Transformations as between the text of the myth and the performance of the real life kava ceremony

(i) *In the myth.* The murderer half-brothers of the victim are identical to the kava makers.
In the ritual. The matāpule and the kava maker are separate individuals, physically separated, but the kava maker acts under the instructions of the matāpule.

(ii) *In the myth.* The murdered victim who later becomes Tuʻi Tonga is identical to the kava.
In the ritual. The presiding chief, a descendant of a Tuʻi Tonga, is physically separated from the kava. However, the first action in the ceremony is to present the *kava* plants and food to the presiding chief and then remove them from him (*supra*, p. 244).

If we accept the mythical identification of matāpule with kava maker and of Tuʻi Tonga with kava, then it follows that, in the real life ceremonial, the four main elements are related as:

kava maker : kava : : matāpule : Tuʻi Tonga (presiding chief).

B. *Main transformations and identifications in the stories about the island of ʻEueiki* (Bott I; Gifford I–IV; Gifford V)

Preliminary comments
Of the numerous contrasts between Bott I and Bott II (tabulated on pp. 257–8) the following seem especially significant:

	BOTT I	BOTT II
4. the victim is	female ugly	male beautiful
14/15. the victim is reconstituted as	*two* plants: sweet sugar cane from the foot or intestines; bitter kava from the head	the human Tuʻi Tonga

In *Figure 3* it has been proposed that the two plants should be interpreted as the lawful (sweet) and unlawful (bitter) aspects of the Tuʻi Tonga Fefine's sexual personality. An alternative possibility, suggested by the above tabulation, is that the sweet and bitter plants correspond to male and female aspects of the Tuʻi Tonga title. The ambiguity cannot be resolved without 'intuition'. It seems likely in any case that both the mythology and the ritual has here been modified by 'modern' influences.

The sugar cane and the kava are opposed not only as sweet and sour but also as stalk and root, and I would guess that the sugar cane once grew, neither from the foot nor the 'intestines' of the victim but from her vagina. In the ritual, the sugar cane serves as a prototype food offering (*supra*, p. 244). All modern accounts of the kava ceremonial imply that the drinking of the prepared kava is now of far greater ritual significance than the distribution or consumption of the food, but there is evidence that at one time the food entitlement of individual participants was very important (Gifford, 1929, p. 162). This change of emphasis may be due to the fact that in the pre-Christian era the offering of food had pagan religious significance (*supra*, p. 260); it could also reflect the fact that the three prime titles of Tuʻi Tonga, Tuʻi Tonga Fefine, and Yuʻi Kanokupolu were all combined in the single person of Queen Salote (*supra*, p. 243).

That the symbolic allocation of the kava and the sugar cane is as in *Figure 3* and not the other way round is supported by Gifford (1929, p. 159) where it is reported that when the Tuʻi

Tonga was ill the kava would be described as 'diluted', and that a special kava, accompanied by prayers for a son, was performed when the Tu'i Tonga's consort was confined. Furthermore Gifford (1929, p. 162) seems to imply that claims for personal precedence in the *'alofi* circle on the part of individual matāpule and minor chiefs on account of genealogical connection (through women) with the presiding chief were based on particular entitlements to food rather than particular entitlements to drink.

Another binary opposition that occurs in the ritual is that between the right and left sides of the *'alofi* circle (*supra*, p. 209). This distinction is linked with the allocation of titles to two 'moieties' (Kauhalalalo, Kauhalauta), but this does not seem to be linked with the sweet/bitter opposition or with any other feature of the mythology and I shall not attempt an analysis.

It has already been noted that the myths in the Bott I group appear to be heavily loaded with the theme of incest, but it needs to be emphasized that if the stories are taken to refer to titles rather than to individuals the incestuous elements follow almost automatically from the principles of positional succession. Just as in the classical ancient Egyptian case where Horus and Osiris stood in positional succession, Isis's relation to Horus is that of mother, wife, or sister according to viewpoint, so also with these Tongan stories: Nua is mother-sister-wife-daughter of the Tu'i Tonga.

I. Transformations occurring within the mythology itself.

(i) The leprous girl from 'Eueiki, who is the daughter of a matāpule (or of a total stranger) is converted into the two plants of the kava ritual, kava and sugar cane.

(ii) The beautiful girl from 'Eueiki becomes the mother of the Tu'i Tonga.[8]

(iii) As a result of incest the Tu'i Tonga Fefine become the mother and 'wife' of the Tu'i Tonga.[9]

(iv) But Nua, the mother and 'wife' of the Tu'i Tonga is also mother of Fasiapule, a matāpule.

The *explicit* mythical statement that the relationship between the Tu'i Tonga and matāpule titles is that of 'half-brother through a common mother' thus has the added *implicit* component that, through incest, the common mother is the Tu'i Tonga Fefine.

II. Transformations as between the text of the myth and the performance of the real life kava ceremony.

  (i) *In the myth.* 'Eueiki produces two girls one leprous, one beautiful. The leprous girl is converted into two plants one 'poisonous' (kava) one sweet (sugar cane).
  In the ritual. A distinction is made between the drink (kava) and the food (sugar cane). Distinctions are also made between the passive role of the presiding chief and the active role of the matāpule.

THE KAVA AS SACRIFICE

In my schematic analysis of the two myths I have referred to the killing as a 'murder'. Is it legitimate to see this killing as sacramental and to call it a 'sacrifice'? Is the relation between kava myth and kava ritual a charter for a symbolic killing, in the same way as the myth of the Last Supper provides the Christian with a charter for a symbolic meal that commemorates a 'full, perfect and sufficient sacrifice?'

General theories about the 'meaning of sacrifice' fall into three types. First there are versions of Robertson-Smith's 'communion theory', which was designed to fit the 'sacrifice' of the Christian mass into a wider universal class. Here the sacrificial victim is, at the moment of slaughter, identified with the deity. The eating of the meat of the sacrifice is deemed an essential element in the rite; the congregation shares a collective guilt in participating in god murder and ritual cannibalism; this collective guilt is an 'atonement', it makes the members of the congregation aware of themselves as a collectivity that has jointly sinned yet jointly assimilated itself to god. The views of Durkheim and of Freud both have much in common with this basic thesis of Robertson-Smith.

Second, 'gift theories of sacrifice' presume that in making a sacrifice the donor is offering a gift to his deity in order to compel the god to make a counter gift in return. Though sociologically unsophisticated, this type of generalization often corresponds closely to the ethnographic facts. Often enough this is what native informants say that they are doing. However, this 'theory' evades the basic problem: even if we were to concede that it is, in some way, 'sensible' for a human being to want to make a gift to his deity, how could it possibly be sensible that the form of this gift should be the killing of an animal?

The third class of theory derives from Hubert and Mauss. This emphasizes the sacramental aspect of the sacrificial performances. A sacrifice serves to 'make the donor sacred', i.e. it improves his mystical condition; if he is ill he is made well, if he is in a state of sin he is freed from his sin. This theory is, in some respects, the opposite of that postulated by Robertson-Smith. Where Robertson-Smith laid stress on the symbolic identification of the victim and the deity, the Hubert and Mauss theory emphasizes the identification of the victim with the donor. By killing the victim the sacrificer alters its mystical condition; but if donor and victim are identical this also alters the mystical condition of the donor. The ideology is mixed up with the apparently self-contradictory notion that although cleanliness is a superior state to dirtiness, potency (power) is often felt to be dirty. A sick person is one who is 'contaminated' by mystical power; if he is to be made well he must be cleansed of that contamination by separating the dirty from the sterile. In a sacrifice, the killing of the victim separates the life potency from the cadaver. In a curiously inverted sense it is a 'purification' of both the dead animal and the living human being.

These theories are not necessarily mutually exclusive. If sacrifice constitutes a 'gift' from man to god, it also constitutes an atonement by which man and god are momentarily bound together and, in this moment of coalescence, it makes little difference to the ideology whether the bond itself – namely the sacrificial victim – is felt to be identified with the deity, or with the donor, or with both at once. In the language of structural analysis the victim 'mediates' the opposition between deity and donor.

If these theories are applied to the Tongan material that has so far been considered, several details seem particularly relevant.

(i) In real life 'kava can be presented ceremonially only by a matāpule; even a titled chief can present kava to the Queen only through a matāpule' (Gifford, 1929, p. 140).

Therefore, on the sacrifice analogy: the kava mediates the opposition between the matāpule as donor and the presiding chief as recipient. The matāpule titles in real life belong to the descendants of foreigners, and they are persons whose relationship to the Tuʻi Tonga is comparable to that of the foreigner 'husbands' of the Tuʻi Tonga Fefine (*supra*, p. 246) [10] and of the mythical 'Fijian' (maternal) half-brother Fasiapule (*supra*, p. 252).

(ii) In Bott I and its variants stress is placed on the fact that the parents of the leper girl pay reverential respect to their royal visitor. In Gifford I the rank status of Fevanga, the girl's father, is expressly specified as that of 'attendant (*takanga*) to the Tuʻi Tonga'. That is to say, he is a matāpule (see Gifford, 1929, p. 140). The mythical kava-leper girl is therefore again an offering that mediates the opposition between a matāpule as donor and a Tuʻi Tonga as recipient.

(iii) In contrast, in Bott II, the victim's elder half-brothers are both the donors and the recipients of the sacrifice. There is no opposition that can be 'mediated'; on the contrary the donor-recipients of the offering carry their identification with the victim so far that they devour him. But here again it turns out that the ritual of the kava has established a relationship between matāpule and Tuʻi Tonga.

This treatment of the material, both ritual and mythical, implies the following triads of 'mediated oppositions':

Opposed categories		*Mediating third term*
X	Y	Z
donor	receiver	gift
matāpule	presiding chief	kava
foreigner	Tongan	{ wife to foreigner { sister to Tongan
sister's husband	younger brother	elder sister
half-brother	half-brother	{ Bott I common mother { Bott II common father
Rank derived from both parents	Title derived from father	Ancestral Tu'i Tonga Fefine

In each of the three columns X, Y, and Z any one of the items is the symbolic equivalent of any other.

THE PROBLEM OF CHRISTIAN INFLUENCE

So finally we return once more to the initial problem of ritual interpretation. In the performance of the kava ceremonial as described above (pp. 207–15) what is really going on? When the matāpule order the distribution of the kava, what is it that is being distributed? Can we ignore the Christian context noted (p. 242)? Is the Eucharistic flavour just accidental?

Bott II explicitly exhibits the Tu'i Tonga being produced by a kava rite, yet structural analysis implies an identification of the kava with the female principle of rank derived from an ancestral Tu'i Tonga Fefine.

Whether we follow the 'overt' implications of the mythology or resort to a structuralist interpretation we are only offered three alternatives as to what the kava 'symbolizes':

Kava is: *either*

The body of the leprous daughter of the matāpule mystically transformed (as in Bott I)

or

The body of the Tu'i Tonga himself mystically transformed (as in Bott II)

or

Some mystical (incestuous) combination of the male

and female potencies of the Tu'i Tonga and the Tu'i
Tonga Fefine (as in *Figure 3*, p. 261).

The last alternative is no more metaphysical then the normal
Christian assertion that, in the Mass, the bread and the wine
become the body and blood of Jesus Christ and, in some
mystical sense, a manifestation of his purifying potency.

This homology with the Christian Mass seems to me too
striking to be ignored, but how should we explain it? Does it
arise from a subliminal influence of Christian ideas working
on the minds of recent Tongan mythographers (*supra*, p. 242), or
does it represent a direct parallel between traditional Christianity and traditional Polynesian thought at a structural level
of apprehension? As to the first of these alternatives, we have
evidence that, in at least one detail, the mythology has under-
gone a recent modification to keep it in line with a modification
of the ritual. Bott I says that the leper girl on 'Eueiki was
pounded to death; it thus fits the modern procedure of pounding the kava root. But Bott tells us that the substitution of
pounding for chewing in the actual ritual is a recent innovation
(*supra*, p. 244).

Evidence of this kind is bound to raise doubts about how far
we can regard *any* of the mythology as traditionally authentic,
but my own view, for what it is worth, is that the Christian
era modifications of pre-Christian materials have not been
substantial. It is rather that the more or less accidental fit
between certain themes in Polynesian kinship ideology and
certain aspects of the Christian dogma of the Virgin Birth have
provided a favourable climate for the survival of a very un-
Christian body of mythology.

In my own words, the kava ceremonial reduced to its most
skeletal form may be described as follows:

> A semi-poisonous food substance (the kava plant) is first identified
> with the Presiding Chief, then it is removed from him and ritually
> processed according to the instructions of the Presiding *Matāpule*
> so as to convert it into a sacramental drink which is then imbibed
> by all the principal title holders present.

There is a *direct* parallel between this ritual performance and the theme of cannibalism in Bott II. The parallel is also very Christian. The sacramental kava is the 'body and blood of the sacrificed man-god'.

But the mythology of Bott I suggests a different pattern, for in the latter case the emphasis is on paired oppositions rather than assimilation, and on incestuous and non-incestuous sex relations between men and women rather than on love-hate relationships between men.

In the real life ceremonial the *'alofi* circle is in two halves and the semi-circle of the presiding chief stands in polar opposition to the semi-circle of the kava bowl (Bott, *Figure 2*, p. 209).

Considering the sequence as a whole, both in its ritual and in its mythological aspects the following paired relationships are implied, with the qualification, already noted (p. 264), that the (apparent) relative secularity of food as against drink may be a recent modification:

Ritual oppositions		Mythological
Chief's semi-circle	kava bowl semi-circle	oppositions
matāpule : chief	kava maker : kava	
secular : sacred	food : drink	sugar cane : kava
		non-poisonous : poisonous
		beautiful : leprous
		son : daughter
		male : female

This patterning of ritual and mythological ideas exists in a secular context in which there is a real life 'contradiction' by which, although titles pass from fathers to sons, sisters rank higher than brothers (*supra*, p. 246).

It is an arrangement that provides the framework for a ritual enactment of a marked ambivalence in the relationship between the presiding chief and the presiding matāpule (*supra*, p. 262). The *manifest* behaviour in the ritual is one of friendly gift-giving, but the implications of the mythical background are that there is an undercurrent of jealousy and hate (*supra*, p. 258) and that the assembled matāpule are only willing to recognize the potency of ritual chieftainship because they are concerned to assimilate that potency to themselves.

For those who are prepared to give any credence at all to this style of analysis the general significance of the ceremony has by now become very obvious, indeed it has been indicated already at several points during the course of this essay.[11]

When the male titleholders sitting in the '*alofi* circle drink the kava and receive the distributions of sugar cane these are sacramental foods in the same sense as are the bread and wine of the Christian Mass. At a mystical level they are the equivalent of the divine potency that distinguishes the Tuʻi Tonga and the Tuʻi Tonga Fefine from ordinary mortals.

Of the two substances, it is the kava rather than the sugar cane that now carries real sacramental value and the significance of this fact is to be found in the circumstance that not only are the Tuʻi Tonga descended from an original incestuous relationship between a male and female Tuʻi Tonga but that the matāpule are likewise so descended. 'A great aristocrat is one descended, preferably through a line of elder sisters, from the elder sister of the Tuʻi Tonga' (Bott, p. 218).

By the ritual drinking of kava the titleholder concerned reaffirms his aristocratic status, he assimilates to himself once again the magical, matrilineally inherited, potency of his divine ancestors. By so doing he asserts his equality, or even his superiority, to the personal status of his presiding chief.

When one considers that in Christian theology, Jesus is divine by filiation from the Father but human and royal by an ambiguous filiation through the mother, it is not after all surprising that the kava mythology, in its modern form, despite the hints of cannibalism and incest, should make mystical. sense to devout Christians.

FINAL NOTE ON METHOD

Let me return to my initial thesis. The analysis that I have presented employs a combination of 'structuralist' and 'functionalist' techniques. In so far as I use functionalist assumptions I have operated intensively within a very narrow range of ethnographic data and I have adhered to the Malinowskian dogma that myth and ritual are two aspects of the same thing. But I have combined this orthodoxy with many features of structuralist procedure and I believe that the outcome is to be preferred to either a functionalist or a psychoanalytical interpretation of the more usual sort because it depends much less on intuition. Even so my argument might be criticized as superficial. Even if Bott were to agree that the mystical identity between the kava on the one hand and the potency of the Tu'i Tonga Fefine on the other has now been established (as I think perhaps she does), she might still argue that the concatenation, in such a context, of themes of cannibalism and incest is too suggestive to be ignored and that, at this 'deeper' level, the Freudian approach adds insights that neither functionalism nor structuralism can provide. On this issue I am not fully persuaded one way or the other. Certainly the convergence between Bott's Freudian approach and my own structural analysis seems very striking. But it was Audrey Richards's *Chisungu* that first convinced me that these matters are far more multivalent than I had once supposed, so it is to Audrey that I now offer this essay in uncertain analysis.

NOTES

1. In terms of our value system it might further appear that the younger half-brother is in each case 'illegitimate', but Dr Bott assures me that this would not be the case according to Tongan idiom.

2. 'The basic meaning of the term mātāpule seems to be sister's husband (M.S.)' (Gifford, 1929, p. 29). Hence it is a term of respect. As a *title*, it denotes the ceremonial attendant of a chief. Titles are hereditary in the male line and in most cases the patri-lienages that own matāpule titles are of 'foreign' origin, e.g. they are supposed to have come from Fiji or Samoa.

3. The Tu'i Tonga Fefine held office until death so that she might be, on occasion, the reigning Tu'i Tonga's father's sister.

4. Eua is the smallest of the inhabited islands of the Tongan group. 'Eueiki is ordinarily uninhabited and, as is well known to all Tongans, it is very difficult to land there because of the nature of the reef (Bott, personal communication).

5. Bott comments that this notion of 'illegitimacy' is modern. Formerly 'in the bush' meant 'of low rank', i.e. the offspring of a temporary liaison between an important man and a woman of low status. The child of a liaison between two aristocrats of comparable status would not be described in this way (cf. p. 246).

6. Bott, p. 216. 'There are other linguistic links with the idea of kava as a poison. *Kavafisi* and *kavahaha* are creepers used as fish poisons. The word "*kavahia*" means to be nauseated.'

7. Cf. note 5. 'Aho'eitu has a human mother and a heavenly father.

8. One explicit tradition asserts that the child of Nua, the girl from 'Eueiki, was named Uanga and that this Uanga succeeded as Tu'i Tonga (Gifford, 1924, p. 49).

9. Gifford (1924, p. 46), which records the incest of Tu'itātui with his sister Latūtama, implies that the child of this liaison was named Talamata and that Talamata succeeded as Tu'i Tonga. Gifford (1929, p. 53) assumes that Uanga and Talamata are two names for the same historical individual.

10. Although the 'original' Tu'i Lakepa is supposed to have been a Fijian who was elder sister's husband to a Tu'i Tonga this title is not now considered to carry *matāpule* rank (Bott, personal communication; cf. Gifford, 1929, p. 34).

11. Firth (1970, pp. 199–233) gives an account of kava ritual and myth in Tikopia which can usefully be compared with the analysis given above. In Tikopia, as in Tonga, there are two main versions of the mythology but the roles are reversed. A healthy boy replaces the leper girl; a female spirit who 'dies' in childbirth and then survives as the Female Deity of Tikopia replaces the male 'Aho'eitu who is murdered and then survives as the Tu'i Tonga. The Tikopia libate their kava; the Tongans drink theirs. It may be noted that the appearance of the Female Deity in the Tikopia pattern is consistent not only with the function attributed to the Tu'i Tonga Fefine in this present paper but also with other characteristics of the Female Deity to which I have drawn attention elsewhere (Leach, 1961, p. 21).

REFERENCES

BOTT, E. 1968. 'Psychoanalysis and Ceremony'. In J. D. Sutherland (ed.), *The Psychoanalytic Approach*, pp. 52–77. London: Baillière, Tindall, & Cassell. See pp. 205–37 in this volume. (Page references in text above refer to pages in *this* volume.)

FIRTH, R. 1970. *Rank and Religion in Tikopia*. London: Allen & Unwin.

GIFFORD, E. W. 1924. *Tongan Myths and Tales*. B. P. Bishop Museum Bulletin No. 8. Honolulu.

GIFFORD, E. W. 1929. *Tongan Society*. B. P. Bishop Museum Bulletin No. 61. Honolulu.

HUBERT, H. & MAUSS, M. 1909. 'Essai sur la nature et la fonction du sacrifice' in *Mélanges d'histoire des religions*. Paris: Felix Alcan. Translation 1964. *Sacrifice: Its nature and function*. London: Cohen & West.

LEACH, E. R. 1961. *Rethinking Anthropology*. London: Athlone Press.

LÉVI-STRAUSS, C. 1963. *Structural Anthropology*. New York: Basic Books.

MARINER, W. 1818. *An Account of the Natives of the Tonga Islands*. (2nd edn.) 2 vols. (John Martin ed.). London: J. Murray.

RICHARDS, A. I. 1956. *Chisungu: A girls' initiation ceremony among the Bemba of Northern Rhodesia*. London: Faber & Faber.

WILLIAMSON, R. W. 1939. *Essays in Polynesian Ethnology* (R. Piddington ed.). Cambridge: Cambridge University Press.

ROBERTSON-SMITH, W. 1927. *Lectures on the Religion of the Semites*. (3rd edn.) London: A & C Black.

A rejoinder to Edmund Leach

ELIZABETH BOTT

I find myself captivated by the intellectual elegance of Dr
Leach's analysis. I accept as plausible the series of symbolic
links establishing the mystical identity between kava on the
one hand and descent from women on the other, and, with a
little misgiving, descent from the Tu'i Tonga Fefine in particular. The symbolic linking of Kava (the leprous girl of 'Eueiki)
with Nua (the beautiful spirit girl of 'Eueiki) seems indisput-
able, and the two Nua are the Tu'i Tonga's daughter, his
mother, and his wife. (Nua 1 is the daughter of Lo'au who is
equated/confused with the Tu'i Tonga. Nua 1 is also the wife
of Tu'i Tonga Momo and the mother of Tu'i Tonga Tu'itātui.
Nua 2, the spirit girl of 'Eueiki, marries Tu'i Tonga Tu'itātui.)
Kava is equivalent to the Tu'i Tonga's sister only through an
indirect link: Kava = Nua = Tu'i Tonga's wife = Latūtama,
the sister of Tu'i Tonga Tu'itātui. Assuming that Nua 1 is the
mother of Latūtama as well as the mother of Tu'i Tonga
Tu'itātui, which the myth does not explicitly state, the link
between kava and the sister of the Tu'i Tonga is more direct,
for then Kava = Nua = mother of Latūtama.

All this fills in much more adequately what Leach rightly
calls my 'wild guessing' about the links between the 'Aho'eitu
myth and the kava myth. And from it follows the conclusion
that whereas the seating of the ceremony expresses the fixed
and theoretically unchanging relationships of *titles* to one
another, the making and drinking of kava reaffirms the aristo-

cratic status of the title*holders* and their mystical assimilation
to their divine ancestress, the Tu'i Tonga Fefine.

Of the many equivalences that can be established, it seems
to me plausible that the kava itself embodies not only the
divine ancestress, the Tu'i Tonga's sister, but also the Tu'i
Tonga. Kava and sugar cane grow out of the earth-buried
body of the murdered leper girl. But 'Aho'eitu grows out of
the body of an earth-woman, and is then chewed, spat out
and mixed with water as if he himself were kava. Out of this
grows the Tu'i Tonga, so that when the kava is ritually consumed, what is being assimilated is not only the leper girl/Nua/
daughter/mother/wife/sister of the Tu'i Tonga, but also the
Tu'i Tonga himself. Thus the kava making and drinking would
express the mystical union of man and woman, the derivation of
man from woman and woman from man, and the insoluble
puzzle of the first ancestor.

There is a detail that neither Leach's analysis nor mine
fully explains. In the kava ceremony of the Tu'i Kanokupolu
and Ha'a Ngata, which was the type observed by Mariner,
Gifford, and my husband and me, the sugar cane (or pork) is
distributed to the kava drinkers, but they do not eat it. The
kava drinkers summon their 'grandchildren of high rank'
(*mokapuna 'eiki*) to take it away. According to the kava myth
both the sugar cane and the kava plant grew out of the body
of the murdered leper girl, but the sugar cane grew out of a
lower part of the body. I agree with Leach that the ritual and
mythological oppositions establish sugar cane as secular/food/
non-poisonous/beautiful/son/male/of lower rank – many of
these being attributes concerning titles and the relationships of
political authority and obligations that titles involve. Further,
the Tongan word for the food presented to the kava drinkers is
fono, which is a homonym for a political meeting at which a
chief gives orders to his people. It looks as if there is a paradoxical difference between the female substance (kava) and
the male substance (fono) that grow out of the leper girl/
beautiful boy. The female substance is of higher rank than the

male substance but can be consumed. The male substance is of lower rank but can only be consumed by those of higher rank than the kava drinkers. The male substance is thus simultaneously 'lower' and 'higher', just as brothers are simultaneously lower and higher than their sisters – lower in rank but greater in political power.

On one occasion I observed a kava ceremony of the 'King of the Second House' (Tu'i Fale Ua or Tu'i Pelehake), to which title the last Tu'i Tonga is said to have bequeathed his kava rites. In this ceremony the chief ate his *fono*. So did the Falefā, the titles of the four mythical half-brothers of 'Aho'eitu, and so did certain other 'foreign' matāpule who are said to have been specifically exempted from the *tapu* of eating in the presence of the Tu'i Tonga. Unfortunately I did not discover whether the King of the Second House ate his *fono* in his capacity as Tu'i Tonga or in his capacity as King of the Second House. Cook is the only authority I have found who gives a description of the Tu'i Tonga's kava ceremony, and he does not include this detail. The present-day eating of the *fono* in the kava ceremony of the 'King of the Second House' may therefore mean either a ritual repetition of the original eating up of 'Aho'eitu, or, more probably, a symbolic statement to the effect that only titles that are either (a) the embodiment of the Tu'i Tonga or (b) ritual outsiders can assimilate themselves directly to the male principle of the Tu'i Tonga/Tu'i Tonga Fefine.

What of Leach's claim that structuralist analysis is 'intuition free'? In the sense that the analysis uses as data only texts, ceremonies, and abstractions of organizational principles, it is relatively free from contamination either by the observer's or the informants' imputations of meaning and feeling to behaviour. Fieldwork becomes unnecessary, except that one must have a little contact with informants in order to collect texts, observe the ceremonies, and abstract the organizational principles. The analysis requires familiarity with and acceptance of the condensations, displacements, representation by reversal, and the symbolic equivalences peculiar to the logic of what Freud called the primary process, but such familiarity is now so general among western intellectuals that acceptance of primary process thinking can hardly be said to require intuition. The ability to analyse it is another matter, and clearly Dr Leach has a considerable gift for such analysis.

But can one disprove or prove a structuralist interpretation more readily than a psychoanalytic or functionalist one? I doubt it. So many equivalences can be established that one can arrive at a considerable range of possible interpretations- and the choice of one rather than another depends on 'feel' as well as logic.

I find structuralist analysis exciting because it shows how an understanding of primary process thinking can be applied to the cultural products of many societies, and because it indicates the universality of a small number of logical problems: How did man begin? How are the two sexes related to each other? What does death mean? and so on.

I find myself dissatisfied with the approach on two counts. (1) It places exclusive emphasis on the logical/cognitive aspect of the basic human dilemmas, evidently regarding their emotional aspects as irrelevant or uninteresting. (2) The logic is insufficiently linked with social behaviour. It is like a purely formal analysis of dreams, revealing their peculiar logic and a few of the universal intellectual problems with which they deal' but showing little of the specific anxieties and defences that an understanding of each dream can elucidate. 'The interpretation of dreams is the royal road to a knowledge of the unconscious activities of the mind,' Freud said in the early days of psycho, analysis, but he did not regard the analysis of them as an end in itself, which structuralist anthropologists seem to be in danger of doing. But, even with this danger, it is refreshing to have some emphasis on universals again after two generations of functionalist particularism.

I think there is a marked similarity in the methods used in applying the concepts of all three frames of reference – functionalist, structuralist, and psychoanalytic. All three have been developed in an attempt to interpret facts in certain situations and all three have then been used to illuminate facts in other situations, usually with some modification of the frame of reference in the process. I object to Leach's statement that psychoanalytic concepts are 'dogma', meaning that they have no relation to observed facts. They have been developed to explain observed facts, and the development has led to a much more complete understanding of cognitive, perceptual, and emotional processes in human beings than existed beforehand. I do not think this considerable body of constructs needs to be re-established every time a new bit of data is looked at any more than I would expect Leach or Lévi-Strauss to re-examine for each new social context the notion, for example, that 'the other world' is a place where everything stands on its head.

The content of the three frames of reference is of course different. The functionalist frame of reference purports to be entirely social, though it makes certain 'crude' and sometimes implicit assumptions about human nature. The structuralist frame of reference makes certain assertions about human cognitive processes. The psychoanalytic frame of reference makes a very similar set of assertions about certain types of cognitive process, but sets them in a wider interpretive framework. Leach does not distinguish between primary and secondary process thinking, a differentiation that becomes important when one tries to link analysis of cognitive aspects of behaviour with analysis of its perceptual and emotional aspects. Nor, of course, does the structuralist frame of analysis lead one to concepts of anxiety, defence, or to the reasons for keeping certain ideas, both individual and cultural, in a partially understood form. I think it is the extreme intellectualism of structuralism that is so limiting, but, paradoxically, it is also the main source of its appeal.

It is very difficult to frame hypotheses from any of the three conceptual systems in a form that can be proved or disproved. Acceptance or rejection rests on whether or not the hypotheses illuminate the facts, which in turn depends on many factors, including the preferences and prejudices of the reader. My own preferences and prejudices lead me to accept Leach's structuralist interpretations of the kava ceremony and myths, for they link and illuminate facts that were not as adequately linked before. I find his interpretations elegant, though restricted. But I also find plausible my own interpretation that the kava ceremony and myths are statements about emotional and social as well as logical/cognitive problems.

Thus, even though my original paper was not written with Audrey Richards's work in mind, her writings and my personal contact with her have obviously influenced my thinking. In particular, I find myself in agreement with her stress on the importance of the problem one is studying instead of adherence to the somewhat arbitrary demarcations of disciplines that now form the traditional definitions of university departments. This is not to condone confusion of level of conceptual analysis, though it suggests the wisdom of keeping an open mind on whether the current fashion in defining levels of analysis is the most useful. Like Audrey Richards, I am wary of single explanations of ritual behaviour, however elegant. As she says in concluding her analysis of *chisungu*, the girls' initiation rite among the Bemba (1956, p. 169), 'Single explanations of ritual behaviour, however satisfying to the observer, seem to me to deny the nature of symbolism itself and its use in human society to express the accepted and approved as well as the hidden and denied, the rules of society and the occasional revolt against them, the common interests of the community and the conflicting interests of different parts of it.' This later addition to the dialogue between myself and Dr Leach is given here in recognition of this agreement and in tribute to her work.

Appendix

EDMUND LEACH

The following supplementary analysis is the result of discussion between the editor and the author.

Patrilineal structures of the type represented by the reduced model shown in *Figure I* are quite familiar and have been extensively discussed in a polemical body of literature that emphasizes, as a rule, the ambiguous relationship between ϵ and his mother's brother α. In a society that stresses the theme of perpetual succession the relationship between the structural cross-cousins (β/ϵ) is interchangeable with that of mother's brother/sister's son (α/ϵ). Much of the argument deployed in Radcliffe-Brown (1924) and connected literature, as cited in Goody (1969), could be relevant to the Tongan case, and indeed Tonga features in that literature (cf. Goody, 1969, p. 81).

Figure I

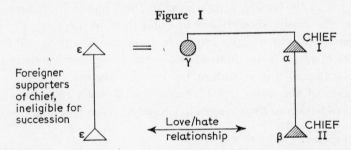

A comparable matrilineal structure is that made famous by Malinowski's discussion of the relation between the Trobriand chief and his sons and heirs. It can be represented by *Figure II*.

Figure II

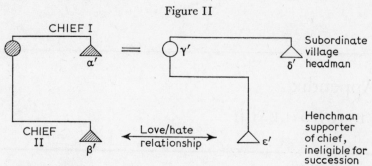

The Tongan structure corresponds to that of *Figure I* but with the special characteristic that, because γ has explicitly higher personal rank than α, ε may be of higher personal rank than β, even though β is politically superior.

The relationship between the titles of β and ε is that of chief to matāpule. The base meaning of the term matāpule is 'sister's husband' (see note 2, p. 274). Thus the terminology corresponds to ε/α in *Figure I*. But, in the mythology and in the kava ceremonial, the relationship between β and ε is that of 'half-brother through a common mother'. If we apply this equivocation to *Figure I*, then it is at once apparent that the common mother must be γ, which is precisely the outcome of the full-scale analysis, which is developed around text *Figure 3* (p. 261).

In assessing the relationship between this analysis and that advanced by Goody with regard to the Tongan institution of *fahu*, the reader should bear in mind that, in the case of kava ceremonial, the relationships are those of the titles and not those of actual individuals. The claims of ε against β are strictly mythological and it cannot possibly be argued that 'the exclusion of the sister's children from succession is in flagrant contradiction to their claims in property' (Goody, 1969, p. 81).

REFERENCES

RADCLIFFE-BROWN, A. R. 1924. The mother's Brother in South Africa. *South African Journal of Science* **21**: 542–55.

GOODY, J. R. 1969. The Mother's Brother and the Sister's Son in West Africa. In *Comparative Studies in Kinship*. London: Routledge.

Bibliography of the principal writings of Audrey Richards

P. H. GULLIVER

ABBREVIATIONS

EAISR   East African Institute of Social Research
JAA   *Journal of African Administration*
JRAI   *Journal of the Royal Anthropological Institute*
JRAS   *Journal of the Royal African Society*
PRAI   *Proceedings of the Royal Anthropological Institute*
SAJS   *South African Journal of Science*

1932. *Hunger and work in a savage tribe: a functional study of nutrition among the southern Bantu*. London, Routledge.
Anthropological problems in northeastern Rhodesia. *Africa* **5**: 123–44.
An anthropologist in Northern Rhodesia. *The Listener*.

1934. Mother right among the central Bantu. In E. E. Evans-Pritchard *et al.* (eds.): *Essays presented to C. G. Seligman*. London, Kegan Paul, pp. 267–79.

1935. The village census in the study of contact problems. *Africa* **8**: 20–33.
Tribal government in transition. *JRAS* **34**, supplement Oct.
Preliminary notes on the Babemba of north-eastern Rhodesia. *Bantu Studies* **9**: 225–53.
A modern movement of witchfinders. *Africa* **8**: 448–61.
From bush to mine. *Geographical Magazine*.
Urbanising the native. *Spectator* June.

1936. The life of Bwembya, a native of Northern Rhodesia. In M. Perham (ed.): *Ten Africans*. London, Faber & Faber, pp. 17–40.

(With E. M. Widdowson.) A dietary study in north-eastern Rhodesia. *Africa* **9**: 166–96.

1937. Reciprocal clan relationships among the Bemba of north-eastern Rhodesia. *Man* **37**: 188–93.

1938. The village census in the study of culture contact. In *Methods of study of culture contact in Africa*. London, International Institute of African Languages & Cultures (Memo. XV), pp. 46–59.

1939. Land, labour and diet in Northern Rhodesia: an economic study of the Bemba tribe. London, Oxford University Press for International Institute of African Languages & Cultures.

The development of field work methods in social anthropology. In F. C. Bartlett *et al.* (eds.): *The study of society*. London, Routledge and Kegan Paul.

1940. The political system of the Bemba of north-eastern Rhodesia. In M. Fortes & E. E. Evans-Pritchard (eds.): *African political systems*. London, Oxford University Press, pp. 83–120.

Bemba marriage and modern economic conditions. Livingstone, Rhodes-Livingstone Institute (Rhodes-Livingstone Paper No. 4).

1943. Bronislaw Kaspar Malinowski. *Man* **43**: 1–4.

1944. Practical anthropology in the life-time of the African Institute. *Africa* **14**: 289–300.

Pottery images or *mbusa* used at the chisungu ceremonies of the Bemba people of north-eastern Rhodesia. *SAJS* **41**: 444–58.

1947. Colonial problems as a challenge to the social sciences. London, Anti-Slavery & Aboriginees Protection Society.

Social research in the colonial field. *Pilot Papers* **2**: 26–38.

1949. Colonial future: the need for facts. *Spectator* February.

1950. Huts and hut-building among the Bemba. *Man* **50**: 87–90; 101–9.

Some types of family structure among the central Bantu. In A. R. Radcliffe-Brown & D. Forde (eds.): *African systems of kinship and marriage*. London, Oxford University Press, pp. 207–51.

1951. The present day recruitment of chiefs in Buganda. In *Report of the Astrida Conference* 1951. Kampala, EAISR.

The Bemba of north-eastern Rhodesia. In E. Colson & M. Gluckman (eds.): *Seven tribes of British Central Africa*. London, Oxford University Press for Rhodes-Livingstone Institute, pp. 164–93.

1952. (With A. B. Mukwaya.) Discussion on the difference between Busoga and Buganda system of chiefs. In *Conference Papers*. Kampala, EAISR.

Some preliminary suggestions on the determinants of clan and lineage structures, and the present day recruitment of chiefs in Buganda. In Inst. pour la Recherche sci. en Afr. Centrale. *C. R. des travaux du seminaire d'Anthropologie Sociale*. July 1951.

1953. Anthropological research in East Africa. Transactions of the New York Academy of Sciences. **16**: 44–9.

East African conference on colonial administration [position of the lower chiefs]. *JAA* **5**: 62–5.

1954 Economic development and tribal change: a study of immigrant labour in Buganda. Cambridge, Heffer for EAISR. (Edited, and contributed several chapters.)

(With P. Reining.) Report on fertility survey in Buganda and Buhaya, 1952. In F. Lorimer (ed.): *Culture and human fertility*. Paris, UNESCO, pp. 351–403.

1955. Ganda clan structure, some preliminary notes. In *Conference Papers*. Kampala, EAISR.

The tribal kingdom of Uganda. *Times British Colonies Review* **20**.

1956. Chisungu: a girl's initiation ceremony among the Bemba of Northern Rhodesia. London, Faber & Faber.

1957. The concept of culture in Malinowski's work. In R. Firth (ed.): *Man and culture: an evaluation of the work of Bronislaw Malinowski*. London, Routledge & Kegan Paul, pp. 15–31.

The human problems of Africa. *Corona* **9**: 137–40.

1958. A changing pattern of agriculture in East Africa: the Bemba of Northern Rhodesia. *Geographical Journal* **124**: 302–14.

Tribal groups in Kenya. *Times British Colonies Review* **21–2**.

1959. East African chiefs: a study of political development in some Uganda and Tanganyika tribes. London, Faber & Faber, New York, Praeger. (Edited, and contributed several chapters.)

1960. Social mechanisms for the transfer of political rights in some African tribes. *JRAI* **90**: 175–90.

The Bemba, their country and diet. In S. & Ph. Ottenberg (eds.): *Cultures and societies of Africa.* New York, Random House, pp. 96–109.

1961. Land, labour and diet in Northern Rhodesia. London, Oxford University Press. (2nd reprint, with new foreword and bibliography.)

Agnes Winifred Hoernle, 1885–1960. *Man* **61**: 35.

Anthropology on the scrap-heap? *JAA* **13**: 3–10.

African kings and their royal relatives. *JRAI* **91**: 135–50.

1962. Constitutional problems in Uganda. *Political Quarterly* **33**: 360–9.

Chisungu. *Problèmes sociaux congolais* **59**: 83–112.

Tribe and nation in East Africa. *The Round Table* June.

1963. Some effects of the introduction of individual freehold into Buganda. In D. Biebuyck (ed.): *African agrarian systems.* London, Oxford University Press for International African Institute, pp. 267–80.

Introduction. P. C. W. Gutkind: *The royal capital of Buganda.* The Hague, Mouton & Co.

The pragmatic value of magic in primitive societies. *PRAI* **39**: 340–347.

1964. Foreword; Authority patterns in traditional Buganda; Traditional values and current political behaviour; Epilogue. In L. A. Fallers (ed.): *The king's men.* London, Oxford University Press for EAISR.

Freedom, Communications and Transport. In David Bidney (ed.): *The concept of freedom in Anthropology.* The Hague, Mouton & Co.

1965. The adaptation of universities to the African situation. *Minerva.*

1966. The changing structure of a Ganda village: Kisozi 1892-1952. Nairobi, East Africa Publishing House for EAISR (EA, Studies No. 24).

Multi-tribalism in African urban areas. *Civilisations* **16**: 354–64.

1967. African systems of thought: an Anglo-French dialogue. *Man* (ns) **2**: 286–98.

Presidential address to the conference of the African Studies Association of the United Kingdom held at Edinburgh, 21–24 September 1966. *African Affairs* **66**: 40–54.

1969. The multicultural states of East Africa. Montreal, McGill-Queen's University Press for Centre for Developing Areas Studies (Keith Collard Lectures, series 3).

Keeping the king divine. *PRAI*: 23–5.

Characteristics of ethical systems in primitive human society. In F. J. Ebling (ed.): *Biology and ethics.* London, Academic Press (Institute of Biology Symposia No. 18), pp. 23–32.

Socialization and contemporary British Anthropology. In P. Mayer (ed.): *Socialization: the approach from Social Anthropology.* ASA Monograph 8. London, Tavistock.

Bronislaw Malinowski. In T. R. Raison (ed.): *The Founding Fathers of Social Science.* London, Penguin. First published in *New Society* July 1963.

Index